330

D1423891

# Understanding
# Economic
# Growth

- · Macro-level
- · Industry-level
- · Firm-level

palgrave
macmillan

OECD

**PALGRAVE MACMILLAN** is the global academic imprint of the Palgrave Macmillan division of St. Martin's Press, LLC and of Palgrave Macmillan Ltd. Macmillan® is a registered trademark in the United States, United Kingdom and other countries. Palgrave is a registered trademark in the European Union and other countries.

Houndmills, Basingstoke, Hampshire RG21 6XS, and
175 Fifth Avenue, New York, N.Y. 10010
Companies and representatives throughout the world.

ISBN 1–4039–4146–7 hardback
ISBN 1–4039–4147–5 paperback

A catalogue record for this book is available from the British Library.

A catalog record for this book is available from the Library of Congress.

10   9   8   7   6   5   4   3   2   1
13  12  11  10  09  08  07  06  05  04

OECD Publishing is a department of the Organisation for Economic Co-operation and Development (OECD). It furthers the OECD's objective of disseminating widely the results of its research on economic and social issues arising from a globalised world, its statistical gathering activity, as well as the conventions, guidelines and standards agreed by its members.

The OECD member countries are: Australia, Austria, Belgium, Canada, the Czech Republic, Denmark, Finland, France, Germany, Greece, Hungary, Iceland, Ireland, Italy, Japan, Korea, Luxembourg, Mexico, the Netherlands, New Zealand, Norway, Poland, Portugal, the Slovak Republic, Spain, Sweden, Switzerland, Turkey, the United Kingdom and the United States.

The opinions expressed and arguments employed in this publication are the sole responsibility of the authors and do not necessarily reflect those of the OECD or of the governments of its member countries.

# Foreword

The end of World War II marked the beginning of a long period of prosperity in most countries now members of the OECD. For nearly three decades, known to historians as the "thirty glorious years", growth remained exceptionally strong and in many countries per capita incomes tended to catch up with American levels. This period of affluence did much to give credence to the idea that, in a very open international environment, economic catch-up was virtually automatic.

The history of the past two decades tempered to a great extent that initial enthusiasm. In the major countries of continental Europe, per capita incomes stopped converging towards American levels as of the early 1980s, before falling in relative terms throughout the 1990s. Japan has suffered a similar reversal of fortune during the past 15 years.

With the benefit of hindsight, it now appears that the very substantial acceleration in productivity seen in the United States since 1995 has not spread to the other OECD countries as widely as might have been hoped. This disappointing performance has been worsened in Europe by often misguided labour market policies. Originally designed to discourage labour supply in the hope to reduce unemployment, these policies have only managed to depress employment rates and per capita incomes. However, in the last few years large countries such as Australia, the United Kingdom and Canada, as well as a number of smaller OECD countries, have been highly successful in regaining momentum towards economic convergence. All in all, it is now clear that living standards do not converge automatically and that technical progress is not "exogenous". As the new growth theories strongly suggest, it depends in fact on the quality of national institutions and public policies.

Moving from theory to practice and gaining in the process a better understanding of the real determinants of growth, here are the reasons which prompted the OECD to launch a long-term research project resulting today in the publication of this book. Through hard work, countless international comparisons and highly sophisticated quantitative analyses, the authors of "Understanding Economic Growth" have unearthed a rich set of findings. While it would be illusory to summarise them in a few lines, it is possible however to stress a few important lessons that will help the conduct of pro-growth policies in OECD countries.

The work underpinning this publication stresses the crucial importance of human capital and R&D in achieving growth. Econometric analysis points, for instance, to the number of years of study having a strong influence on economic growth, and also to the very appreciable impact of private sector R&D.

The authors also examine the role of new information and communication technologies in the recent acceleration in productivity growth in the United States and certain OECD countries. Their role appears to be very important, but does seem to depend a great deal, in turn, on the regulatory and institutional framework in which technological innovation takes place. There is, in particular, empirical evidence that the opening up of product and services markets and the flexibility of the regulatory framework contribute significantly to technological catch-up and also facilitate the birth of small, highly innovative firms.

As the book amply demonstrates, this does not mean that one can overlook the contribution that sound macroeconomic policies – low and stable inflation, moderate tax burdens, openness to international trade – make to economic growth.

I trust that this publication will enable students and professionals interested in growth issues to become acquainted with recent, innovative work. It will, I hope, contribute to a better understanding of the main economic challenges of today and help clarify the debate on the long-term growth of our economies.

Jean-Philippe Cotis
*OECD Chief Economist*

# Table of Contents

Chapter 3

## Industry-level analysis
### Market dynamics and productivity

Chapter 4

## Firm-level analysis
### Dynamics, productivity and policy settings    70

**Table of Contents**

List of Tables

## Table of Contents

List of Figures

Table of Contents

# Overview

Differences in the growth performances of OECD countries during the 1990s revived the debate over the underlying causes of economic growth. This debate prompted the OECD to undertake a number of in-depth studies into this issue. The main theme can be expressed in a simple question: what has driven economic growth in OECD countries in recent decades? Following on from this, what effects, if any, have other developments – not least the spread of information technology (IT) – had on the determinants of overall economic growth? How, and how much, do government policies and other aspects of the business environment contribute to long-term growth, and what policies should therefore be advocated? And, finally, what impact has restructuring within and between industries had on overall growth performances?

## Macro-level analysis

Growth in GDP per capita across OECD countries has shown widening disparities. These disparities were driven by higher than average growth rates in some catch-up countries (*e.g.* Korea and Ireland), but also by high growth rates in some relatively affluent countries, such as the United States, Canada, Australia, the Netherlands and Norway, and low growth rates in much of continental Europe and Japan.

### Labour utilisation

Cross-country disparities are, at least partially, related to differences in the patterns of labour utilisation and skill upgrading of the workforce. In particular, most of the countries that experienced an acceleration in Gross Domestic Product (GDP) per capita growth also recorded an increase in labour utilisation. Conversely, most countries where employment stagnated, or even declined, saw a deterioration in growth, as labour productivity growth was not able to make up for poor employment performance. Furthermore, in most countries the up-skilling of the workforce played a significant role in boosting labour productivity. However, in those with poor employment performance, this partially resulted from higher unemployment among low skilled workers.

### Technological progress

There are also some new factors behind these growth disparities. In particular, multi-factor productivity (MFP), taken as a proxy for disembodied (*i.e.* not incorporated in improvements in the quality of the capital stock) technological change, accelerated in a number of OECD countries, most notably in the United States and Canada, but also in some smaller economies (*e.g.* Australia, Ireland). The contribution of IT to aggregate productivity growth appeared initially to be disembodied.

This resulted from rapid technological progress within the IT-producing industry itself. Since the mid- to late-1990s, an increasing contribution to embodied productivity growth seems to have stemmed from greater use of highly productive IT equipment by other industries. Not surprisingly, MFP growth accelerated somewhat later in those OECD countries without a sizeable IT-producing industry.

All in all, growing disparities in growth trends over the 1990s seem to result from a combination of "traditional" factors – mostly related to the efficiency of labour market mechanisms – and "new economy" elements reflecting the size of IT-producing industries, but also the pace of adoption of this technology by other industries. The evidence tends to indicate that the ability of countries to innovate in expanding industries and to adopt leading technologies is also influenced by national policy and institutional settings, which help to shape business conditions for existing firms and new entrepreneurial activities.

## *Macroeconomic policies*

Empirical analysis suggests that stability-oriented macroeconomic policies have a fairly substantial impact on economic output. Reductions in the variability of inflation tend to have a direct positive impact on growth, while the main effect of the level of inflation is felt through investment. Similarly, high levels of taxation and government spending seem to affect growth both directly and indirectly through investment. Analysis suggests that high taxes tend to reduce output growth, with the combined effect of a one percentage point increase in the overall tax rate amounting to a decline in the level of output of about 0.6-0.7%. Moreover, the study also finds evidence that spending on R&D can have a substantial effect on both the level and the rate of growth of total output, and that education and training play a key role in explaining differences in growth performances. Finally, a high degree of exposure to foreign trade was found to have a significant positive impact on output growth.

# Industry-level analysis

Having examined relative growth performances at the aggregate level, it is important to assess the role played by developments within individual industries and the reallocation of resources across industries and firms. This industry-level analysis sheds further light on issues that the earlier macro-level analysis may fail to capture, such as the effects of specific policies – including product market regulations and trade restrictions – on industry performance. Likewise, differences in growth patterns at the industry level may also point to variations in the extent to which countries are benefiting from broader economic changes, or from the potential offered by new technologies.

Overview

**Macro-level analysis**

*Macroeconomic policies*

**Industry-level analysis**

### Multi-factor productivity (MFP)
*Multi-factor productivity growth is the growth that remains once productivity gains from changes in the volume and quality of inputs to production have been accounted for. Ideally, particularly when averaged over several of years, it reflects productivity gains from "disembodied" technological change, i.e. technological change that does not emerge directly from the technological sophistication of machinery and equipment used to produce goods and services but from other processes. For instance, the interconnection of computers via the Internet and e-mail has allowed people to work in new and more productive ways. The more people that are connected, the greater the potential of the network to increase productivity (hence, so-called "network" economies).*

### *Strict regulations*

The empirical results indicate a negative direct effect of product market regulations on productivity. Moreover, if the interaction of regulation with the technology gap is also considered, the results point to an even stronger indirect effect via the slower adoption of existing technologies. Strict regulations seem to have a particularly detrimental effect on productivity the further a country is from the technology frontier, possibly because they reduce the scope for knowledge spillovers. The results also provide some insight into the potential effects of policy reforms on the long-run level of MFP. In particular, a reduction in the stringency of product market regulations could, on this evidence, substantially reduce the productivity gap in countries such as Greece, Portugal and Spain in the long run.

### *Industrial relations and labour legislation*

Results suggest that the nature of industrial relations does not matter per se, but that it may negatively affect productivity via its interactions with employment protection legislation (EPL). Indeed, there is evidence that the negative impact of EPL on productivity only applies to countries with an intermediate degree of centralisation/co-ordination, *i.e.* where sectoral wage bargaining is predominant, but without national co-ordination. By contrast, EPL is not found to influence productivity in either highly centralised/co-ordinated or decentralised countries.

## Firm-level analysis

Finally, we must examine the micro determinants of economic growth by focusing on the reallocation of resources within narrowly defined industries, resulting from the expansion of more productive firms, the entry of new firms and the exit of obsolete ones. A key finding of this firm-level analysis is that a large fraction of aggregate labour productivity growth is driven by what happens in each individual firm, whilst shifts in market shares from low to high productivity firms seem to play only a modest role. The analysis also points to a significant and broadly similar degree of "firm churning" amongst OECD countries. More specifically, the high correlation between entry and exit rates across industries suggests a process of "creative destruction", in which a large number of new firms displace a large number of inefficient firms. However, the failure rate for new entrants, especially small firms, is high, which suggests that "creative destruction" also involves a great deal of market experimentation. Nonetheless, surviving firms tend to grow rapidly towards the average efficient size.

## Regulation and entrepreneurial activity

Analysis suggests that weak regulation encourages entrepreneurial activity in both the US and in Europe. However, US entrant firms appear to be smaller and less productive than their European Union counterparts, but grow faster when successful. The econometric results presented in this study offer some rationale for these differences. Indeed, they support the view that strict regulations on entrepreneurial activity, as well as high costs of adjusting the workforce, negatively affect the entry of new firms. Thus, in the United States, low administrative costs of start-ups and not unduly strict regulations on labour adjustments are likely to stimulate potential entrepreneurs to start on a small scale, test the market and, if successful with their business plan, expand rapidly to reach the minimum efficient scale. In contrast, higher entry and adjustment costs in Europe may stimulate a pre-market selection of business plans with less market experimentation. In addition, the more market-based financial system may lead to a lower risk aversion to project financing in the United States, with greater financing possibilities for entrepreneurs with small or innovative projects, often characterised by limited cash flows and lack of collateral.

Overview

**Firm-level analysis**

*Regulation
and entrepreneurial activity*

*Technology*

## Technology

There is no evidence in the available data that one policy model dominates the other in terms of aggregate performance. However, in a period of rapid diffusion of a new technology, greater experimentation may allow new ideas and forms of production to emerge more rapidly, thereby leading to a faster process of innovation and technology adoption. This seems to be confirmed by the strong contribution to overall productivity made by new firms in IT-related industries. In this context, easing regulations may stimulate firm entry and, via this channel, may ultimately lead to higher productivity growth.

# Chapter 1

Chapter

Growth performances
in OECD countries

**Measuring growth:
analytical framework**

*Role of labour*

**The contribution of IT
to growth**

**Key conclusions**

# Key questions

- **How have growth trends
  differed across OECD
  countries in recent years?**

- **To what extent
  are the different growth
  experiences due
  to "traditional" factors
  (catch-up through capital
  deepening and differences
  in labour utilisation) versus
  "new economy" influences?**

# Growth performances
## in OECD countries

Economic growth performances among OECD countries varied considerably during the 1990s, with a few countries – including the US – experiencing significantly stronger growth than others.
In some countries (e.g. Ireland and Korea), strong rates of expansion appear to have been at least partly the result of the familiar catch-up process enjoyed by most of the western European economies in the two decades following the Second World War.

However, rapid growth in the US cannot be attributed to catch-up effects. Instead, the phase of powerful economic growth experienced in the US until 2001 led many commentators to speculate that a "new economy" had emerged in which economic performance was being enhanced by the spread of IT. This, it is argued, produced an unusual combination of strong output and productivity growth, together with falling unemployment and low inflation. These patterns are all the more surprising for a country already at the technology frontier in many industries, and were not repeated in most other affluent OECD economies.

Indeed, in the 1990s, the large continental European countries and Japan experienced slow economic growth and rising, or persistently high, unemployment.

# Measuring growth: analytical framework

Growth is determined by a variety of macroeconomic policy and structural conditions, and thus differs significantly among countries. Growth performances have therefore continued to vary widely even between economies at similar stages of economic advancement [● → Table 1.1]. In order to disentangle the relative importance of these various influences on growth, this study adopted a theoretical framework in which growth was seen as the combination of three different forces:

- technological progress;
- a convergence process towards the country-specific steady state path of output per capita;
- shifts in the steady state path that can arise from changes in policy and institutions, as well as investment rates and changes in human capital inputs.

The analysis used various specifications, from a standard growth equation that considered only the impact of the convergence process and the accumulation of physical capital through increasingly complex formulations adding in the effects of investment in human capital (education) and various policy-related or other structural influences on growth. The analysis was conducted across 21 OECD countries for the period 1971-98, with the choice of countries mainly determined by the availability of data.

The growth disparities can only be understood by examining the fundamental determinants of economic growth throughout the OECD countries. It should be noted that cross-country comparisons of economic performance are complicated by a number of measurement issues, including different approaches used in calculating the value of economic output and the size of the stock of machinery and equipment. However, differences in measurement are unlikely to account for more than a modest proportion of the observed differences in growth rates between countries. In the US, for example, the use of chain weighted indexes (as opposed to fixed-weighted indexes) to calculate GDP has tended to understate economic growth in recent years. This has been more or less offset, however, by the US practice of using "hedonic" price measures, which has tended to boost estimates of real GDP during the same period.

These measurement differences have therefore roughly cancelled each other out. Moreover, in the short term, differences in growth rates are partly a function of the economic cycle: it is obviously misleading to compare growth in an economy that is at the height of a boom with that of an economy in the midst of recession. As a result, much of the

## Growth performances in OECD countries

### Measuring growth: analytical framework

## Catch-up effects

*The concept of "catch-up" effects is that less developed economies experience faster growth in output per head, partly by adopting the working practices, capital equipment and technologies of more advanced countries. Moreover, economies with less well-educated workforces appear likely to derive proportionately greater returns to investment in education and training. This should lead to a process in which the less advanced economies initially grow more rapidly, but that economic growth rates slow as they catch up with the more advanced countries.*

analysis of economic growth in this study utilises estimates of underlying or trend growth rates, adjusted for cyclical fluctuations.

In calculating figures for real GDP – *i.e.* the volume of output – statistical agencies need to strip out the effects of changes in prices. This is normally done at a disaggregated level, adjusting figures for the value of output of individual products or groups of products for changes in the prices of these products. The resulting indexes of real output of the individual components of GDP must then be added back together to arrive at an index for overall GDP in real terms. This is done by weighting the components together according to their shares in overall output, but there are various approaches to calculating these weights, notably using fixed-weighted indexes or chain-weighted indexes (**see definitions on pages 20 and 22**).

Economic growth in the major OECD economies generally decelerated in the 1990s, continuing a well-established trend. However, growth performances varied widely between individual countries, with the US and some smaller economies (including Australia, Ireland and the Netherlands) showing stronger growth rates while others, mainly the large continental European countries and Japan, continued to decelerate. Economic output, usually gauged by Gross Domestic Product (GDP), which is a measure of the total value of production in an economy in any given year, is partly a function of the inputs employed. Additions to the labour force, for example, increase productive capacity, as does investment in new machinery and equipment. Economic growth in the US averaged 3.2% per year in 1990-2000, while GDP per head of population rose at an average rate of much less than this (2.2%). This indicates that some of the superior performance of the US economy in terms of absolute GDP growth was simply a reflection of a rapidly rising population. This was in turn partly the result of net inward migration, which boosted the total US population by around 0.3% per year during 1990-2000. However, inward migration also added to population growth in the major European countries, though less significantly, during this period. Moreover, output per capita, which strips out the effects of both immigration and natural population growth, still rose at a faster rate in the US than in the other large OECD economies during the 1990s, particularly in the second half of the decade. This therefore still leaves open the question of why the US economy performed better.

## Role of labour

As noted above, increases in economic output can partly be explained by increases in inputs, mainly capital and labour. Growth is affected not only by the increase in overall population, which obviously boosts the labour supply, but also by changes in the structure of the population. Changes in the size of the labour force and the employment rate therefore go some way towards explaining differences in GDP growth rates between countries. Generally speaking, those economies with low

---

**Growth performances in OECD countries**

**Measuring growth: analytical framework**

*Role of labour*

---

**Hedonic price measures**

*Hedonic price measures adjust the market prices of goods to take account of changes in the characteristics of goods. Hedonic measures are most notably being used at the present time to take account of the rapid pace of change in computer hardware and software.*

Table 1.1

# Uneven growth of GDP across OECD countries

Average annual rates of change, 1970-2000

| | Actual growth of GDP | | | |
|---|---|---|---|---|
| | 1970-1980 | 1980-1990 | 1990[1]-2000 | 1996-2000 |
| United States | 3.2 | 3.2 | 3.2 | 4.2 |
| Japan | 4.4 | 4.1 | 1.3 | 0.7 |
| Germany[3] | 2.7 | 2.2 | 1.6 | 2.0 |
| France | 3.3 | 2.4 | 1.8 | 2.9 |
| Italy | 3.6 | 2.2 | 1.6 | 2.1 |
| United Kingdom | 1.9 | 2.7 | 2.3 | 2.9 |
| Canada | 4.3 | 2.8 | 2.8 | 4.4 |
| Austria | 3.6 | 2.3 | 2.3 | 2.7 |
| Belgium | 3.4 | 2.1 | 2.1 | 3.2 |
| Denmark | 2.2 | 1.9 | 2.3 | 2.8 |
| Finland | 3.5 | 3.1 | 2.2 | 5.3 |
| Greece | 4.6 | 0.7 | 2.3 | 3.7 |
| Iceland | 6.3 | 2.7 | 2.6 | 4.6 |
| Ireland | 4.7 | 3.6 | 7.3 | 10.4 |
| Luxembourg | 2.6 | 4.5 | 5.9 | 7.1 |
| Netherlands | 2.9 | 2.2 | 2.9 | 3.8 |
| Norway[4] | 4.4 | 1.5 | 2.8 | 2.6 |
| Portugal | 4.7 | 3.2 | 2.7 | 3.6 |
| Spain | 3.5 | 2.9 | 2.6 | 4.1 |
| Sweden | 1.9 | 2.2 | 1.7 | 3.3 |
| Switzerland | 1.4 | 2.1 | 0.9 | 2.2 |
| Turkey | 4.1 | 5.2 | 3.6 | 3.1 |
| Australia | 3.2 | 3.2 | 3.5 | 4.2 |
| New Zealand | 1.6 | 2.5 | 2.6 | 2.2 |
| Mexico | 6.6 | 1.8 | 3.5 | 5.6 |
| Korea | 7.6 | 8.9 | 6.1 | 4.3 |
| Hungary | .. | .. | 2.3 | 4.7 |
| Poland | .. | .. | 3.6 | 4.9 |
| Czech Republic | .. | .. | 1.5 | 0.1 |
| Slovak Republic | .. | .. | 4.6 | 3.6 |
| *Weighted averages:* | | | | |
| EU15 | 3.0 | 2.4 | 2.0 | 2.9 |
| OECD24[5] | 3.4 | 3.0 | 2.5 | 3.2 |
| *Standard deviation:* | | | | |
| EU15 | 0.92 | 0.86 | 1.62 | 2.19 |
| OECD24[5] | 1.17 | 0.96 | 1.38 | 1.92 |

1. 1991 for Germany and Hungary, 1992 for Czech Republic, 1993 for Slovak Republic.
2. 1991 for Germany, 1992 for Czech Republic and Hungary, 1993 for Slovak Republic.
3. Western Germany before 1991.

| Actual growth of GDP per capita | | | | Trend growth of GDP per capita | | |
|---|---|---|---|---|---|---|
| 1970-1980 | 1980-1990 | 1990$^2$-2000 | 1996-2000 | 1980-1990 | 1990$^2$-2000 | 1996-2000 |
| 2.1 | 2.2 | 2.2 | 3.3 | 2.1 | 2.3 | 2.8 |
| 3.3 | 3.5 | 1.1 | 0.5 | 3.3 | 1.4 | 0.9 |
| 2.6 | 2.0 | 1.3 | 2.0 | 1.9 | 1.2 | 1.7 |
| 2.7 | 1.8 | 1.4 | 2.6 | 1.6 | 1.5 | 1.9 |
| 3.1 | 2.2 | 1.4 | 1.9 | 2.3 | 1.5 | 1.7 |
| 1.8 | 2.5 | 1.9 | 2.4 | 2.2 | 2.1 | 2.3 |
| 2.8 | 1.5 | 1.7 | 3.5 | 1.4 | 1.7 | 2.6 |
| 3.5 | 2.1 | 1.8 | 2.6 | 2.1 | 1.9 | 2.3 |
| 3.2 | 2.0 | 1.8 | 3.0 | 2.0 | 1.9 | 2.3 |
| 1.8 | 1.9 | 2.0 | 2.4 | 1.9 | 1.9 | 2.3 |
| 3.1 | 2.7 | 1.8 | 5.0 | 2.2 | 2.1 | 3.9 |
| 3.6 | 0.2 | 1.9 | 3.5 | 0.5 | 1.8 | 2.7 |
| 5.2 | 1.6 | 1.6 | 3.4 | 1.7 | 1.5 | 2.6 |
| 3.3 | 3.3 | 6.4 | 9.2 | 3.0 | 6.4 | 7.9 |
| 1.9 | 3.9 | 4.5 | 5.7 | 4.0 | 4.5 | 4.6 |
| 2.1 | 1.6 | 2.2 | 3.2 | 1.6 | 2.4 | 2.7 |
| 3.8 | 1.1 | 2.2 | 2.0 | 1.4 | 2.0 | 2.2 |
| 3.4 | 3.1 | 2.5 | 3.2 | 3.1 | 2.8 | 2.7 |
| 2.5 | 2.6 | 2.5 | 4.0 | 2.3 | 2.7 | 3.2 |
| 1.6 | 1.9 | 1.4 | 3.2 | 1.7 | 1.5 | 2.6 |
| 1.2 | 1.5 | 0.2 | 1.8 | 1.4 | 0.4 | 1.1 |
| 1.8 | 2.8 | 1.8 | 1.5 | 2.1 | 2.1 | 1.9 |
| 1.5 | 1.7 | 2.3 | 3.0 | 1.6 | 2.4 | 2.8 |
| 0.5 | 1.9 | 1.2 | 1.4 | 1.4 | 1.2 | 1.8 |
| 3.3 | -0.3 | 1.7 | 4.2 | 0.0 | 1.6 | 2.7 |
| 5.8 | 7.6 | 5.1 | 3.3 | 7.2 | 5.1 | 4.2 |
| .. | .. | 3.4 | 5.1 | .. | 2.3 | 3.5 |
| .. | .. | 3.5 | 4.9 | .. | 4.2 | 4.8 |
| .. | .. | 1.6 | 0.2 | .. | 1.7 | 1.4 |
| .. | .. | 4.4 | 3.5 | .. | .. | .. |
| | | | | | | |
| 2.6 | 2.1 | 1.7 | 2.6 | 2.0 | 1.8 | 2.2 |
| 2.5 | 2.3 | 1.8 | 2.6 | 2.2 | 1.9 | 2.2 |
| | | | | | | |
| 0.70 | 0.85 | 1.39 | 1.88 | 0.79 | 1.35 | 1.56 |
| 1.02 | 0.81 | 1.21 | 1.72 | 0.74 | 1.17 | 1.37 |

4. Mainland only.
5. Excluding Czech Republic, Hungary, Korea, Mexico, Poland and Slovak Republic.

Source: OECD (2001), OECD Economic Outlook, No 70.

or falling labour utilisation rates experienced a slowdown in the growth of GDP per head due to the resulting decline in productive capacity. However, in most OECD countries, the impact of changes in the proportion of the population of working age over the past decade has been fairly modest, with the notable exceptions of Turkey and Ireland. In the latter case, a reversal of the traditional pattern of net outward migration helped to boost output growth during the 1990s. Changes in employment rates, in contrast, have had a more significant influence on growth in GDP per head in most countries, though their impact varies widely from country to country. Employment rates added considerably to growth in GDP per capita in Ireland, the Netherlands and Spain, but subtracted from growth in Finland, Sweden and Turkey [● · Fig.1.1].

Stripping out the effects of the economic cycle, changes in population size and structure and shifts in the employment rate leaves us with a crude measure of labour productivity, GDP per employee, that accounts for at least half of growth in GDP per capita in most countries during the 1990s. However, output is also influenced by changes in hours worked per employee, which have generally declined over the past decade. Reductions in the length of the average working week, either as a result of legislation or collective labour agreements, have been combined with the increasing trend towards part-time work, which has resulted partly from higher female participation in the labour force. Labour productivity per hour worked has consequently risen faster than the productivity measure based on the number of employees. Compared with the previous decade, hourly labour productivity picked up in a number of countries, including the United States, Australia, Norway, Portugal, Germany, Finland and Sweden, while it declined in the other countries.

However, these changes were accompanied by different employment patterns across countries. Amongst the G-7 economies, significant employment increases in the United States (as well as in Canada and Japan, but with no acceleration in productivity) contrasted sharply with declines in Germany and Italy. Even stronger contrasts in employment patterns were found amongst some smaller countries. As indicated above, strong upward trends in employment rates in Ireland, the Netherlands and Spain compare with declines in Finland, Sweden and Turkey.

As well as changes in the quantity of labour used in the production process, variations in labour quality, in terms of education, experience and skill levels, clearly have an impact on output per employee. These variations are difficult to measure, and the contribution of changes in "human capital" to economic growth is consequently difficult to disentangle from the effects of other factors. However, in a bid to approximate this effect, it is possible to construct a measure of labour input (measured in "efficiency units") that sums the numbers of workers each weighted by their relative wage according to level of education.

## Growth performances in OECD countries

### Measuring growth: analytical framework

*Role of labour*

### Fixed-weighted indexes

*The simplest approach is to use weights derived from the shares of individual components in total output in a fixed base year. The base year is usually changed every five years or so to take account of changes in the price structure in the economy. However, this approach suffers from "substitution bias" in that for years after the base year it tends to overstate the contribution made by sectors where prices are falling and output is consequently increasing more rapidly. Fixed weight GDP measures therefore tend to show more rapid growth rates in the years following the base year.*

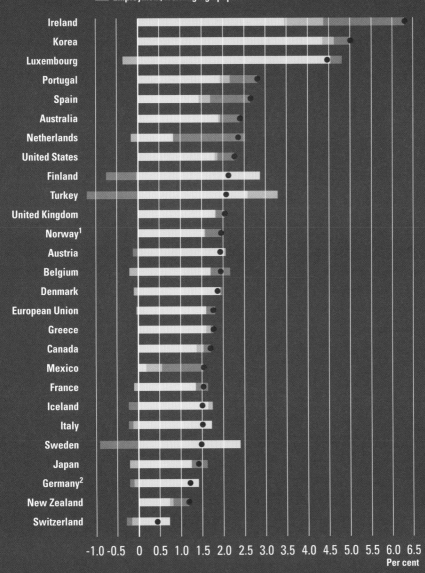

Fig. 1.1

## Components of GDP growth per capita

Trend series, average annual percentage change, 1990-2000

● GDP per capita growth

Contribution to GDP per capita growth from trend changes in:

▊ GDP per person employed
▊ Working-age population/total population
▊ Employment/working-age population

Ireland
Korea
Luxembourg
Portugal
Spain
Australia
Netherlands
United States
Finland
Turkey
United Kingdom
Norway¹
Austria
Belgium
Denmark
European Union
Greece
Canada
Mexico
France
Iceland
Italy
Sweden
Japan
Germany²
New Zealand
Switzerland

-1.0 -0.5  0  0.5  1.0  1.5  2.0  2.5  3.0  3.5  4.0  4.5  5.0  5.5  6.0  6.5

Per cent

1. Mainland only.
2. 1991-2000.

The reasoning behind this is that employees with different skill or educational levels are likely to contribute to productive activity to differing degrees, but that data on these relative productivity levels are not available. Using wage rates to define these relative contributions assumes that wage differentials provide a reasonable proxy for relative productivity, which is open to question. However, because the approach is applied consistently for all of the countries analysed, it does allow cross-country comparisons and sheds some light on the impact of changes in the quality of labour inputs.

The results of this exercise are shown in ●‒ Fig.1.2, and indicate that in some countries, particularly in Europe, an increase in the general educational level of the labour force has had a positive impact on output per employee. However, in many cases the improvement in the general educational standard of employees has come at the expense of higher unemployment among the low-skilled. That is, the improvement partly results from weak labour market conditions that have encouraged employers to concentrate on the recruitment of better-educated staff while dismissing or not employing those with fewer skills. In contrast, tight labour market conditions in Ireland and the Netherlands have resulted in a widening of the employment base, as labour shortages have obliged employers to take on low-skilled workers. As a result, the average educational level of employees has declined in these countries, and compositional changes in the workforce have had a negative effect on overall labour productivity growth.

Growth performances
in OECD countries

**Measuring growth:
analytical framework**

*Role of labour*

## Chain-weighted indexes

*This approach uses weights that are based on the geometric mean of prices in the current year and the previous year. It therefore takes account of changes in relative prices between consecutive years, and avoids "substitution bias". It also tends to result in lower calculations of GDP growth rates (relative to the fixed-weight approach).
It is, however, more complicated to apply and suffers from the drawback that, due to the use of geometric means, the calculated components of GDP are not additive.*

# Focus on IT

## The contribution of IT to growth

The economic impact of IT is closely linked to the extent to which different IT technologies have diffused across OECD economies. This is partly because IT is a network technology; the more people and firms that use the network, the more benefits it generates. The diffusion of IT currently differs considerably between OECD countries, since some countries have invested more or have started earlier to invest in IT than other countries.

A core indicator of IT diffusion is the share of IT in investment. Investment in IT establishes the infrastructure for the use of IT (the IT networks) and provides productive equipment and software to businesses. While IT investment has accelerated in most OECD countries over the past decade, the pace of that investment differs widely. The data show that IT investment rose from less than 15% of total non-residential investment in the early 1980s, to between 15% and 30% in 2001. In 2001, the share of IT investment was particularly high in the United States, the United Kingdom, Sweden, the Netherlands, Canada and Australia [●→ Fig. 1.3]. IT investment in many European countries was substantially lower than in the United States.

The rapid growth in IT investment has been fuelled by a rapid decline in the relative prices of computer equipment and the growing scope for the application of IT. Due to rapid technological progress in the production of key IT technologies, such as semi-conductors, and strong competitive pressure in their production, the prices of key technologies have fallen by between 15 and 30% annually, making investment in IT attractive to firms. The benefits of lower IT prices have been felt across the OECD, as both firms investing in these technologies and consumers buying IT goods and services have benefited from lower prices. The lower costs of IT are only part of the picture; IT is also a technology that offers large potential benefits to firms, *e.g.* in enhancing information flows and productivity.

A second determinant of the economic impacts associated with IT is the size of the IT sector, *i.e.* the sector that produces IT goods and services. Having an IT-producing sector can be important, since IT production has been characterised by rapid technological progress and has been faced with very strong demand. The sector has therefore grown very fast, and made a large contribution to economic growth, employment and exports. Moreover, having a strong IT sector may help firms that wish to use IT, since the close proximity of producing firms might have advantages when developing IT applications for specific purposes. In addition, having a strong IT sector should also help to

Growth performances
in OECD countries

**The contribution of IT to growth**

Fig. 1.2

## Enhancements in human capital contribute to labour productivity growth

Average annual percentage change, 1990-2000

● Trend growth in GDP per person employed

Contribution to growth in GDP per person employed[1] from changes in:
- Hourly GDP per efficient unit of labour
- Hours worked
- Human capital

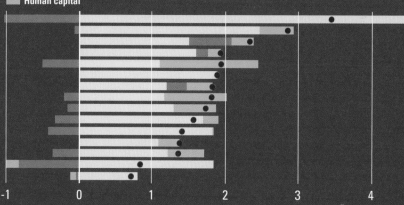

1. Based on the following decomposition: growth in GDP per person employed = (changes in hourly GDP per efficient unit of labour) + (changes in average hours worked) + (changes in human capital).
2. 1990-1999.
3. Mainland only.
4. 1991-2000.

Fig. 1.3

## IT investment in selected OECD countries

As a percentage of non-residential gross fixed capital formation, total economy

- 1980
- 1990
- 2001[1]

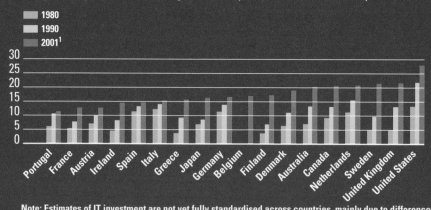

Note: Estimates of IT investment are not yet fully standardised across countries, mainly due to differences in the capitalisation of software in different countries. See Ahmad (2003)
1. Or latest available year.

Source: OECD Productivity Database.

Fig. 1.4

## Share of the IT sector in value added, non agricultural business sector, 2000

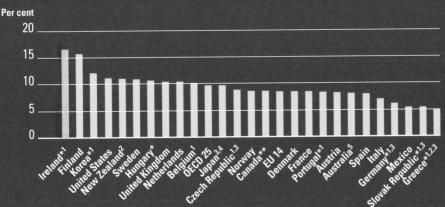

Per cent

* 1999 ** 1998
1. Excludes rental of IT (ISIC 7123).
2. Includes postal services.
3. Excludes IT wholesale (ISIC 5150).
4. Includes only part of computer-related activities.
5. 2000-2001.

Source: OECD (2002), Measuring the Information Economy, www.oecd.org/sti/measuring-infoeconomy

Fig. 1.5

## IT use varies widely across sectors: information technology as a percentage of all stock of equipment and software, United States, 2001

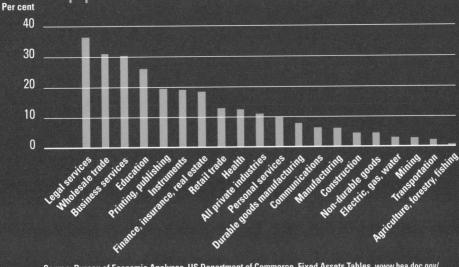

Per cent

Source: Bureau of Economic Analyses, US Department of Commerce, Fixed Assets Tables, www.bea.doc.gov/

generate the skills and competencies needed to benefit from IT use. And it could also lead to spin-offs, as in the case of Silicon Valley or in other high technology clusters.

In most OECD countries, the IT sector is relatively small, although it has grown rapidly over the 1990s. In 2000, value added in the IT sector represented between 4% and 17% of business sector value added [● Fig.1.4]. Moreover, about 6-7% of total business employment in the OECD area can be attributed to IT production. Trade in IT has also grown very rapidly, growing from just over 12% of total trade in 1990, to almost 18% in 2000 [❶ 1].

## Growth performances in OECD countries

### The contribution of IT to growth

A third factor that affects the impact of IT in different OECD countries is the distribution of IT across the economy. In contrast to Solow's famous remark "*You see computers everywhere but in the productivity statistics*" [❶ 2]; computers are, in fact, heavily concentrated in the service sector. ● Fig.1.5 shows evidence for the United States. It shows the share of the total stock of equipment and software that is accounted for by IT equipment and software (excluding communications equipment). The graph shows that more than 30% of the total stock of equipment and software in legal services, business services and wholesale trade consists of IT and software. Education, financial services, health, retail trade and a number of manufacturing industries (instruments and printing and publishing) also have a relatively large share of IT capital in their total stock of equipment and software. The average for all private industries is just over 11%. The goods-producing sectors (agriculture, mining, manufacturing and construction) are much less IT-intensive; in several of these industries less than 5% of total equipment and software consists of IT.

The relative distribution of IT investment across sectors for other OECD countries is not very different for other OECD countries [❶ 3]; services sectors such as wholesale trade and financial services are typically the most intensive users of IT. This may suggest that any impacts on economic performance might be more visible in the services sectors than in other parts of the economy. Nevertheless, IT is commonly considered to be a general-purpose technology, as all sectors of the economy use information in their production process, which implies that all sectors might be able to benefit from the use of IT.

❶ 1 OECD (2002),
*Measuring the Information Economy*,
2002, www.oecd.org/sti/
measuring-infoeconomy

❶ 2 Solow, R.M. (1987),
"We'd Better Watch Out",
*New York Times*, July 12,
Book Review, No. 36.

❶ 3 Pilat, D.
F. Lee and B. van Ark (2002),
"Production and use of ICT:
A sectoral perspective on productivity growth in the OECD area",
*OECD Economic Studies*, No. 35.

## Growth performances in OECD countries:
# Key conclusions

- The production and utilisation of new technologies was found to explain a large part of the increased productivity in a number of countries (e.g. United States, United Kingdom, Sweden).

- Policies of certain countries to reintegrate low-skilled workers resulted in a widening of the employment base and increased potential growth. However, one side effect of this improved employment performance was to depress temporarily productivity growth.

# Key questions

- **How important are education and other aspects of "human capital" to growth?**

- **What contribution does innovation make?**

- **What impact do macroeconomic policies and conditions, such as inflation and trade, have on economic growth?**

# Chapter 2

# Macro-level analysis

## The role of economic policy and other structural factors

In examining the main drivers of long-term economic growth, there is a potentially significant role for economic policy and other determinants of the economic environment within which firms operate in explaining differences in growth performance.

The following section examines the impact of human capital, R&D activity, macroeconomic and structural policy settings, trade policy and financial market conditions on economic efficiency.

In addition, it provides an assessment of the indirect impact of these factors on growth via their impact on investment spending.

Examining the links between these factors and growth also helps to gauge the medium-term growth outlook for countries that have changed their policy settings in recent years, and for whom the full effects of these reforms may not yet have materialised.

# Basic determinants of growth

## Education

The magnitude of the impact of human capital on growth found in this analysis might be interpreted as suggesting that the economy-wide returns to investment in education may be larger than those experienced by individuals. If this were the case, it could be through spillover effects, such as a positive link between education levels and advances in technology, through which human capital may not only affect the level of long-run output per capita, but may also have more persistent effects on its growth rate. Expenditures on education and training could therefore have a more permanent impact on the growth process if high skills and training go hand-in-hand with the process of innovation, leading to a faster rate of technological progress, or if a highly skilled workforce eases the adoption of new technologies. Advances in technology indeed often have strong links with education, especially at the higher level. Thus, education may not only make a contribution to growth via improvements in the quality of the workforce but also a contribution via innovation. If this is the case, policies aimed at encouraging individuals to engage in education for longer periods would clearly be beneficial to the economy as a whole, rather than just to the individuals concerned.

However, there are some caveats to this interpretation of the results. First, the impact of education may be overestimated because the indicator of human capital may be acting partially as a proxy for other variables. The indicators of human capital used in the analysis are relatively crude and somewhat narrow, taking little account of the quality aspects of formal education or other important dimensions of human capital, such as on-the-job training. Finally, extending the period of formal education may not be the most efficient way of providing workplace skills, and this aspect of education must also be balanced against other goals of education systems. Thus, for those countries at the forefront of education provision, the growth dividend from further increases in formal education may be less marked than that implied in this analysis.

## Innovation

At the macroeconomic level, innovation contributes to the three drivers of output growth: capital, labour and multi-factor productivity (MFP). Countries that registered above-average growth performance in the 1990s generally drew more people into employment; accumulated more capital; improved the quality of their workforces; and, in many cases, improved MFP. The contribution of innovation to MFP growth has long been recognised: increased MFP reflects greater overall efficiency in the use of labour and capital and is driven by technological and non-technological innovation – improved management practices, organisational changes, and improved ways of producing goods and services in response to evolving consumer and societal needs. However, innovation also creates new products that become part of the capital stock used by firms in generating their own economic output. Companies in the IT sector, which have been the most dynamic component of business investment and have made significant contributions to economic growth in many fast-growing economies, have experienced extremely high rates of technological innovation in the past decade. Similarly, improvements in the quality of the workforce are often a response to the needs of firms that were innovative in the development and/or adoption of new technologies.

The importance of innovation in driving growth can be seen in comparisons of various indicators of innovation's contribution to growth rates. Countries that experienced accelerated rates of growth in MFP between the 1980s and 1990s (Australia, Canada, Denmark, Finland, Ireland, New Zealand, Norway, Sweden, the United States) tended to have above-average rates of growth in patenting. This held true even for the United States, which had a high patenting rate even at the beginning of the 1990s and might have been expected to face greater difficulties in increasing its rate of patenting and its rate of growth. Of course, patents do not measure innovation directly, but by sampling an important fraction of inventive activity they can provide useful insight into innovative performance. The growing rate of patenting and the rising share of high-technology goods in trade among OECD countries further suggest that innovation plays an increasingly important role in economic growth.

Expenditure on R&D can be considered as an investment in knowledge that can translate into new technologies and more efficient ways of using existing resources. Insofar as it is successful in these respects, it is therefore plausible that higher R&D expenditure would result in higher growth rates. The potential benefits from new ideas may not accrue fully to the innovators themselves due to spillover effects, implying that without policy intervention the private sector would probably engage in less R&D than is socially optimal. This can justify some government involvement, both through direct provision and funding, but also through indirect measures such as tax incentives and protection of intellectual property rights to encourage private-sector R&D.

Overall expenditure on R&D as a share of GDP has risen somewhat since the 1980s in most countries [● → Fig.2.1], largely reflecting increases in R&D in the business sector, which accounts for the majority of expenditure in this area in most OECD countries. On the contrary, publicly financed business-sector R&D has declined over the past decade [▯ → 1].

## Macro-level analysis

### Basic determinants of growth

*Innovation*

▯ → 1 OECD (2001),
OECD *Science, Technology and Industry Scoreboard – Towards a Knowledge-Based Economy.*

[2a] David, P.A.,
B.H. Hall, and A.A. Toole (1999),
"Is Public R&D a Complement
or Substitute for Private R&D?
A Review of the Econometric Evidence",
NBER Working Papers, No. 7373.

[2b] Guellec, D.
and B. van Pottelsberghe (2000),
"The Impact of Public R&D
Expenditure on Business R&D",
OECD STI Working Papers,
No. 2001/4.

## Macro-level analysis

### Basic determinants of growth

*Deregulation and investment*

## Technology spillover

*Partly due to data
limitations, some of the
beneficial impact of
technological development
is felt through channels
that are difficult to quantify.
Publicly funded basic
research, for example, may
provide the foundations for
more specific, production-
related research activity in
industry that has a more
direct impact on growth.
"Spillover" or "technology
transfer" effects are also
part of the catch-up process
that is thought to boost
growth in less developed
economies. These are
encouraged by foreign
direct investment and other
activities that lead to better
technology or improved
management practices
being imported from more
developed economies.*

An important policy consideration is whether public and private R&D are complements or substitutes, *i.e.* whether government spending on R&D adds to total investment in this area, or simply replaces activities that would otherwise have been undertaken by the private sector. Available empirical literature gives conflicting answers: a number of studies support the complementarity hypothesis, but others cite instances where publicly funded R&D displaces private investment [2]. A final consideration with respect to the role of public-sector R&D is that it is often directed at making improvements in areas such as defence and medical research, where the impact on output growth is indirect and could take some time to filter through. All in all, these considerations suggest that when taking R&D activity into account as an additional form of investment, the possible interactions between different forms of R&D expenditure and different forms of financing should also be considered.

The empirical results support previous evidence suggesting a significant effect of R&D activity on the growth process. Furthermore, regressions including separate variables for business-performed R&D and that performed by other institutions (mainly public research institutes) suggest that it is the former that drives the positive association between total R&D intensity and output growth. Indeed, the analysis suggests that public R&D has a negative impact on output growth, which would appear to support the "crowding-out" argument that public-sector R&D investment simply displaces private-sector activity. However, there are avenues for more complex effects that regression analysis cannot identify. For example, while business R&D is likely to be more directly targeted towards innovation and implementation of new production processes (leading quickly to improvements in productivity), other forms of R&D (*e.g.* in energy, health and university research) may not raise technology levels significantly in the short run. They may, though, generate basic knowledge with possible "technology spillovers". The latter are difficult to identify, not least because of the long lags involved and the possible interactions with improvements in human capital and other influences on growth.

### *Deregulation and investment*

In the past decade the rate of GDP growth has been remarkably different amongst OECD countries. One of the most striking and often cited comparisons is the one between the US with a 4.3% average GDP growth in the second half of the 1990s and large continental European economies (Germany, Italy and France) with 2% average growth. One commonly held explanation of these differences is that stricter regulation of markets has prevented faster growth in many European countries especially during the nineties. Various measures of product market regulation are negatively related to investment, which is, of course, an important engine of growth.

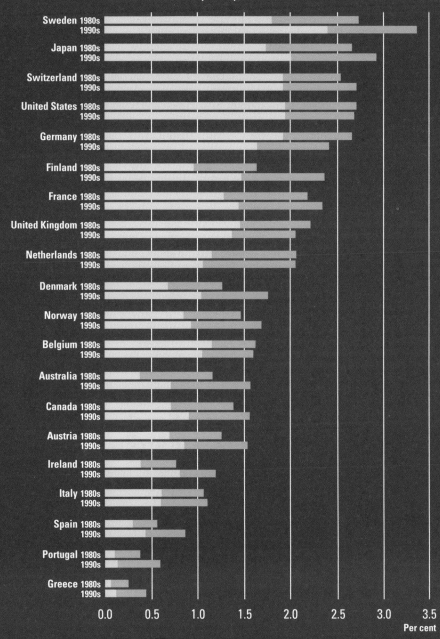

Fig. 2.1

**Private and public R&D budgets: business R&D has risen, government R&D budgets have declined**

Total expenditure on R&D as a percentage of GDP, 1980s and 1990s

■ Business-enterprise expenditure on R&D
■ Non-business-enterprise expenditure on R&D

Sweden 1980s / 1990s
Japan 1980s / 1990s
Switzerland 1980s / 1990s
United States 1980s / 1990s
Germany 1980s / 1990s
Finland 1980s / 1990s
France 1980s / 1990s
United Kingdom 1980s / 1990s
Netherlands 1980s / 1990s
Denmark 1980s / 1990s
Norway 1980s / 1990s
Belgium 1980s / 1990s
Australia 1980s / 1990s
Canada 1980s / 1990s
Austria 1980s / 1990s
Ireland 1980s / 1990s
Italy 1980s / 1990s
Spain 1980s / 1990s
Portugal 1980s / 1990s
Greece 1980s / 1990s

0.0   0.5   1.0   1.5   2.0   2.5   3.0   3.5

Per cent

In the last decade or so, most OECD countries have experienced some form of regulatory reforms (deregulation for short) implying entry liberalisation and privatisation. However, the timing, extent, nature, and starting point varies across countries. For instance, the United States started deregulating earlier than most, having begun in the seventies. In 1977, 17% of US GDP was produced by fully regulated industries, and by 1988 this total had been cut to 6.6% of GDP. Other early and decisive reformers include New Zealand and the United Kingdom, while Italy and France have been laggards.

We rely on these diverse histories to study the effects of regulatory reforms in sectors that have traditionally been most heavily sheltered from competition and have witnessed, at different times and to different degrees, some form of deregulation and privatisation in various countries. Specifically, we look at the effects of regulation on investment in the transport (airlines, road, freight and railways), communication (telecommunications and postal) and utilities (electricity and gas) sectors. We measure regulation with different time-varying-indicators that capture entry barriers and the extent of public ownership, among other things.

We find that regulatory reforms have had a significant positive impact on capital accumulation in the transport, communication, and utilities industries. In particular, liberalisation of entry in potentially competitive markets seems to have had the largest and most significant impact on private investment. The effect of privatisation is less clear-cut. On the one hand privatisation may lead to more profit opportunities for private firms; on the other hand public enterprises may over-invest if they pursue political objectives and/or if managers are not constrained by the discipline imposed by capital markets. There is also evidence that the marginal effect of deregulation on investment is greater when the policy reform is large and when changes occur starting from levels of regulation that are already low. In other words, small changes in a heavily regulated environment are not likely to produce much of an effect.

## Policy and institutional determinants of growth

In recent years most OECD countries have made significant steps towards low inflation and improved public finances. A number of studies have shown that these moves towards more stability-oriented macroeconomic policies have been beneficial, at least for a while. Three issues have received particular attention: the benefits of maintaining low and stable inflation, the impact of government deficits on private investment, and the possibility that an overly large public sector can have a negative impact on growth (due partly to the heavy tax burden required to finance high government expenditure).

### Macro-level analysis

**Policy and institutional determinants of growth**

### Hurdle rate

*The rate of return on an investment that businesses or individuals require in order to undertake that investment. High inflation and interest rates tend to raise hurdle rates, as the rate of return needs to be higher than the cost of borrowing or the return from using available funds for other purposes (such as deposits or other low-risk investments).*

## Inflation

The usual arguments for lower and more stable inflation rates include reduced uncertainty and enhanced efficiency of the price mechanism. Inflation can be considered as a tax on investment, as low levels of inflation may reduce the profit margin required before businesses will undertake an investment project (the so-called "hurdle rate" for investment). Low inflation could therefore have a positive impact on the accumulation of physical capital.

Theoretically, inflation could also have an effect on capital accumulation via its impact on economic uncertainty, as low inflation generally means more stable inflation and lower price volatility. Reduced uncertainty may, in turn, result in more stable output growth and improve the environment for private-sector investment decisions. Notably, if investment is irreversible (*i.e.* once a machine has been put in place it has no alternative use), then more stable output growth might prompt firms to raise their capital expenditure.

In testing these arguments, a simple comparison of inflation rates and growth rates for OECD countries suggests that the link between the level of inflation and output growth is not very strong [● ⋯ Fig.2.2]. The same is true of the relationship between the variability of inflation and changes in average growth rates from the 1980s to the 1990s [● ⋯ Fig.2.3]. In this latter case however, there are two clear outliers (Ireland and Greece) that weaken the relationship. Excluding these two countries, there is a rough negative relationship. Other things being equal, in countries that achieved a significant reduction in the variability of inflation, growth held up better than in others during the 1990s.

However, the empirical analysis suggests that these simple observations understate the relationship between inflation and growth, partly because they take no account of the influence of other factors. In fact, the OECD growth study shows that the variability of inflation is an important negative influence on output per capita. This supports the hypothesis that uncertainty about price developments affects growth via its impact on economic efficiency, for example by leading to a sub-optimal choice of potential investment projects with lower average returns. Conversely, the effect of the level of inflation is less clear-cut: in the trade-augmented specifications of the model, the level of inflation seems to have a negative and significant impact on the steady state level of GDP per capita, probably via its impact on competitiveness. However, when the trade variable is excluded, this relationship breaks down. The instability of the relationship between the level of inflation and growth may simply be a reflection of the fact that inflation is currently low in many OECD countries, and is therefore not producing the kind of distortions in the allocation of resources that are thought to retard growth. Indeed, economic theory lends some support to the idea that the link between inflation and growth is likely to be more uncertain at low levels of inflation [🔲→3]. On the one hand, it could be argued that further reductions in inflation, even towards zero inflation (or more stringently, price stability), would produce further benefits [🔲→4]. On the other hand, negative effects on growth may emerge due to nominal wage rigidities creating market inefficiencies [🔲→5].

There is also robust evidence that high inflation has a negative indirect impact on growth via its effect on investment. In contrast to the analysis of the direct effects on growth, the results suggests that it is the level of inflation, rather than its variability, that has the more significant negative impact on investment. This is probably because it leads to a shift in the composition of investment towards less risky, but also lower return, projects. This finding is consistent with the view that uncertainty about inflation, as captured by its variability, mainly influences growth via distortions in the allocation of resources (as discussed above), rather than by discouraging capital spending, while high levels of inflation reduce savings and investment.

## Fiscal policy

Most types of government expenditures probably have some impact on economic growth, either directly (for example through the accumulation of capital in housing, urban infrastructure, transport and communications) or indirectly by affecting incentives to invest in the private sector. All have to be financed. Analysing the impact of these expenditures on growth is not straightforward, in part because the mechanisms may be complex and slow to operate in some cases. Moreover, there is some evidence that the causation goes the other way, in that demand for government services such as health, education and law and order tends to rise as economies become more affluent. Growth could, therefore, influence the level of government expenditure, rather than the other way around.

In situations where public consumption or social transfers are financed by government deficits, a traditional argument for a more restrictive fiscal policy is to reduce the crowding out effects on private investment. Also, if fiscal policy is seen as being at odds with the objectives of monetary policy, the efficacy of the latter could be undermined, leading to higher interest rates and pressures on exchange rates. Where taxes are raised to support government spending, they may distort incentives, reduce the efficient allocation of resources and dampen output growth in the short term. At worst, according to some growth models allowing for endogenous growth effects, they may have a long-lasting negative

## Macro-level analysis

**Policy and institutional determinants of growth**

*Fiscal policy*

🔲→3a Edey, M. (1994), "Costs and Benefits From Moving from Low Inflation to Price Stability", *OECD Economic Studies*, No. 23.

3b Bruno, M. and W. Easterly (1998), "Inflation Crises and Long-run Growth", *Journal of Monetary Economics*, Vol. 41.

🔲→4 Feldstein, M. (1996), "The Costs and Benefits of Going from Low Inflation to Price Stability", *NBER Working Papers*, No. 5469.

🔲→5 Akerlof, G.A., W.T. Dickens and G.L. Perry. (1996), "The Macroeconomics of Low Inflation", *Brookings Papers on Economic Activity*, Vol. 1.

Fig. 2.2

## Level of inflation and economic growth

Average growth and median inflation in equal-sized samples
of annual inflation and growth data

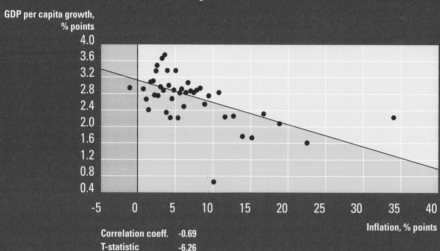

Correlation coeff.   -0.69
T-statistic          -6.26

Note: Individual observations across countries and time are first ranked by the level of inflation. These ranked observations, coupled with corresponding data on growth in GDP per capita growth rates, were then divided into successive groups of 20 observations. The points shown in the figure represent the median inflation of each group and the corresponding average growth in GDP per capita.

Fig. 2.3

## Variability of inflation and growth between the 1980s and 1990s

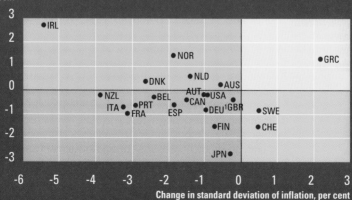

Correlation coeff. -0.32
T-statistic        -1.49

1. Western Germany before 1991.

impact. In any event, these negative effects may be more evident where expenditure is financed by so-called "distortionary taxes" and where public expenditure focuses on areas not directly related to growth.

The bottom line from the literature is that there may be both a "size" effect of government intervention as well as specific effects stemming from the financing and composition of public expenditure. At a low level, the productive effects of some components of public expenditure are likely to be beneficial for output growth. However, government expenditure, and the taxes required to finance it, may reach levels where the negative effects on efficiency start to dominate. This could reflect the extension of government involvement into activities that might be more efficiently carried out by the private sector, and/or misguided or inefficient systems of transfers and subsidies.

## Macro-level analysis

### Policy and institutional determinants of growth

*Fiscal policy*

Between the 1980s and 1990s the size of the public sector tended to increase in most OECD countries, as did government gross liabilities, although the most recent years have seen some reversal of this trend. Notwithstanding these latter developments, in 1999 the share of total government expenditure in GDP was still in the range of 40-50% in a number of OECD countries. Moreover, less than a fifth of expenditure is typically allocated to areas more directly related to growth (*e.g.* schooling, infrastructure and R&D), and in a number of countries, the share of these "productive" expenditures has declined over the past decade [ ● → Table 2.1].

The empirical analysis considered three main aspects of the impact of fiscal policy on growth:

## Distortionary taxes

*Distortionary taxes affect the economic choices of households and firms, notably with respect to the level and composition of their (human and physical) capital investment. By contrast, non-distortionary taxes are more neutral. Non-distortionary taxes mainly relate to taxation on domestic goods and services, while distortionary taxes include taxation on income and profits, as well as taxation on payroll and manpower.*

- the overall "size" effect;
- the role of the tax structure on the one hand and the composition of expenditure on the other;
- and an analysis of the direct and indirect effects of these policy variables, by separately testing their significance for private investment and, directly, for growth itself.

The results of the empirical analysis tentatively support the hypothesis that the size of government has a detrimental impact on growth. The overall tax burden is estimated to have a negative impact on output per capita and, controlling for this factor, an additional negative effect is found for systems that rely heavily on direct taxes. These results provide some support for the idea that increases in taxes as a result of high government spending could have an overall negative impact on output per capita, by influencing the efficiency of resource allocation across different investment projects. The composition of expenditures also appears to be important: as both government consumption and investment seem to have a positive impact on output per capita, this implies that the type of expenditure omitted from this analysis, *i.e.* public transfers, is behind the negative effects detected for total financing.

There is also some evidence that the extent of public sector involvement in the economy may be negatively associated with the rate of accumulation of private capital, suggesting a further indirect impact on economic growth via its effect on investment.

## International trade

Aside from the benefits of exploiting comparative advantages, economic theory suggests that there may be additional gains from trade arising through economies of scale, exposure to competition and the diffusion of knowledge. Past progress in reducing tariff barriers and dismantling non-tariff barriers has almost certainly opened up opportunities to gains from trade.

However, OECD countries already have a generally open stance towards trade, suggesting that the volume of trade conducted depends at least partly on patterns of growth (and, to some extent, geography, size and transport costs) rather than just on tariff and non-tariff barriers. For this reason, the intensity of trade variable used in the empirical analysis should be considered more as an indicator of trade exposure – capturing features such as competitive pressures – rather than one with direct policy implications. Moreover, the empirical analysis also has to take into account the fact that small countries are naturally more exposed to foreign trade, regardless of their trade policy or competitiveness, while competitive pressures within large countries to a great extent stem from domestic competition. To better reflect overall competitive pressures, the indicator of trade exposure was therefore adjusted for country size.

●⇢ Fig.2.4 plots country differences in this "corrected" measure of trade exposure and its evolution over the past decade. As expected, although significant differences remain across the board, exposure to foreign trade has increased in OECD countries, possibly fostering technology transfer and growth. The analysis suggests that an increase in trade exposure of 10 percentage points – which is roughly the change that has actually been observed over the past two decades in the OECD sample – could lead to an increase in steady-state output per capita of 4%.

## The financial system

Financial systems play a role in the growth process because they are key to the provision of funding for capital accumulation and the diffusion of new technologies. A well-developed financial system:

- mobilises savings, by channelling the small-denomination savings of individuals into profitable large-scale investments, while offering savers a high degree of liquidity;
- reduces the risks to individual savers by allowing diversification of investments;

Table 2.1

**Expenditures contributing directly to growth**
Percentage

| | A Education | | B Transport and communicati• | |
|---|---|---|---|---|
| | 1985 | 1995 | 1985 | 1995 |
| Australia | 14.6 | 13.2 | 10.1 | 8.3 |
| Austria | 9.6 | 9.5 | 3.3 | 2.1 |
| Belgium | 12.7 | .. | 8.7 | .. |
| Canada | 13.0 | .. | 5.4 | .. |
| Denmark | 11.3 | 11.7 | 4.0 | 3.0 |
| France[1] | 10.5 | 10.7 | 2.9 | 1.9 |
| Germany | 9.5 | 7.6 | 4.3 | 3.4 |
| Iceland | 13.0 | 12.3 | 9.0 | 7.6 |
| Ireland[1] | 10.6 | 12.2 | 4.5 | 5.0 |
| Italy | 10.0 | 8.9 | 7.7 | 4.6 |
| Japan | 12.8 | 10.8[4] | .. | .. |
| Korea | 17.8 | 18.1 | 7.1 | 9.6 |
| Netherlands | 9.9 | .. | .. | .. |
| New Zealand | .. | 13.3[4] | .. | .. |
| Norway | 12.0[3] | 13.7 | 6.6[3] | 5.9 |
| Portugal[2] | 8.7 | 13.3 | 3.6 | 4.8 |
| Spain | 8.8 | 10.3 | 6.3 | 6.0 |
| Sweden | .. | .. | .. | .. |
| Switzerland | 19.7 | .. | 11.4 | .. |
| United Kingdom | 10.2 | 12.1 | 3.2 | 3.6 |
| United States | .. | .. | .. | .. |

1. 1993 instead of 1995.
2. 1992 instead of 1995.
3. 1988.
4. 1994.
5. 1984.
6. 1986.
7. 1987.

| C R&D | | A+B+C | | Share of total government outlays in GDP | | |
|---|---|---|---|---|---|---|
| 1985 | 1995 | 1985 | 1995 | 1985 | 1995 | 2000 |
| 2.1[5] | 2.2[4] | 26.8 | 23.6 | 38.0 | 35.7 | 32.6 |
| 1.2 | 1.4 | 14.1 | 13.0 | 50.3 | 52.5 | 47.9 |
| 0.9 | .. | 22.3 | .. | 57.1 | 50.2 | 46.7 |
| 1.5 | .. | 19.8 | .. | 45.2 | 45.0 | 37.7 |
| 1.2 | 1.2 | 16.4 | 15.9 | 54.2[3] | 56.6 | 49.9 |
| 2.3 | 1.8 | 15.7 | 14.4 | 51.9 | 53.5 | 51.0 |
| 2.2 | 1.8 | 16.0 | 12.9 | 45.6 | 46.3 | 43.3 |
| 1.6 | 2.5 | 23.6 | 22.4 | 35.3 | 39.2 | 38.5 |
| 0.8 | 0.8 | 15.9 | 18.0 | 50.7 | 38.0 | 29.3 |
| 1.2 | 1.0 | 18.8 | 14.5 | 49.7 | 51.1 | 44.4 |
| 1.8 | 1.9 | .. | .. | 29.4 | 34.4 | 36.6 |
| .. | 2.7 | .. | 30.4 | 17.6 | 19.3 | 23.1 |
| 1.8 | .. | .. | .. | 51.9 | 47.7 | 41.6 |
| .. | 1.3[1] | .. | .. | 51.8[6] | 38.6 | 38.6 |
| 1.6 | 1.6 | 20.2 | 21.3 | 41.5 | 47.6 | 40.8 |
| 0.5[5] | 0.9 | 12.9 | 19.0 | 39.9 | 41.3 | 40.8 |
| 0.7 | 0.9 | 15.8 | 17.1 | 39.7 | 44.0 | 38.8 |
| 1.7 | 1.7 | .. | .. | 60.4 | 61.9 | 52.7 |
| .. | .. | .. | .. | .. | .. | .. |
| 2.0 | 1.5 | 15.5 | 17.2 | 40.5[7] | 42.2 | 37.0 |
| 4.1 | 2.8 | .. | .. | 33.8 | 32.9 | 29.9 |

- reduces the costs of acquiring and evaluating information on prospective projects, for example through specialised investment services;
- helps to monitor investments to reduce the risk of resource mismanagement. All these services are likely to contribute to economic growth but there could, in theory, also be opposite effects. For example, lower risk and higher returns resulting from diversification may prompt households to save less.

Unfortunately, the range of suitable indicators to allow an analysis of the impact of the financial sector on growth is limited. In this study, two indicators were considered:

- total claims of deposit money banks on the private sector, which measures the degree of financial intermediation via the banking system.
- stock market capitalisation (the value of listed shares), which is an imperfect indicator of the ease with which funds can be raised on the equity market. However, both indicators point to significant development in the financial systems of most OECD countries between the 1980s and the 1990s [● → Fig.2.5].

The results of the analysis point to a robust link between stock market capitalisation and growth, but, somewhat counter-intuitively, show a negative relationship between private credit provided to the private sector and growth. However, the banking credit indicator is not independent from other monetary variables, being strongly related to money supply and demand conditions. A more suitable model that also includes an inflation variable points to a positive relationship between private credit and growth. Overall, these results provide general support to the notion that the level of financial development influences growth, over and above its potential effect on investment. This perhaps points to a greater capacity of more developed financial systems to channel resources towards projects with higher returns.

Finally, financial development might also positively affect investment. As in the growth analysis, the indicator of credit provided by the banking sector appears to be only weakly associated with investment, while the stock market capitalisation has a stronger effect. These results are consistent with a number of empirical studies attempting to explain cross-country differences in growth across a broad range of countries (including OECD and non-OECD economies), which have concluded that financial development plays a significant role [■ → 6].

## Macro-level analysis

### Policy and institutional determinants of growth

*The financial system*

■ → 6a Levine, R. (1997), "Financial Development and Economic Growth: Views and Agendas", *Journal of Economic Literature*, Vol. 35, No. 2.

6b Levine, R., N. Loayza and T. Beck (2000), "Financial Intermediation and Growth: Causality and Causes", *Journal of Monetary Economics*, Vol. 46, No. 1.

6c Temple, J. (1999), "The New Growth Evidence", *Journal of Economic Literature*, Vol. 37, No. 1.

## The overall impact

The results of the previous section can be used to assess the effect of a given change in a policy or institutional variable on steady-state output per capita. Two important caveats need to be borne in mind in this exercise. First, as discussed above, it has been assumed that the policy and institutional variables affect only the level of economic efficiency and not its steady-state growth rate: the magnitude of the growth effects of some policy changes may, therefore, possibly be underestimated. Second, the calculations should only be taken as broad indications, given the variability of coefficients across the specifications and interaction effects between variables that may be important but cannot be taken into account.

Bearing in mind the illustrative nature of this exercise, the estimated direct effects (derived from the growth equations that control for the level of investment) and indirect effects (derived by combining the effect on investment with that of the latter on output per capita) of policy variables are as follows [● · Table 2.2]:

- The point estimate for the variability of inflation suggests that a reduction by 1 percentage point in the standard deviation in inflation – *i.e.* about one half of the reduction recorded on average in the OECD countries from the 1980s to the 1990s – could lead to a 2% increase in long-run output per capita.

- The effect of the level of inflation mainly works through investment: a reduction of one percentage point – *i.e.* one-fourth of that recorded in the OECD between the 1980s and 1990s – could lead to an increase in output per capita of about 0.13%, over and above what could emerge from any accompanying reduction in the variability of inflation.

- Taxes and government expenditures seem to affect growth both directly and indirectly through investment. An increase of about one percentage point in the overall tax level – *i.e.* slightly less than has been observed over the past two decades in the OECD sample – could be associated with a direct reduction of about 0.3% in output per capita. If the investment effect is taken into account, the overall reduction would be about 0.6-0.7%.

- A persistent 0.1 percentage point increase in R&D intensity (an increase of about 10% with respect to average R&D intensity) would have a long-run effect of raising output per capita by 1.2% under the "conservative" interpretation of

Fig. 2.4

## Increasing exposure of several OECD countries to foreign trade

Size-adjusted exposure to foreign trade, 1980s and 1990s

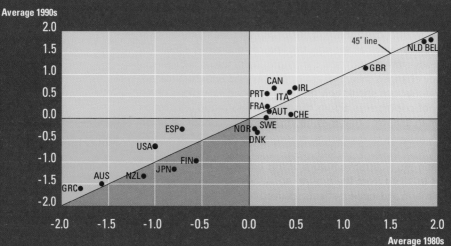

Note: The indicator of exposure to foreign trade is a weighted average of export intensity and import penetration, adjusted for country size (i.e. it is the residual from the regression of the weighted average of export intensity and import penetration on population size). The data reported in the figure are standardised to ease cross-country comparison.

Fig. 2.6

## The contribution of investment in IT capital to GDP growth

Percentage points contribution to annual average GDP growth, total economy

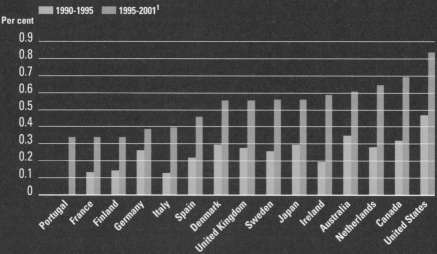

1. Or latest available year, i.e. 1995-2000 for Denmark, Finland, Ireland, Japan, Netherlands, Portugal and Sweden.
Note: See Schreyer et al. (2003) for methodological details.

Source: OECD estimates based on OECD Productivity Database.

Fig. 2.5

## Developments in financial systems

Panel A. Deposit money banks credit to the private sector as percentage of GDP.

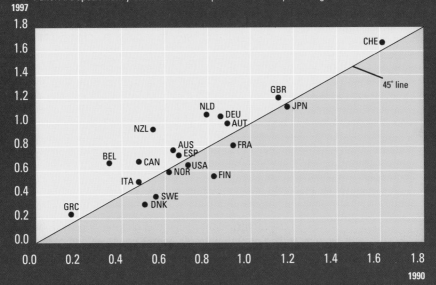

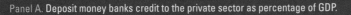

Panel B. Stock market capitalisation as percentage of GDP.

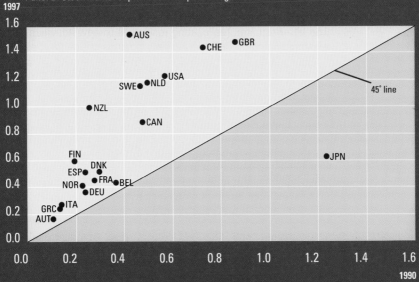

Source: World Bank.

the estimation results. However, in the case of R&D it is perhaps more appropriate to consider the results as reflecting a permanent effect on growth of GDP per capita (*i.e.* a fall in R&D intensity is not likely to reduce the steady-state level of GDP per capita but rather reduce technical progress). If the R&D coefficient is taken to represent growth effects, a 0.1 percentage point increase in R&D could boost output per capita growth by some 0.2%. These estimated effects are large, perhaps unreasonably so, but nevertheless point to significant externalities in R&D activities.

• Finally, an increase in trade exposure of 10 percentage points – about the change observed over the past two decades in the OECD sample – could lead to an increase in steady-state output per capita of 4 per cent.

Although the factors identified in this chapter appear to be crucial to understanding growth patterns across countries and over time, there are a number of additional determinants that could not be directly analysed. In particular, in the current period, characterised by a process of adaptation to information and communication technologies, a number of other policy and institutional factors are also likely to play a key role by influencing the ability of markets to adapt to the new technologies. The latter requires reallocating resources to new activities, reshaping existing firms and discovering new business opportunities. The next chapter will look at these institutional and policy factors, exploring their impact on the performance of industries and individual firms.

Table 2.2

**Estimated impact of changes in institutional
or policy factors on output per capita[1]**

| Variable | Impact on output per working age person (per cent)[2] | | | Order of magnitude with respect to OECD experience (1980s-90s)[3] |
|---|---|---|---|---|
| | Effect via economic efficiency | Effect via investment | Overall effect | |
| Inflation rate (fall of 1% point) | | 0.4 to 0.5 | 0.4 to 0.5 | About 1/4 of the observed fall |
| Variability of inflation (1% point fall in SD of inflation) | 2.0 | | 2.0 | About 1.5 times the observed fall |
| Tax burden[4] (increase of 1% point) | -0.3 | -0.3 to -0.4 | -0.6 to -0.7 | About 2/3 of the observed increase |
| Business R&D intensity[4] (increase of 0.1% points) | 1.2 | | 1.2 | About the increase observed |
| Trade exposure[4] (increase of 10% points) | 4.0 | | 4.0 | About the increase observed |

1. The values reported in this table are the estimated long-run effects on output per working-age person of a given policy change. The range reported reflects the values obtained in different specifications of the growth equation.

2. The direct effect refers to the impact on output per capita over and above any potential influence on the accumulation of physical capital. The indirect effect refers to the combined impact of the variable on the investment rate and by that channel, on output per capita.

3. Average change from the 1980 average to the 1990 average in the sample of 21 OECD countries, excluding new members as well as Iceland, Luxembourg and Turkey.

4. In percentage of GDP.

# The contribution of IT at the macro level

Evidence of the role of IT investment is primarily available at the macroeconomic level, *e.g.* from Colecchia and Schreyer [▓▶ 7] and Van Ark, *et al* [▓▶ 8]. Both studies show that IT has been a very dynamic area of investment, due to the steep decline in IT prices which has encouraged investment in IT, at times shifting investment away from other assets. While IT investment accelerated in most OECD countries, the pace of that investment and its impact on growth differed widely.

For the countries for which data are available, growth accounting estimates show that IT investment typically accounted for between 0.3 and 0.8 percentage points of growth in GDP per capita over the 1995-2001 period [● ▶ Fig.2.6]. The United States, Australia, the Netherlands and Canada received the largest boost; Japan and the United Kingdom a more modest one, and Germany, France and Italy a much smaller one. Software accounted for up to a third of the overall contribution of IT investment to GDP growth in OECD countries.

The results of these two cross-country studies have been confirmed by many studies for individual countries, which are summarised in ● ▶ Table 2.3. National studies may differ from the results shown in ● ▶ Fig.2.6, due to differences in measurement. France and the United States, for instance, use specially designed "hedonic" deflators for computer equipment: these deflators adjust prices for key quality changes induced by technological progress, like higher processing speed and greater disk capacity. They tend to show faster declines in computer prices than conventional price indexes, and that means more rapid growth in real terms. As a result, countries that use hedonic indexes are likely to record faster real growth in investment and production of information and communications technology (IT) than countries that do not use them. This faster real growth will translate into a larger contribution of IT capital to growth performance.

The method used in the work by Colecchia and Schreyer [▓▶ 7] and Van Ark, *et al.* [▓▶ 8] adjusts for these differences. They are therefore more comparable than the results of individual national studies. Nevertheless, the national studies typically show the same countries as experiencing a large impact of IT investment on growth, notably Australia, Canada, Korea, the United Kingdom and the United States.

The impact of IT investment on economic growth has not ended with the recent slowdown. While IT investment has slowed down over the past year, technological progress in the production of computers, *i.e.* the release of increasingly powerful computer chips, is projected to continue for the foreseeable future.

---

## Macro-level analysis

**The contribution of IT at the macro level**

---

▓▶ 7 Colecchia, A. and P. Schreyer (2001), "The Impact of Information Communications Technology on Output Growth", *OECD STI Working Papers*, No. 2001/7.

▓▶ 8 van Ark, B., R. Inklaar and R.H. McGuckin (2002), "'Changing gear' Productivity, ICT and Services: Europe and the United States", Research Memorandum GD-60, Groningen Growth and Development Centre.

Table 2.3

## The impact of IT investment on GDP growth results from national studies

| Country | GDP growth | | Labour prod. growth | | Contribution of IT | | Notes | |
|---|---|---|---|---|---|---|---|---|
| | 1990 1995 | 1995 2000 | 1990 1995 | 1995 2000 | 1990 1995 | 1995 2000 | | |
| **United States** | | | | | | | | |
| Oliner and Sichel (2002) | .. | .. | 1.5 | 2.3 | 0.5 | 1.0 | 1991-95 | 1996-2001 |
| Jorgenson, et al. (2002) | 2.5 | 4.0 | 1.4 | 2.7 | 0.5 | 1.0 | 1990-95 | 1995-99 |
| BLS (2002) | .. | .. | 1.5 | 2.7 | 0.4 | 0.9 | 1990-95 | 1995-2000 |
| **Japan** | | | | | | | | |
| Miyagawa, et al. (2002) | .. | .. | 2.2 | 1.4 | 0.1 | 0.4 | 1990-95 | 1995-98 |
| Motohashi (2002) | 1.7 | 1.5 | .. | .. | 0.2 | 0.5 | 1990-95 | 1995-2000 |
| **Germany** | | | | | | | | |
| RWI and Gordon (2002) | 2.2 | 2.5 | 2.6 | 2.1 | 0.4 | 0.5 | 1990-95 | 1995-2000 |
| **France** | | | | | | | | |
| Cette, et al. (2002) | 0.5 | 2.2 | 1.6 | 1.1 | 0.2 | 0.3 | 1990-95 | 1995-2000 |
| **United Kingdom** | | | | | | | | |
| Oulton (2001) | 1.4 | 3.1 | 3.0 | 1.5 | 0.4 | 0.6 | 1989-94 | 1994-98 |
| **Canada** | | | | | | | | |
| Armstrong, et al. (2002) | 1.5 | 4.9 | .. | .. | 0.4 | 0.7 | 1988-95 | 1995-2000 |
| Khan and Santos (2002) | 1.9 | 4.8 | .. | .. | 0.3 | 0.5 | 1991-95 | 1996-2000 |
| **Australia** | | | | | | | | |
| Parhann, et al. (2001) | .. | .. | 2.1 | 3.7 | 0.7 | 1.3 | 89/90-94/95 | 94/95-99/00 |
| Simon and Wardrop (2002) | 1.8 | 4.9 | 2.2 | 4.2 | 0.9 | 1.3 | 1991-95 | 1996-2000 |
| Gretton, et al. (2002) | .. | .. | 2.2 | 3.5 | 0.6 | 1.1 | 89/90-94/95 | 94/95-99/00 |
| **Belgium** | | | | | | | | |
| Kegels, et al. (2002) | 1.5 | 2.8 | 1.9 | 1.9 | 0.3 | 0.5 | 1991-95 | 1995-2000 |
| **Finland** | | | | | | | | |
| Jalava and Pohjola (2002) | .. | .. | 3.9 | 3.5 | 0.6 | 0.5 | 1990-95 | 1996-99 |
| **Korea** | | | | | | | | |
| Kim (2002) | 7.5 | 5.0 | .. | .. | 1.4 | 1.2 | 1991-95 | 1996-2000 |
| **Netherlands** | | | | | | | | |
| Van der Wiel (2001) | .. | .. | 1.3 | 1.5 | 0.4 | 0.6 | 1991-95 | 1996-2000 |

▣┄▸ 9a McKinsey (2001),
*US Productivity Growth 1995-2000:*
*Understanding the Contribution*
*of Information Technology*
*Relative to Other Factors,*
McKinsey Global Institute, October.

9b Gordon, R.J. (2003),
"Hi-Tech Innovation and Productivity Growth:
Does Supply Create Its Own Demand?",
*NBER Working Papers,* No. 9437.

## Macro-level analysis

### The contribution of IT at the macro level

Technological progress is also continuing at a rapid pace in other IT technologies, such as communications technologies. This implies that quality-adjusted IT prices will continue to decline, thus encouraging IT investment and further productivity growth. The level of IT investment is likely to be lower than that observed prior to the slowdown, however, in particular in the United States, as the 1995-2000 period was characterised by some one-off investment peaks, *e.g.* investments related to Y2K and the diffusion of the Internet [▣┄▸ 9].

## Macro-Level analysis:
# Key conclusions

- Sound macro-policy settings are conducive
  to higher growth paths. In particular,
  the reduction in the levels of inflation
  in most OECD countries could have stimulated
  the accumulation of physical capital
  in the private sector and, through this channel,
  had a positive bearing on output.

- Empirical evidence lends some support
  to the notion that the overall size of government
  in the economy may reach levels
  that hinder growth.

- Research and development activities undertaken
  by the business sector seem to have high social
  returns, while no clear-cut relationship
  could be established between R&D activities
  and growth undertaken by governments
  and universities. There are, however,
  possible interactions and international spillovers
  that the regression analysis cannot identify.
  Moreover, certain public R&D
  (e.g. energy, health and university research)
  may in the long run generate basic knowledge,
  with possible "technology spillovers".

- Empirical evidence also confirms the importance
  of financial markets and open trading systems
  for growth, both by helping to channel resources
  towards the most rewarding activities,
  and in encouraging investment.

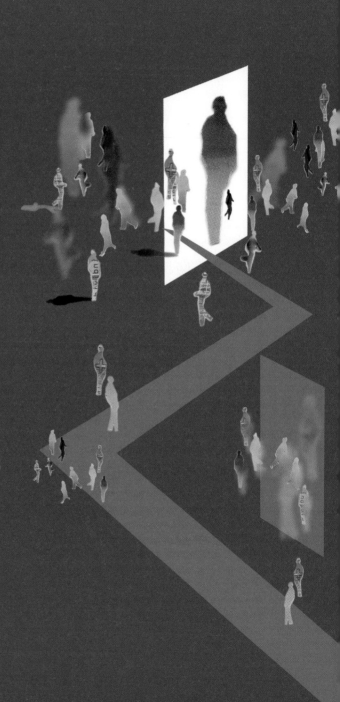

# Chapter 3

## Industry-level analysis

# Key questions

- **What are the factors that affect industry-level productivity and how do they relate to multi-factor productivity (MFP)?**

- **How do institutional settings and labour market policies affect growth?**

- **Is there any correlation between product market regulations and productivity?**

# Industry-level analysis

## Market dynamics and productivity

Assessing the role of policy and institutions
in determining long-term growth cannot be limited
to aggregate analysis. It also requires an exploration
of the role played by developments within individual industries
and the reallocation of resources across industries and firms.

Indeed, the macro-level analysis in the previous chapter
may fail to capture the effects of specific policies
– such as product market regulations and trade restrictions –
on industry performance. Likewise, differences in growth
patterns at the industry level may also point to variations in
the extent to which countries are benefiting from broader
economic changes, or from the potential offered by new
technologies.

For example, as discussed in Chapter 1, technological change
has enabled rapid productivity growth in the IT-producing
industry and, most recently, in IT-using industries, but there
are considerable variations in the degree to which countries
have benefited from these opportunities.

This chapter is devoted to an exploration of these aspects of
growth by using industry-level data.

# Industry growth

### *Structure and labour*

From a long-term historical perspective, structural shifts have been an important factor in generating growth. Historically, resources have been switched from low-productivity agricultural sectors to more productive manufacturing industries. More recently, of course, there has been a rapid expansion of the service sector. However, in the short and medium-term, data seems to suggest that a substantial contribution to overall productivity growth also comes from productivity changes within industries, rather than as a result of significant shifts of employment across industries. This can be seen in ●⋯ Fig.3.1, which presents a decomposition of labour productivity growth in the business sector into three elements:

- An "intra-sectoral effect", measuring productivity growth within industries;

- A "net-shift effect", measuring the impact on productivity of the shift in employment between industries;

- And a residual third effect, the "interaction effect". This effect is positive when sectors with growing productivity have a rising employment share or when industries with falling relative productivity decline in size. It is negative when industries with growing relative productivity decline in size or when industries with falling productivity grow in size.

The results of these calculations show that the intra-industry effect is the most important contributor to productivity growth in the non-farm business sector [●⋯ Fig.3.1]. The net-shift effect also makes an important contribution, due notably to the increased size of the business services sector, but its impact seems to fade out during the 1990s. The interaction effect tends to be negative for most countries. These results are confirmed by looking at manufacturing only: employment shifts across manufacturing industries played a very modest role in most countries.

The evidence that productivity growth is more than ever a matter of performance improvement within industries is perhaps not surprising, as around 70% of value added in the countries covered is already in services. However, other OECD economies, including Ireland and Japan as well as some low-income countries, have much smaller service sectors, suggesting that there may be further scope for structural change.

Fig. 3.1

## Decomposition of aggregate labour productivity growth into intra-sectoral productivity growth and inter-sectoral employment shifts

Non-farm business sector

■ 1973-1982    ■ 1982-1991    □ 1991-1999

Annual compound growth rate of labour productivity

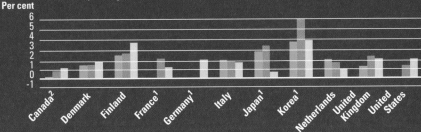

Intra-sectoral effect: productivity growth within sectors

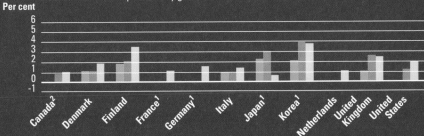

Net-shift effect: employment shifts between sectors

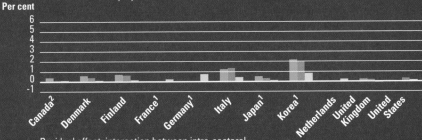

Residual effect: interaction between intra-sectoral productivity growth and inter-sectoral employment shifts

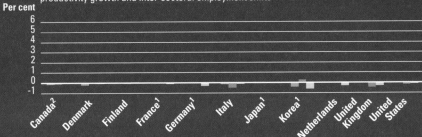

1. 1991-1998 instead of 1991-1999.
2. 1991-1996 instead of 1991-1999.

### Growth and labour

Labour productivity growth differs significantly across industries within each country. Notably, the manufacturing sector contributed around half of overall productivity growth in the 1990s in several countries, including most major economies, although it accounts for only around 20% of total employment. More interestingly, however, the contribution to productivity growth of specific industries varies across the major OECD economies [●→ Fig.3.2]. In the United States, manufacturing and service industries that are most closely related to IT, either in terms of IT production or IT use (*e.g.* machinery and equipment in manufacturing and trade and financial activities in the service sector) made a strong contribution to the acceleration in labour productivity growth from the first to the second half of the 1990s. Europe and Japan did not enjoy this contribution from IT-related industries, and their aggregate labour productivity growth remained fairly stable or even declined. This wide variance of industry productivity growth rates and industry composition across countries may reflect different policy and regulatory settings that affect incentives to innovate and move to rapidly growing, but also potentially more uncertain, activities.

**Industry-level analysis**

**Industry growth**

*Growth and labour*

**Empirical analysis**

## Empirical analysis

OECD industry-level data was used to investigate the effect of institutions and regulations on multi-factor productivity growth, *i.e.* the productivity growth that remains once both capital and labour have been accounted for. Similar to the macroeconomic regressions described earlier, "catch-up" was controlled in the analysis. In this case it was measured by a variable proxying distance from the technological frontier (indicated by the most productive country). This framework allows exploration of not only direct effects of institutions and regulations on efficiency but also indirect influence via the speed of catch-up.

The empirical analysis covers 23 industries in manufacturing and business services in 18 OECD countries over the period 1984-1998. The catch-up term is proxied by the difference between the MFP level in a particular industry and the highest level amongst all countries for that industry. Albeit crude, this measure broadly confirms expectations about which countries and regions tend to be at the forefront of technology in certain fields: the United States and Japan were often at the frontier in most industries over the period considered, but a number of European countries were also close to it when taking into account their lower levels of hours worked. The comparison of MFP levels also suggests that in only a few cases does the identity of the frontier remain constant, which implies that some countries "leapfrogged" others in terms of technology leadership in most industries. What matters for productivity growth, however, is the distance from the technological frontier – which captures the potential for technology transfer – rather than the identity of the frontier itself.

Fig. 3.2

## Contribution of IT-related industries to labour productivity growth

Percentage changes in value added per person employed, 1989-1995 and 1995-1999

- **IT-using industries[1]**
- **Machinery and equipment**
- **Other industries**

Panel A. 1989-1995

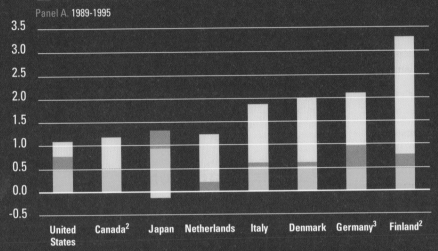

Panel B. 1995-1999

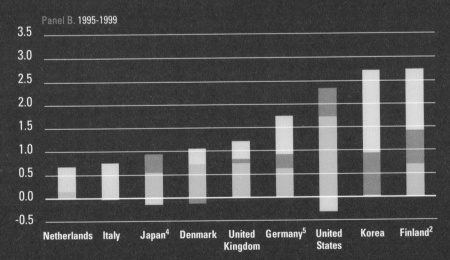

1. Wholesale and retail trade, repairs; finance, insurance, real estate and business services.
2. Value added per hour worked.
3. 1991-1995.
4. 1995-1998.
5. 1995-1997.

### Market conditions

The issue of market conditions can be investigated using manufacturing data, for which appropriate statistical information on market structures and technology regimes can be computed. For this analysis, manufacturing industries were classified into two broad categories: low-tech and high-tech industries. The results point to a strong and highly significant effect of technology catch-up for low-tech industries, whereas this effect is not statistically significant in high-tech industries. However, this latter group is rather heterogeneous and was consequently sub-divided further into two groups: high concentration and low concentration. The results suggest a significant convergence in highly concentrated high-tech industries, but no convergence in low-concentrated industries. These findings are consistent with the idea that firms operating in low-tech industries tend to share the same technology, so that spillover effects may be significant. In contrast, such spillover effects are likely to be less marked where the evolution of technology stimulates product or process diversification.

# Policies, institutions and productivity

This section analyses three factors, all directly or indirectly influenced by policies and institutions, that may affect industry-level productivity:

- the degree of competition in the product market;
- institutional settings in the labour market;
- innovation in the business sector, which are at least partially influenced by policy intervention, either directly by publicly financed R&D, or indirectly by tax rebates on R&D expenditure.

### Competition

Different arguments can be advanced to suggest that greater competition is likely to lead to stronger MFP. In weakly competitive markets, there are relatively few opportunities for comparing firms' performances, and firm survival is not immediately threatened by inefficient practices. Therefore, slack and the sub-optimal use of factor inputs can persist. However, the empirical evidence supporting these arguments is still fairly limited, partly due to the difficulty of measuring competitive pressures. Traditional indicators of product market conditions, such as mark-ups, industry concentration indexes or market shares, have various shortcomings. For example, high productivity firms may gain market shares and enjoy innovation rents in an environment that is still highly competitive. More broadly, recent research shows that the relationship between these indicators and product market competition is not straightforward. Furthermore, they fail to provide a direct link to policy or regulation, making it difficult to draw policy conclusions. The empirical analysis in this study is, therefore, based on some of the potential policy determinants of competition rather than on direct measures of it.

The empirical results indicate a negative direct effect of product market regulations on productivity, whatever indicator is considered. However, if the interaction of regulation with the technology gap is also considered, the results point to an even stronger indirect effect via the slower adoption of existing technologies: strict regulations seem to have a particularly detrimental effect on productivity the further the country is from the technology frontier, possibly because they reduce the scope for knowledge spillovers.

The empirical results also provide some insight into the potential effects of policy reforms on the long-run level of MFP. In particular, a reduction in the stringency of product market regulations may substantially reduce the productivity gap in countries such as Greece, Portugal and Spain in the long run. This assessment only takes into account the indirect effect of regulatory reform on the process of technology adoption, but does not include the potential effect of such a reform on increased R&D activity.

## Labour

Although labour market regulations are primarily designed to ensure socially desirable outcomes, some of them can affect the costs of implementing measures aimed at improving efficiency. For example, restrictions on hiring and firing are often found to reduce incentives for internal efficiency by hindering labour adjustments. At the same time, bargaining systems may affect the way the gains from process and product innovation are distributed between firms and workers. Systems that favour the sharing of innovation rents with workers (for instance by increasing the bargaining power of insiders or tying negotiations to enterprise performance) may inhibit innovative activity by reducing the expected returns from innovations. Conversely, systems that favour the appropriation of rents by firms, for instance by co-ordinating individual bargaining processes at the industry or nationwide level, and compressing wages of skilled workers, may increase incentives to innovate [◼□··1].

## Innovation and R&D

The way R&D affects productivity in high-tech industries appears to depend on the concentration of the industry. The results of OECD analysis show that there is no significant effect of R&D on productivity in low-concentration high-tech industries, but a strong effect in highly concentrated industries. High-tech industries with low concentration are often characterised by "creative destruction" with technological ease of entry and a major role played by new firms in innovation. Returns to R&D in these industries may be short lived, and are likely to be driven by the need to engage in product differentiation to maintain/acquire

---

### Industry-level analysis

**Policies, institutions and productivity**

*Labour*

*Innovation and R&D*

◼□··1 Teulings, C. and J. Hartog (1998), *Corporatism or Competition? Labour Contracts, Institutions and Wage Structures in International Comparison,* Cambridge University Press.

market shares. By contrast, high-tech but concentrated industries are generally characterised by "creative accumulation", with the prevalence of large, established firms and the presence of barriers for new innovators. Returns to R&D in these industries are, therefore, likely to be larger than in low concentration ones, possibly leading to persistent technological leadership.

## The impact of policy and institutions on R&D activity

The direct effects of policy and institutions on MFP are likely to be combined with indirect effects stemming from their influence on R&D activity. For example, if product market regulations protect firms from competition, then firms may have little drive to develop new processes and products. Or, labour market regulations or certain types industrial relations may not be conducive to the changes in work practices or personnel that are needed to make the fruits of R&D worth implementing. There are indeed already both theoretical and empirical studies supporting the idea that certain forms of product regulation may curb incentives to engage in innovation. Likewise, a few studies argue that high costs of adjusting the workforce may indeed have important consequences for the profitability of innovation. The following describes some recent OECD evidence on the issue.

The OECD work is based on regression analysis which explores what factors explain differences R&D intensity (expressed as the ratio of business-performed R&D expenditure to sales) across countries and industries. Alongside a number of control variables (such as human capital), the analysis gauges the impact of a number of variables. Indicators of product market regulation used in the analysis include: measures of state control and administrative regulation (administrative barriers to start-ups, features of the licensing and permit system, etc.), indicators of tariff and non-tariff barriers, plus an indicator of global protection of intellectual property rights (IPRs). Import penetration is used as a proxy for competitive pressures not captured by the regulatory indicators. A control for the average size of firms captures the possible bias in R&D intensity across industries and countries due to different accounting practices between large and small firms and has been proved to play an important role in the literature [2].

The regression results confirm the positive association between R&D intensity and the average size of firms in each industry, a commonly reported result. More interestingly, R&D activity tends to increase with trade openness, perhaps pointing to the existence of positive international knowledge spillovers. Indeed, trade openness tends to increase product variety in domestic markets and induces imitation by domestic producers and the latter often requires spending on R&D [3]. The degree of protection of IPRs also appears to have a significant positive effect on R&D intensity.

[2a] Griliches, Z. (1990) "Patent Statistics as Economic Indicators: A Survey", *Journal of Economic Literature*, Vol. 28.

2b Geroski, P.A. (1991) *Market Dynamic and Entry*, Basil Blackwell.

[3] Cohen, W. and D. Levinthal (1989), "Innovation and Learning: The two Faces of R&D", *Economic Journal*, Vol. 99.

Concerning the role of regulation, the results point to a negative effect of non-tariff barriers and state control on R&D. By contrast, trade tariffs as well as barriers to entrepreneurship are positively associated with R&D intensity. This seemingly contradictory result may in fact make sense. While trade restrictions tend to add to foreign competitors' costs without changing the incentive to innovate amongst domestic firms, they may also curb imports and the possible knowledge spillovers related to them. This latter effect is likely to be stronger for non-tariff barriers than for tariffs because they have greater impact on the diffusion of products and, eventually, the possibility of imitation by domestic firms. The positive associations between barriers to entrepreneurship and R&D might be due to the fact that these barriers, by discouraging entry, may contribute to increasing returns from innovation.

The regression results show that R&D intensity decreases with the stringency of EPL and increases with the degree of co-ordination in industrial relations. Initial results suggested that both variables acted independently on R&D. However, the true picture appears to be more complex. At any given level of EPL and co-ordination in industrial relations, their combination appears to have a positive effect on R&D intensity in high-tech industries and a negative effect in low-tech industries. The rationale for this result is that in low-tech industries the scope for expansion is often limited and innovation often leads to downsizing and reshuffling of the workforce and may, therefore, be discouraged by legislation hindering labour adjustments. By contrast, in high-tech industries, co-ordination tends to partly offset the negative influence of EPL, by pushing firms towards greater recourse to in-house training.

## Industry-level analysis

**Policies, institutions and productivity**

*The impact of policy and institutions on R&D activity*

# Focus on IT

## The contribution of IT at the industry level

The impact of IT at the industry level is seen mostly in the IT-producing and IT-using sectors. The IT-producing sector is of particular interest for several countries, as it has been characterised by very high rates of productivity growth, providing a considerable contribution to aggregate performance. ●→ Fig.3.3 shows the contribution of IT manufacturing to productivity growth over the 1990s, distinguishing between the first half of the decade and the second half of the decade. In most OECD countries, the contribution of IT manufacturing to overall labour productivity growth has risen over the 1990s. This can partly be attributed to more rapid technological progress in the production of certain IT goods, such as semi-conductors, which has contributed to more rapid price declines and thus to higher growth in real volumes [◖→4]. However, there is a large variation in the types of IT goods that are being produced in different OECD countries. Some countries only produce peripheral equipment, which is characterised by much slower technological progress and consequently by much smaller changes in prices.

IT manufacturing made the largest contributions to aggregate productivity growth in Finland, Ireland, Japan, Korea, Sweden and the United States. In Finland, Ireland and Korea, close to 1 percentage point of aggregate productivity growth in the 1995-2001 period is due to IT manufacturing. The IT services sector (telecommunications and computer services) plays a smaller role in aggregate productivity growth, but has also been characterised by rapid progress [●→ Fig.3.4]. Partly, this is linked to the liberalisation of telecommunications markets and the high speed of technological change in this market.

The contribution of this sector to overall productivity growth increased in several countries over the 1990s, notably in Canada, Finland, France, Germany and the Netherlands. Some of the growth in the provision of IT services is due to the emergence of the computer services industry, which has accompanied the diffusion of IT in OECD countries. The development of these services has been important in implementing IT, as the firms in these sectors offer key advisory and training services and also help develop appropriate software to be used in combination with the IT hardware.

The IT sector is thus an important driver of the acceleration in productivity growth only in a limited number of OECD countries, notably Finland, Ireland, Japan, Korea, Sweden and the United States. This is because only a few OECD countries are specialised in those parts of the IT sector that are characterised by very rapid technological progress, e.g. the production of semi-conductors. Indeed, much of the production of IT hardware is highly concentrated, because of its large economies of scale and high entry costs. Establishing a new semi-conductor plant cost some USD 100 million in the early 1980s, but as much as USD 1.2 billion in 1999 [◖→5]. And those parts of IT hardware production that can easily

### Industry-level analysis

**The contribution of IT at the industry level**

◖→ 4 Jorgenson D. W. (2001), "Information Technology and the U.S. Economy", *American Economic Review*, Vol. 91, No. 1.

◖→ 5 United States Council of Economic Advisors (2001), *Economic Report of the President*, 2001, United States Government Printing Office, February.

**Fig. 3.3**

## Contribution of IT manufacturing to annual average labour productivity growth

- 1990-1995*
- 1996-2001**

Percentage points

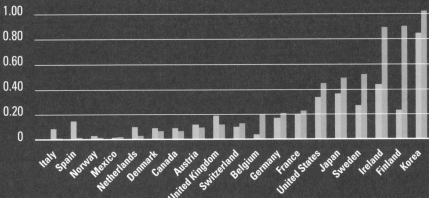

* 1991-95 for Germany; 1992-95 for France and Italy; 1993-95 for Korea.
** 1996-98 for Sweden; 1996-99 for Korea and Spain; 1996-2000 for Belgium, France, Germany, Ireland, Japan, Mexico, Norway and Switzerland.

Source: Pilat, et al. (2002) and OECD STAN Database.

**Fig. 3.4**

## Contribution of IT-producing services to annual average labour productivity growth

- 1990-1995
- 1996-2001

Percentage points

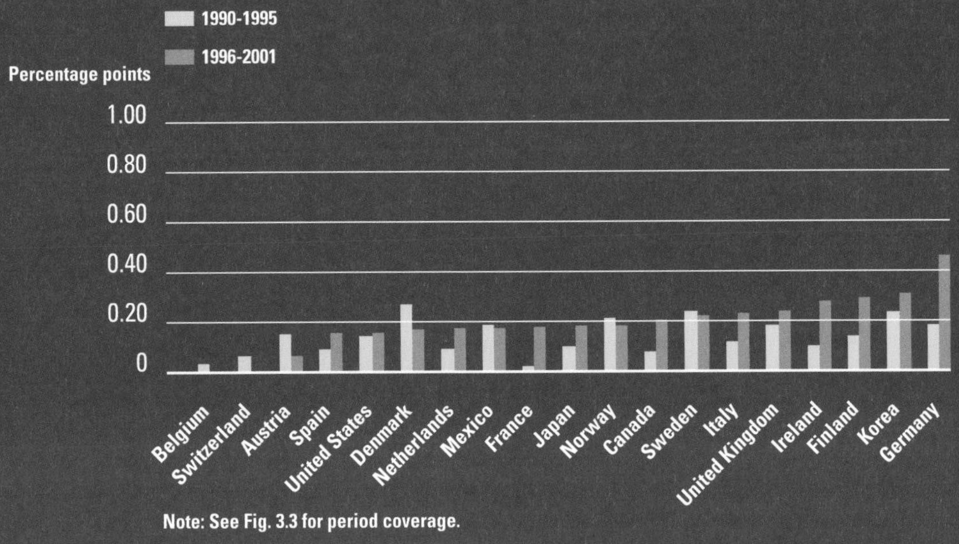

Note: See Fig. 3.3 for period coverage.

Source: Pilat, et al. (2002) and OECD STAN Database.

■□→ 6a McGuckin, R.H.
and K.J. Stiroh (2001),
"Do Computers Make Output
Harder to Measure?",
*Journal of Technology Transfer*, Vol. 26.

6b Pilat, D.
F. Lee and B. van Ark (2002),
"Production and use of ICT:
A sectoral perspective on productivity
growth in the OECD area",
*OECD Economic Studies*, No. 35.

## Industry-level analysis

### The contribution of IT at the industry level

### OECD STAN database

*This database includes
annual measures of output,
labour input, investment
and international trade
from 1970 onward
for OECD countries.
Compatible with other
OECD data bases,
STAN is based on
the International Standard
Industrial Classification
of all Economic Activities,
Revision 3 (ISIC Rev. 3)
and covers all activities
(including services).*

■□→ 7a McKinsey (2001),
*US Productivity Growth 1995-2000:
Understanding the Contribution of Information
Technology Relative to Other Factors*,
McKinsey Global Institute, October.

7b Triplett, J.E.
and B.B. Bosworth (2002),
"'Baumol's Disease' has Been Cured:
IT and Multi-Factor Productivity
in U.S. Services Industries",
paper prepared for Brookings workshop
on services industry productivity,
Brookings Institution, September.

be set up, such as the assembly of PCs, are likely to have fewer technological spin-offs than the high-tech production of semi-conductors. In other words, a hardware sector cannot be set up easily, and only a few countries will have the necessary comparative advantages to succeed in it. In addition, a substantial part of the benefits of IT production has accrued to importing countries and to users, as these have benefited from terms-of-trade effects and an increased consumer surplus.

A much larger part of the economy uses IT in the production process. Indeed, several studies have distinguished an IT-using sector, composed of industries that are intensive users of IT [■□→ 6]. Examining the performance of these sectors over time and in comparison with sectors of the economy that do not use IT can help point to the role of IT in aggregate performance. A more systematic method would be to examine the link between IT use and productivity performance by industry. Unfortunately, the data to engage in such work are still too limited, or available for only a few years. ●→ Fig.3.5 shows the contribution of the key IT-using services (wholesale and retail trade, finance, insurance and business services) to aggregate productivity growth over the 1990s.

The graph suggests small improvements in the contribution of IT-using services in Finland, the Netherlands, Norway and Sweden, and substantial increases in Australia, Canada, Ireland, Mexico, the United Kingdom and United States. The United States has experienced the strongest improvement in productivity growth in IT-using services over the 1990s, which is due to more rapid productivity growth in wholesale and retail trade, and in financial services (securities). This result for the United States is confirmed by several other studies [■□→ 7].

In some countries, IT-using services made a negative contribution to aggregate productivity growth. This is particularly the case in Switzerland in the first half of the 1990s, resulting from poor productivity growth in the banking sector. Poor measurement of productivity in financial services may be partly to blame. The OECD is currently working with member countries to improve methods to capture productivity growth in this sector.

Stronger growth in labour productivity in IT-producing and IT-using industries is partly due to greater use of capital. Estimates of MFP growth adjust for changes in the use of capital and can help to show whether IT-using sectors have indeed generated disembodied technological change. Breaking aggregate MFP growth down into its sectoral contributions can also help to show whether changes in MFP growth should be attributed to IT producing sectors, to IT-using sectors, or to other sectors. ●→ Fig.3.6 shows the contribution of all activities to aggregate MFP growth for the 7 countries for which estimates of capital stock at the industry level are currently available in the OECD STAN database.

Fig. 3.5

## Contribution of IT-using services to annual average labour productivity growth

■ 1990-1995
■ 1996-2001[1]

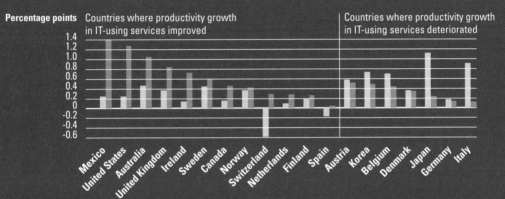

Percentage points

Countries where productivity growth in IT-using services improved

Countries where productivity growth in IT-using services deteriorated

Note: See Fig. 3.3 for period coverage. Estimates for Australia refer to 1996-2001.
1. Or latest available year.

Source: Pilat, et al. (2002) and OECD STAN Database.

Fig. 3.6

## Contributions of key sectors to aggregate MFP growth, 1990-95 and 1996-2001[1]

Contributions to annual average growth rates, in percentage points

■ IT-producing manufacturing    ■ IT-using services    ■ Other activities

Percentage points

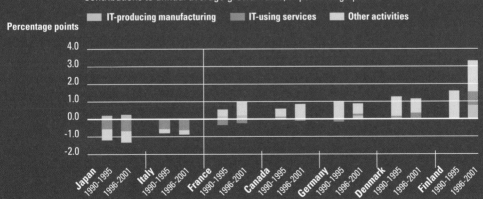

Note: Estimates are based on official estimates of capital stock and sector-specific labour shares (adjusted for labour income from self-employment). No adjustment is made for capital services.
1. Or latest available year, i.e. 2000 for Germany, France and Finland, 1999 for Italy, and 1998 for Japan.

Source: Pilat, et al. (2002) and OECD STAN Database.

● Fig.3.6 shows that IT manufacturing provided an important contribution to the acceleration in productivity growth in Finland. For IT using services, the MFP estimates point to growing contributions to aggregate productivity in Denmark and Finland. In several other countries, MFP growth in the IT-using services was negative over the 1990s.

The OECD STAN database does not yet include capital stock for the United States, which implies that MFP estimates for the United States can not be derived from this source. However, several studies provide estimates of the sectoral contributions to US MFP growth, [● Table 3.1]. The results show considerable variation. Oliner and Sichel [■ 8] found no contribution of non-IT producing industries to MFP growth; Gordon [■ 9] and Jorgenson, Ho and Stiroh [■ 10] found a relatively small contribution, while Baily [■ 11] and the US Council of Economic Advisors [■ 5] found a much more substantial contribution. The differences between the various US studies are partly due to the data sources and methodology used, as well as the timing of various studies.

The problem with some of the studies presented in ● Table 3.1 is that all non-IT producing sectors are combined, and the contribution of the non IT-producing sector to aggregate MFP growth is calculated as a residual. More detailed examination for the United States suggests that this residual is indeed small, but typically made up of a positive contribution from wholesale and retail trade and financial services to MFP growth, and a negative contribution of other service sectors. A recent study by Triplett and Bosworth [■ 7b] finds a relatively strong pick-up in MFP growth in certain parts of the US service sector. They estimated that MFP growth in wholesale trade accelerated from 1.1% annually to 2.4% annually from 1987-1995 to 1995-2000. In retail trade, the jump was from 0.4% annually to 3.0%, and in securities the acceleration was from 2.9% to 11.2%. Combined with the relatively large weight of these sectors in the economy, this translates into a considerable contribution to more rapid aggregate MFP growth of these IT-using services.

There is therefore evidence of strong MFP growth in the United States in IT-using services. More detailed studies suggest how these productivity changes due to IT use in the United States could be interpreted. First, a considerable part of the pick-up in productivity growth can be attributed to retail trade, where firms such as Walmart used innovative practices, such as the appropriate use of IT, to gain market share from its competitors. The larger market share for Walmart and other productive firms raised average productivity and also forced Walmart's competitors to improve their own performance. Among the other IT-using services, securities accounts also for a large part of the pick-up in productivity growth in the 1990s. Its strong performance has been attributed to a combination of buoyant financial markets (*i.e.* large trading volumes), effective use of IT (mainly in automating trading processes) and stronger

## Industry-level analysis

### The contribution of IT at the industry level

■ 8 Oliner, S.D.
and D.E. Sichel (2002),
"Information Technology and Productivity:
Where Are We Now
and Where Are We Going?",
*Federal Reserve Bank of Atlanta Economic Review*, third quarter.

■ 9 Gordon, R.J. (2002),
"Technology and Economic Performance
in the American Economy",
*NBER Working Papers*, No. 8771.

■ 10 Jorgenson, D.W.,
M.S. Ho and K.J. Stiroh (2002),
"Projecting Productivity Growth:
Lessons from the US Growth Resurgence",
*Federal Reserve Bank of Atlanta Economic Review*, third quarter.

■ 11 Baily, M.N. (2002),
"The New Economy:
Post Mortem or Second Wind",
*Journal of Economic Perspectives*,
Vol. 16, No. 2, Spring 2002.

# Table 3.1

## Accounting for the acceleration in US productivity growth, non-farm business sector

| | Oliner-Sichel (2002), 1974-1990 versus 1996-2001 | Gordon (2002), 1972-95 versus 1995-2000 | US Council of Economic Advisors (2001) | Jorgenson, Ho and Stiroh (2002) |
|---|---|---|---|---|
| Output per hour | 0.89 | 1.44 | 1.39 | 0.92 |
| Cycle | n.a. | 0.40 | n.a. | n.a. |
| Trend | 0.89 | 1.04 | 1.39 | 0.92 |
| *Contributions from:* | | | | |
| Capital services | 0.40 | 0.37 | 0.44 | 0.52 |
| IT capital | 0.56 | 0.60 | 0.59 | 0.44 |
| Other capital | −0.17 | −0.23 | −0.15 | 0.08 |
| Labour quality | 0.03 | 0.01 | 0.04 | −0.06 |
| MFP growth | 0.46 | 0.52 | 0.91 | 0.47 |
| Computer sector | 0.47 | 0.30 | 0.18 | 0.27 |
| Other MFP | −0.01 | 0.22 | 0.72 | 0.20 |

Source: Gordon (2002); Jorgenson, Ho and Stiroh (2002); Oliber and Sichel (2002) updated from estimates received from Dan Sichel; Council of Economic Advisors (2001) as updated in Baily (2002).

## Industry-level analysis

### The contribution of IT at the industry level

■□→ 12 OECD (2001),
*The New Economy: Beyond the Hype.*

■□→ 13 Gust, C. and J. Marquez (2002),
"International Comparisons of Productivity Growth: The Role of Information Technology and Regulatory Practices",
*International Finance Discussion Papers,*
No. 727, Federal Reserve Board, May.

■□→ 14a Parham, D.
P. Roberts and H. Sun (2001),
"Information Technology and Australia's Productivity Surge",
Staff Research Paper, Productivity Commission, AusInfo.

14b Simon, J. and S. Wardrop (2002),
"Australian Use of Information Technology and Its Contribution to Growth",
Research Discussion Paper RDP2002-02,
Reserve Bank of Australia, January.

competition [■□→ 7a]. These impacts of IT on MFP are therefore primarily due to efficient use of labour and capital linked to the use of IT in the production process. They are not necessarily due to network effects, where one firm's use of IT has positive spillovers on the economy as a whole.

Spillover effects may also play a role, however, as IT investment started earlier, and was stronger, in the United States than in most OECD countries. Moreover, previous OECD work has pointed out that the US economy might be able to achieve greater benefits from IT since it got its fundamentals right before many other OECD countries [■□→ 12]. Indeed, the United States may have benefited first from IT investment ahead of other OECD countries, as it already had a high level of competition in the 1980s, which it strengthened through regulatory reforms in the 1980s and 1990s. For example, early and far-reaching liberalisation of the telecommunications sector boosted competition in dynamic segments of the IT market. The combination of sound macroeconomic policies, well-functioning institutions and markets, and a competitive economic environment may thus be at the core of the US' success. A recent study by Gust and Marquez [■□→ 13] confirms these results and attributes relatively low investment in IT in European countries partly to restrictive labour and product market regulations that have prevented firms from getting sufficient returns from their investment.

The United States is not the only country where IT use may already have had impacts on MFP growth. Studies for Australia [■□→ 14], suggest that a range of structural reforms have been important in driving the strong uptake of IT by firms and have enabled these investments to be used in ways that generate productivity gains. This is particularly evident in wholesale and retail trade and in financial intermediation, where most of the Australian productivity gains in the second half of the 1990s have occurred.

Industry-Level analysis:
# Key conclusions

- Stringent regulatory settings in the product market, as well as strict employment legislation, have a negative bearing on productivity at the industry level. However, these policy influences depend on a number of factors.

- The impact of regulations and institutions on performance varies, depending on the market and technology conditions in the industry. The burden of strict product market regulations on productivity seems to be greater the larger the technological gap with the industry/country leader: strict regulation hinders the adoption of existing technologies, possibly because it reduces competitive pressures or international technology transfers. In addition, strict product market regulations also have a negative impact on the process of innovation itself.

- The link between employment protection legislation and productivity is also complex. There is evidence to suggest that high hiring and firing costs weaken productivity performance, especially when they are not offset by greater coordination of wage setting and/or internal training, thereby inducing sub-optimal adjustments of the workforce to technology changes and innovation.

- There is considerable variation in the effect of R&D activity on productivity, depending on market structures and technology regimes.

- The increased contribution of IT manufacturing to labour productivity during the 1990s contributed to rapid price declines and higher growth.

# 4

# Key questions

- **What is the contribution of firm dynamics to industry-level productivity growth?**

- **How do firms evolve after market entry? Does this evolution differ in Europe and North America?**

- **What are the policy influences on long-term growth at the firm-level?**

# Chapter 4

# Firm-level analysis

## Dynamics, productivity and policy settings

This chapter takes a further step into the analysis
of the micro-determinants of economic growth
by focusing on the contribution of reallocation of resources
within narrowly defined industries, resulting from the expansion
of more productive firms, the entry of new firms and the exit
of obsolete ones.

The chapter assesses the contribution of firm dynamics
to industry-level productivity growth. As such, it is the first attempt
in the micro-economic literature to study the role of firm dynamics
for a relatively large set of countries and, more importantly,
on the basis of harmonised data.

# Firm growth

The previous chapter showed that overall productivity gains result predominantly from an intra-industry effect. The next natural step is, therefore, to look inside different industries to assess how the reallocation of resources among incumbents, as well as between firms entering and leaving the industry, shapes productivity growth. This process of "creative destruction", whereby new entrants displace obsolescent firms, may be especially important in the current period of diffusion of a new technology, such as IT.

## Creative destruction

*The so-called "creative destruction" in firm behaviour (usually ascribed to Joseph Schumpeter) has long been recognised as of potential importance in understanding economic growth. The distinguishing element of Schumpeter's theory from "standard" theories of firm behaviour is that it recognises heterogeneity amongst producers and that the continual shift in the composition of the population of firms through entry, exit, expansion and contraction may be important in developing and creating new processes, products and markets.*

## *Methodological issues*

The analysis offers a consistent international comparison of firm dynamics and its contribution to aggregate productivity, through the use of specially constructed firm-level data for ten OECD countries (United States, Germany, France, Italy, United Kingdom, Canada, Denmark, Finland, Netherlands and Portugal). These harmonised data are used below to assess the role of entry and exit and reallocation amongst existing firms in total productivity growth. Notwithstanding the efforts made to minimise inconsistencies along different dimensions (*e.g.* sectoral breakdown, time horizon, definition of entry and exit, etc.), some remaining differences have to be taken into account when interpreting the results.

Average productivity growth in an industry can be interpreted as combinations of:

- productivity gains within existing firms;
- increases in the market share of high-productivity firms;
- the entry of new firms that displace less productive ones.

Productivity growth within firms depends on changes in the efficiency and intensity with which inputs are used in production. This source of aggregate productivity growth is therefore associated with the process of technological progress. Shifts in market shares between more productive and less productive companies also affect aggregate productivity trends, as does the reallocation of resources across entering and exiting firms. It should be stressed that this simple taxonomy hides important interactions. The entry of highly productive firms into a given market may stimulate productivity-enhancing investment by incumbents trying to preserve their market shares. Moreover, firms experiencing higher than average productivity growth are likely to gain market shares if their improvement is the result of a successful expansion, while they will lose market shares if their improvement was driven by a process of restructuring associated with downsizing.

There are a number of ways in which aggregate productivity can be decomposed into a within-firm component and different components due to the reallocation of resources across firms. The decompositions reported below refer to the approach developed by Griliches and Regev [■ · 1]. It is applied to both labour and multi-factor productivity (MFP), based on five-year rolling windows for all periods and industries for which data are available.

## Labour productivity growth

●·· Fig.4.1 presents the decomposition of labour productivity growth in manufacturing sectors for two five-year intervals, 1987-92 and 1992-97. It suggests that productivity within each firm accounted for the bulk of overall labour productivity growth. The impact on productivity via the reallocation of output across existing enterprises (the "between" effect) varies significantly across countries and time, but it is typically small. Finally, the net contribution to overall labour productivity growth of the entry and exit of firms (net entry) is positive in most countries (with the exception of western Germany over the 1990s), accounting for between 20% and 40% of total productivity growth.

The entry of new firms has variable effects on overall productivity growth. On the whole, data for European countries show that new firms typically make a positive contribution to overall productivity growth [● · Table 4.1], although the effect is generally of small magnitude. By contrast, entries make a negative contribution in the United States for most industries. Instead, a strong contribution to productivity growth in the United States comes from the exit of low productivity firms. This finding is consistent with further evidence that is presented below, indicating a somewhat different nature of the entry (and exit) process in the United States compared with most other countries.

Although the driving forces of aggregate labour productivity growth differ across countries, a few common patterns can be identified[■ · 2]. In particular, in the industries more closely related to IT, the entry component makes a stronger contribution to labour productivity growth than on average. This is particularly the case in the United States, where the contribution from entrants in IT sectors to labour productivity growth is strongly positive, in contrast to the negative effect observed in most other manufacturing industries. This result suggests an important role for new firms in an area characterised by a strong wave of technological change. The opposite seems to be the case in more mature industries, where a more significant contribution comes from either within-firm growth or the exit of (presumably) inefficient firms.

The decomposition of labour productivity growth in service sectors gives far more varied results than that for manufacturing, no doubt because of the difficulties in properly measuring output in this area of the economy. But, in some broad sectors, *transport and storage, communication* and

**Firm-level analysis**

**Firm growth**

*Labour productivity growth*

■·· 1 Griliches, Z. and H. Regev (1995), "Firm Productivity in Israeli Industry, 1970-1988", *Journal of Econometrics*, Vol. 65.

■·· 2 Scarpetta, S. P. Hemmings, T. Tressel and J. Woo (2002), "The Role of Policy and Institutions for Productivity and Firms Dynamics: Evidence from Micro and Industry Data", *OECD Economics Department Working Papers*, No. 329.

Fig. 4.1

## Components of labour productivity growth in manufacturing

Percentage share of total annual productivity growth of each component[1]

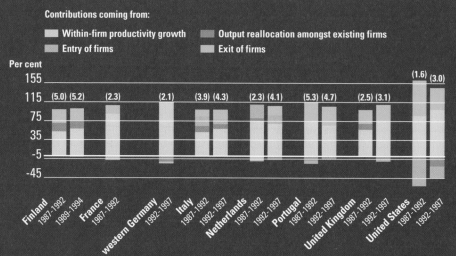

Note: Figures in brackets are overall productivity growth rates (annual percentage change).
1. Components may not add up to 100 because of rounding.

Fig. 4.3

## Components of multi-factor productivity growth in manufacturing

Percentage share of total annual productivity growth of each component[1]

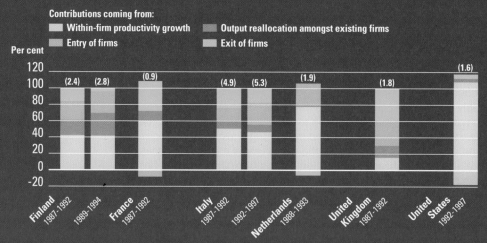

Note: Figures in brackets are overall productivity growth rates (annual percentage change).
1. Components may not add up to 100 because of rounding.

Fig. 4.2

# Components of labour productivity growth in selected service sectors

Percentage share of total annual productivity growth of each component[1]

**Contributions coming from:**

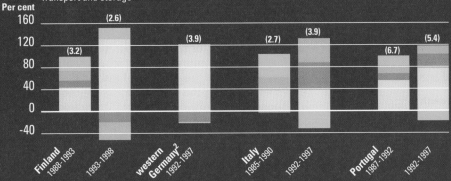

- Within-firm productivity growth
- Output reallocation amongst existing firms
- Entry of firms
- Exit of firms

### Transport and storage

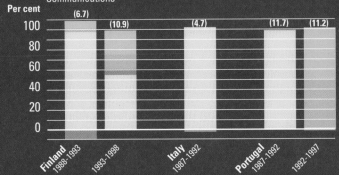

### Communications

### Wholesale and retail trade; restaurants and hotels

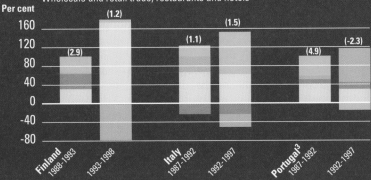

**Note: Figures in brackets are overall productivity growth rates (annual percentage change).**
1. Components may not add up to 100 because of rounding.
2. Transport, storage and communication.
3. Wholesale and retail trade.

*wholesale and retail trade*, the results are qualitatively in line with those for manufacturing [●··Fig.4.2]. The within-firm component is generally larger than that related to net entry and reallocation across existing firms, although in transport and storage, as well as in communication, entering firms seem generally to have higher than average productivity, raising overall aggregate growth.

## Multi-factor productivity

●··Fig.4.3 presents the decomposition of MFP growth in the manufacturing sectors of six countries. It should be stressed at the outset that MFP estimates are less robust than those for labour productivity, because of the difficulty of measuring the stock of capital at the firm level. Bearing this caveat in mind, the decomposition of MFP growth suggests a somewhat different picture from that shown with respect to labour productivity. Thus, although it still drives overall fluctuations, the within-firm component provides a comparatively smaller contribution to overall MFP growth. At the same time, the reallocation of resources across incumbents (*i.e.* the between effect) plays a somewhat stronger role. More importantly, a strong contribution to MFP growth generally comes from net entry. Indeed, the (limited) information available suggests that the entry of new, highly productive firms has made a marked impact on aggregate trends in the more recent past.

By combining information on labour and MFP decompositions it could be tentatively hypothesised that incumbent firms were able to increase labour productivity mainly by substituting capital for labour (capital deepening) or by exiting the market altogether, but not necessarily by markedly improving overall efficiency in production processes. By contrast, new firms entered the market with the "appropriate" combination of factor inputs and new technologies, thus leading to faster growth of MFP.

## Productivity decomposition

The productivity decomposition discussed above is a simple accounting exercise that does not consider possible interactions between its different components. In this regard, some insights may be gleaned from information on the variability of labour productivity within each of the productivity components:

- There is a positive correlation between the entry rate in a given industry and average labour productivity levels; that is to say, highly productive industries are associated with relatively high entry rates. This may reflect new firms putting competitive pressure on incumbents, or that highly productive industries attract more entrants.

Table 4.1

## Analysis of productivity components across industries

Panel A. Proportions of positive contributions to labour productivity growth
across manufacturing industries[1]

| | Total number of observations | Entry contribution % | Exit contribution % | Between component % |
|---|---|---|---|---|
| Finland | 420 | 57 | 93 | 62 |
| France | 126 | 47 | 81 | 40 |
| Italy | 348 | 84 | 89 | 85 |
| Netherlands | 344 | 76 | 77 | 51 |
| Portugal | 211 | 63 | 91 | 49 |
| United Kingdom | 392 | 62 | 92 | 45 |
| United States | 58 | 10 | 98 | 31 |

Panel B. Proportions of positive contributions to labour productivity growth across business services[1]

| | Total number of observations | Entry contribution % | Exit contribution % | Between component % |
|---|---|---|---|---|
| Finland | 24 | 50 | 79 | 46 |
| western Germany | 18 | 56 | 71 | 50 |
| Italy | 227 | 30 | 54 | 29 |
| Portugal | 191 | 39 | 66 | 43 |

Note: These calculations are based on all available data for manufacturing and business services. The time periods considered vary considerably across countries.
1. Number of cases in which the different components made a positive contribution to labour productivity growth (in % of total number of cases).

• Within each country, high productivity industries tend to have a wider dispersion of productivity levels than other industries. Specifically, while most industries, regardless of their aggregate level of productivity, have a number of relatively low productivity firms, high overall productivity in some industries is largely driven by the presence of "exceptional" performers.

# Entry and exit of firms

Firm-level analysis

**Entry and exit of firms**

Since the entry and exit of firms makes a significant contribution to aggregate productivity growth, it is of interest to see how frequently new firms are created and how often existing units close down, across countries and sectors. In fact, a large number of firms enter and exit most markets every year [Panel A of ● · Fig.4.4]. Data covering the first part of the 1990s show firm turnover rates (entry plus exit rates) to be around 20% in the business sector of most countries [Panel B of ● · Fig.4.4]: *i.e.* a fifth of firms are either recent entrants, or will close down within a year.

The industry dimension also makes it possible to compare entry and exit rates and characterise turnover. If entries were driven by relatively high profits in a given industry, and exits occurred primarily in sectors with relatively low profits, there would be a negative cross-sectional correlation between entry and exit rates. However, confirming previous evidence, entry and exit rates are generally highly correlated across industries in OECD countries (this is particularly so when the rates are weighted by employment). This finding suggests a process of "creative destruction", whereby new firms continuously displace obsolete firms.

The variability of turnover rates for the same industry across countries is comparable in magnitude to that across industries in each country. In other words, the observed variability of turnover across countries can be explained both by industry-specific and country-specific effects. Overall, the data suggest a similar degree of "firm churning" in Europe and the United States: with the exception of western Germany and Italy, all countries have higher entry rates than the United States, but differences are small and would, in fact, be even smaller if the different size structure of firms across countries were taken into account.

Regarding industry-specific factors, a general finding (which does not apply to all countries, however) is that turnover rates are somewhat higher in the service sector than in manufacturing [Panel B of ● · Fig.4.4]. At a more detailed level, once country and size effects are controlled for, high technology manufacturing industries and some business-service industries, in particular those related to IT, have higher entry rates than average [● · Fig.4.5].

Fig. 4.4

## High firm turnover rates in OECD countries

Entry and exit rates[1], annual average, 1989-1994

Panel A. Entry and exit rates in total business sector[2]

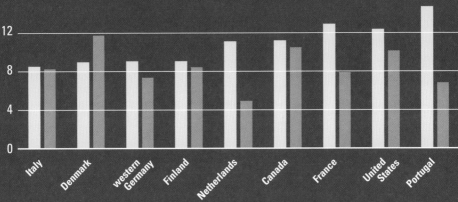

Panel B. Overall firm turnover in broad sectors

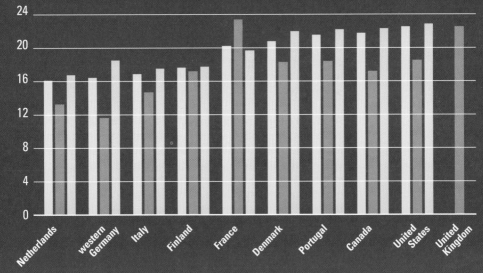

1. The entry rate is the ratio of entering firms to the total population. The exit rate is the ratio of exiting firms to the population of origin. Turnover rates are the sum of entry and exit rates.
2. Total economy minus agriculture and community services.

Some studies have argued that variation in firm entry rates across industries partly relates to differences in product cycles. Some evidence suggests that after commercial introduction of a new product there is an initial phase of rapid firm entry, which is followed by a levelling off and a contraction in the number of firms. For example, the observation of "waves" of entry at different points in time across industries may reflect initial phases in the product cycle. In this context, the high entry rates observed in IT-related industries may reflect the fact that IT products are still in a relatively early phase of their cycles. There is some indirect support for this view: the correlation between ranks of industries (according to their turnover rate) at different points in time is not very high and tends to decline as yearly observations are further apart [● Table 4.2]. Hence, high entry industries at a point in time are not necessarily at the top of the entry ranking of industries ten or even five years later. This result could be read as suggesting that competitive forces in each market change significantly over time because of the maturing of the market in which firms operate.

# Firm survival

The high correlation between entry and exit across industries may be the result of new firms displacing old obsolete units, as well as high failure rates amongst newcomers in the first years of their life. Looking at survival rates, *i.e.* the probability that new firms will live beyond a given age [● Fig.4.6], can help assess this. The survival probability for cohorts of firms that entered their respective market in the late 1980s declines steeply in the initial phases of their life: only about 60-70% of entering firms survive the first two years. Having overcome the initial years, the prospects of firms improve in the subsequent period: those that remain in business after the first two years have a 50 to 80% chance of surviving for five more years. Nevertheless, on average, only about 40 to 50% of firms entering in a given year survive beyond the seventh year.

As in the case of firm turnover, differences in the industry mix across countries could partly cloud the international comparison of survivor rates. After controlling for sectoral composition, survival rates at a four-year horizon appear to be lower in the United States, and even more so in the United Kingdom, than in continental countries. It is important to note that a low survival rate is not necessarily a cause for concern. Entry by new firms may be seen as a process of experimentation and it is in the nature of this process that the failure rate will be high. This is particularly so if new entry leads incumbent firms to increase their efficiency and profitability, as seems to be the case in the United States.

The marked difference in post-entry behaviour of firms in the United States compared with the European countries is partially due to the larger gap between the size at entry and the average firm size of

Table 4.2

## Differences in entry rates across industries do not persist over time

Rank correlation of industry entry rates between different years[1]

|  | Interval | Based on firm entry rates | Based on employment weighted entry rates |
|---|---|---|---|
| United States | 1990-1995 | 0.86 | 0.79 |
| western Germany | 1990-1998 | 0.94 | 0.60 |
|  | 1993-1998 | 0.88 | 0.26 |
| France | 1991-1995 | 0.59 | 0.59 |
| Italy | 1988-1993 | 0.73 | 0.58 |
| Denmark | 1984-1994 | 0.82 | 0.56 |
|  | 1989-1994 | 0.77 | 0.02 |
| Finland | 1990-1997 | 0.27 | -0.02 |
|  | 1993-1997 | 0.20 | -0.02 |
| Netherlands | 1994-1997 | 0.59 | 0.31 |
| Portugal | 1985-1994 | 0.55 | 0.36 |
|  | 1989-1994 | 0.75 | 0.30 |

1. Spearman rank correlation.

Fig. 4.5

## Differences in entry rates across industries

Estimated industry[1] entry rates relative to the total business sector

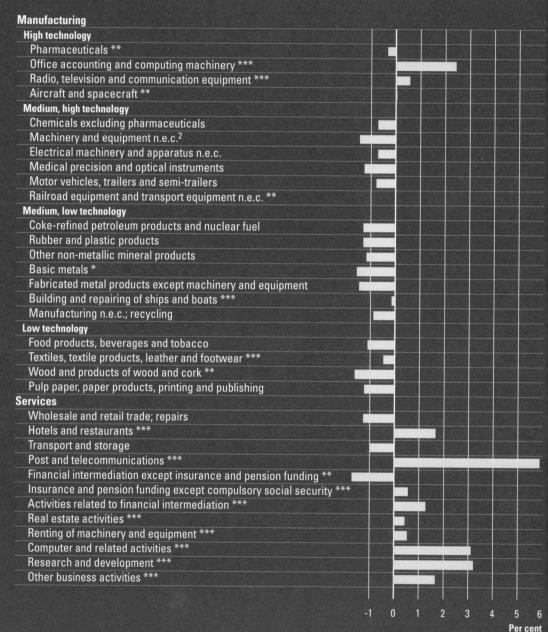

**Manufacturing**

  **High technology**
  Pharmaceuticals **
  Office accounting and computing machinery ***
  Radio, television and communication equipment ***
  Aircraft and spacecraft **

  **Medium, high technology**
  Chemicals excluding pharmaceuticals
  Machinery and equipment n.e.c.[2]
  Electrical machinery and apparatus n.e.c.
  Medical precision and optical instruments
  Motor vehicles, trailers and semi-trailers
  Railroad equipment and transport equipment n.e.c. **

  **Medium, low technology**
  Coke-refined petroleum products and nuclear fuel
  Rubber and plastic products
  Other non-metallic mineral products
  Basic metals *
  Fabricated metal products except machinery and equipment
  Building and repairing of ships and boats ***
  Manufacturing n.e.c.; recycling

  **Low technology**
  Food products, beverages and tobacco
  Textiles, textile products, leather and footwear ***
  Wood and products of wood and cork **
  Pulp paper, paper products, printing and publishing

**Services**
  Wholesale and retail trade; repairs
  Hotels and restaurants ***
  Transport and storage
  Post and telecommunications ***
  Financial intermediation except insurance and pension funding **
  Insurance and pension funding except compulsory social security ***
  Activities related to financial intermediation ***
  Real estate activities ***
  Renting of machinery and equipment ***
  Computer and related activities ***
  Research and development ***
  Other business activities ***

-1  0  1  2  3  4  5  6

Per cent

* indicates significance at 1%, ** at 5% and *** at 10% level.
1. Figures reported are the industry fixed effects in an entry equation that includes country, size and time fixed effect
2. n.e.c.: not elsewhere classified.

Fig. 4.6

## Firm survival rates at different lifetimes[1]

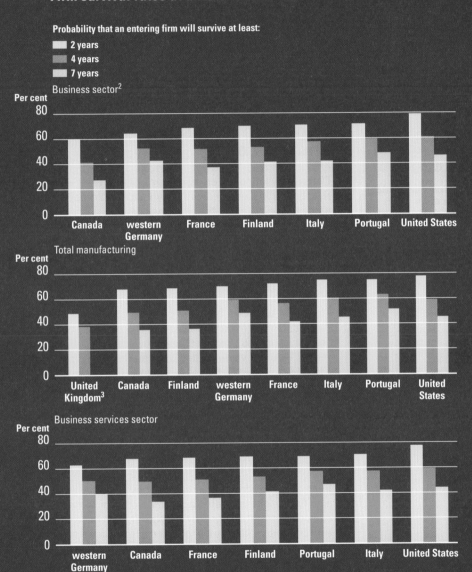

Probability that an entering firm will survive at least:
- 2 years
- 4 years
- 7 years

Business sector[2]

Per cent

Canada · western Germany · France · Finland · Italy · Portugal · United States

Total manufacturing

Per cent

United Kingdom[3] · Canada · Finland · western Germany · France · Italy · Portugal · United States

Business services sector

Per cent

western Germany · Canada · France · Finland · Portugal · Italy · United States

1. Figures refer to average survival rates estimated for different cohorts of firms that entered the market from the late 1980s to the 1990s.
2. Total economy minus agriculture and community services.
3. Data for the United Kingdom refer to cohorts of firms that entered the market in the 1985-1990 period.

incumbents, *i.e.* there is greater scope for expansion amongst young ventures in US markets than in Europe. In turn, the smaller relative size of entrants can be taken to indicate a greater degree of experimentation, with firms starting small and, if successful, expanding rapidly to approach the minimum efficient scale. Firm characteristics at entry are influenced by market conditions (concentration, product diversification, advertising costs etc.) but may also depend on regulations and institutions affecting start-up costs and efficiency-enhancing decisions by existing firms.

# Regulations, institutions and firm entry

Firm-level analysis

**Regulations, institutions and firm entry**

Differences in the observed patterns of firm entry in different countries may be partly explained by policy factors. In order to explore this, the study linked together the firm-level dataset described above with the OECD indicators of regulations and institutional settings. But the decision of a firm to enter the market may depend on a number of additional factors that are not controlled for. In addition, the country coverage is relatively narrow. Therefore, the evidence, and its policy implications, should be viewed as tentative.

The entry equation is based on a theoretical model in which entry depends on the expected (post-entry) profits, net of the costs of entry. The actual proxies used for these two variables are the smoothed growth rate of industry value added, and the smoothed capital intensity (*i.e.* capital stock divided by value added). High capital intensity implies a large share of fixed costs and thus raises entry costs. In this framework, indicators of the stringency of regulations can also influence entrepreneurship. The analysis also accounts for the size effect on firm dynamics (using five size classes, ranging from fewer than 20 employees to more than 500 employees), and allowed us to test whether incentives and disincentives to entry differ according to the size of firms.

Estimated country differences in entry rates are generally statistically significant, but not very large, once control is made for the industry composition of the economy. Moreover, with the exception of Germany and Italy, entry rates are higher in the United States (the reference country in all regressions) than in other countries. The results also suggest a non-linear relationship between entry rates and size: small firms (with fewer than 20 employees) have significantly higher entry rates than the reference group (20-49 employees), while larger firms (50 and more employees) have only marginally lower entry rates.

# Focus on IT

## The contribution of IT at the firm level

A number of studies summarise the early literature on IT, productivity and firm performance (*e.g.* Brynjolfsson and Yang, 1996) [ 3]. Most of these early studies also primarily focus on labour productivity and the return to computer use, not on MFP or other impacts of IT on business performance. Moreover, most of these studies used private sources, since official sources were not yet available. Recent work by statistical offices, using official data, has provided many new insights into the role of IT. To help guide this work with firm-level data, the OECD worked closely with an expert group, composed of researchers and statisticians from 13 OECD countries. This group worked with the OECD Secretariat to generate further evidence on the link between IT and business performance. Their work and that of other researchers is reported in the remainder of this chapter.

There is evidence from many firm-level studies, and from many OECD countries, that IT use has a positive impact on firm performance. These impacts can vary. Fig.4.7 illustrates a typical finding from many firm-level studies that IT-using firms have better productivity performance. It shows that Canadian firms that used either one or more IT technologies had a higher level of productivity than firms that did not use these technologies. Moreover, the gap between technology-using firms and other firms increased between 1988 and 1997, as technology-using firms increased relative productivity compared to non-users. The graph also suggests that some IT technologies are more important in enhancing productivity than other technologies; communication network technologies being particularly important.

The evidence shown in Fig.4.7 is confirmed by many other studies that also point to other impacts of IT on economic performance. For example, firms using IT typically pay higher wages. In addition, the studies show that the use of IT does not guarantee success; many of the firms that improved performance thanks to their use of IT were already experiencing better performance than the average firm. Moreover, the benefits of IT appear to depend on sector-specific effects and are not found equally in all sectors.

There is also evidence that IT can help firms in the competitive process. For the United States, it was found that increases in the capital intensity of the product mix and in the use of advanced manufacturing technologies are positively correlated with plant expansion and negatively with plant exit [ 4]. For Canada, it was found that establishments using advanced technologies gain market share at the expense of non-users [ 5]. Technology users also enjoy a significant labour productivity advantage over non-users, except for establishments that only use fabrication and assembly technologies. Relative labour

### Firm-level analysis

**The contribution of IT at the firm level**

 3 Brynjolfsson, E. and S. Yang (1996), "Information Technology and Productivity: A Review of the Literature", *mimeo,* http://ebusiness.mit.edu/erik/

 4 Doms, M., T. Dunne and M.J. Roberts (1995), "The Role of Technology Use in the Survival and Growth of Manufacturing Plants", *International Journal of Industrial Organization,* Vol. 13, No. 4, December.

 5 Baldwin, J.R. and B. Diverty (1995), "Advanced Technology Use in Canadian Manufacturing Establishments", Working Paper No. 85, Microeconomics Analysis Division, Statistics Canada.

productivity grew fastest in establishments using inspection and communications technologies and in those able to combine and integrate technologies across the different stages of the production process. Technology users were also able to offer higher wages than non-users.

In a recent study for Canada, it was found that a considerable amount of market share is transferred from declining firms to growing firms over a decade [ □ · 6]. At the same time, the growers increase their productivity relative to the declining firms. Those technology users that were using communications technologies or that combined technologies from several different technology classes increased their relative productivity the most. In turn, gains in relative productivity were accompanied by gains in market share. Other factors that were associated with gains in market share were the presence of R&D facilities and other innovative activities.

## Firm-level analysis

### The contribution of IT at the firm level

*Computer networks
play a key role*

□ · 6 Baldwin, J.R. and D. Sabourin (2002), "Impact of the Adoption of Advanced Information and Communication Technologies on Firm Performance in the Canadian Manufacturing Sector", *OECD STI Working Papers*, No. 2002/1.

□ · 7 Atrostic, B.K. and J. Gates (2001), "US Productivity and Electronic Processes in Manufacturing", *CES Working Papers*, No. 01-11, Center for Economic Studies.

□ · 8 Atrostic, B.K. and S. Nguyen (2002), "Computer Networks and US Manufacturing Plant Productivity: New Evidence from the CNUS Data", *CES Working Papers*, No. 02-01, Center for Economic Studies.

□ · 9 Motohashi, K. (2001), "Economic Analysis of Information Network Use: Organisational and Productivity Impacts on Japanese Firms", Research and Statistics Department, METI, *mimeo*.

## *Computer networks play a key role*

Some IT technologies may be more important to strengthen firm performance than others. Computer networks may be particularly important, as they allow a firm to outsource certain activities, to work closer with customers and suppliers, and to better integrate activities throughout the value chain [ □ · 7]. These technologies are often considered to be associated with network or spillover effects. In recent years, more data have become available on this technology. For the United States, for example, a supplement of the Annual Survey of Manufactures provides data on computer network use. Atrostic and Nguyen [ □ · 8] is the first detailed study that directly links computer network use (both Electronic Data Interchange and Internet) to productivity. The study finds that average labour productivity is higher in plants with networks and that the impact of networks is positive and significant after controlling for several production factors and plant characteristics. Networks are estimated to increase labour productivity by roughly 5%, depending on the model specification.

Similar work has been carried out for Japan. The study [ □ · 9] used the Basic Survey on Business Structure and Activities, which provides information about the networks being used by the firm, about certain organisational characteristics of the firm (*e.g.* the degree of outsourcing), and about the occupational structure of the firm. The study finds that the impact of direct business operation networks, such as production and logistic control systems, on productivity is much clearer than that of back office supporting systems, such as human resource management and management planning systems. Firms with networks are also found to have a larger share of white-collar workers and to outsource more production activities.

Fig. 4.7

## Relative labour productivity of advanced technology users and non-users, Canada

Manufacturing sector, 1988 versus 1997

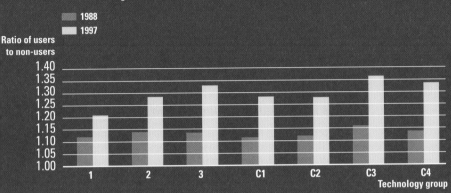

Note: The following technology groups are distinguished: Group 1 (software); Group 2 (hardware); Group 3 (communications); Group C1 (software and hardware); Group C2 (software and communications); Group C3 (hardware and communications); Group C4 (software, hardware and communications).

Source: Baldwin and Sabourin (2002)

Fig. 4.8

## Use of IT network technologies by activity, United Kingdom, 2000[1]

Percentage of all firms, business weighted

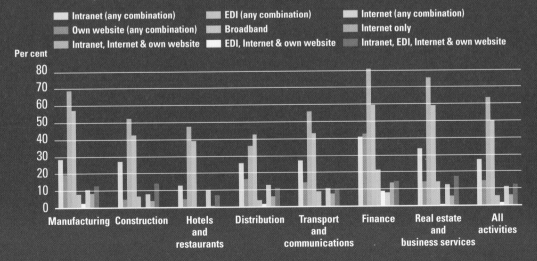

1. Broadband includes xDSL and all other broadband connections.

Source: Clayton and Waldron (2003)

Work in Germany has also focused on computer networks. Bertschek and Fryges [■-- 10] is among the first detailed studies to examine the decision to implement business-to-business (B2B) electronic commerce. It shows that skills and firm size both have a positive and significant impact on e-commerce use. International competition, as measured by exports, also affects the decision to implement B2B, as does the firm's previous use of EDI. The most significant effect is linked to networks; the more firms in an industry that already use B2B, the more likely it is that the firm will also implement B2B.

## Firms in the services sector also benefit from IT

The work with firm-level data is also broadening to the services sector, where IT use is more widespread than in manufacturing. Unfortunately, early studies on IT did not often cover the service sector as the data were poorer. Recently, this has been changing. For example, Doms, *et al.* [■-- 11] constructed a new linked dataset for US retail trade, bringing together a range of different sources. The study's preliminary results show that growth in the US retail sector involves the displacement of traditional retailers by sophisticated retailers introducing new technologies and processes.

The impacts of IT on performance in different sectors of the economy may also be linked to the specific technologies that are being used in different sectors. ● - Fig.4.8 presents evidence for the United Kingdom, which suggests that financial intermediation is the sector most likely to use network technologies, including broadband technology, and also the sector to use combinations of network technologies the most extensively. The combination of several network technologies shows that this sector has intensive users of information and thus has the greatest scope to benefit from IT.

There is also growing evidence for other OECD countries that IT can be beneficial to service sector performance. For Germany, Hempell [■- 12] showed significant productivity effects of IT in the German service sector. Experience gained from past process innovations helps firms to make IT investments more productive. IT investment may thus have contributed to growing productivity differences between firms, and potentially also between countries. For the Netherlands, Broersma and McGuckin [■- 13] used longitudinally linked data from the Annual Survey of Production Statistics to focus on productivity in wholesale and retail trade in the Netherlands. They found that computer investments have a positive impact on productivity and that the impact is greater in retail than in wholesale trade. The study also found that flexible employment practices in retail trade were related to computer use.

■-- 10 Bertschek, I. and H. Fryges (2002), "The Adoption of Business-to-Business E-Commerce: Empirical Evidence for German Companies", *ZEW Discussion Papers,* No.02-05.

## Firm-level analysis

### The contribution of IT at the firm level

*Firms in the services sector also benefit from IT*

■- 11 Doms, M., R. Jarmin and S. Klimek (2002), "IT Investment and Firm Performance in US Retail Trade", *CES Working Papers,* No. 02-14, Center for Economic Studies.

■-- 12 Hempell, T. (2002a), "Does Experience Matter? Productivity Effects of ICT in the German Service Sector", Discussion Papers, No. 02-43, Centre for European Economic Research.

■-- 13 Broersma, L. and R.H. McGuckin (2000), "The Impact of Computers on Productivity in the Trade Sector: Explorations with Dutch Microdata", Research Memorandum GD-45, Growth and Development Centre, June.

■-- 14 Bresnahan, T.F. and S. Greenstein (1996), "Technical Progress and Co-Invention in Computing and the Use of Computers", *Brookings Papers on Economic Activity: Microeconomics.*

## Factors that affect the impact of IT

The evidence summarised above suggests that the use of IT does have impacts on firm performance, but primarily, or only, when accompanied by other changes and investments. Early studies on the rates of return to IT investment suggested that the returns to IT were relatively high compared to other investments in fixed assets. This is commonly attributed to the fact that IT investment is accompanied by many other expenditures in the firm, that are not necessarily counted as investment, for example, expenditure on skills and organisational change. Many empirical studies confirm that IT primarily affects firms where skills have been improved and organisational changes have been introduced. The role of these complementary factors is also raised in the literature on co-invention [ □ · 14], which argues that users help make investment in technologies, such as IT, more valuable through their own experimentation and invention. Without this process of "co-invention", which often has a slower pace than technological invention, the economic impact of IT may be limited. The firm-level evidence also suggests that the uptake and impact of IT differs across firms, varying according to size of firm, age of the firm, activity, etc. This section looks at some of this evidence and discusses the main complementary factors for IT investment.

## IT use is complementary to skills

A substantial number of longitudinal studies address the interaction between technology and human capital, and their joint impact on productivity performance. Although few longitudinal databases include data on worker skills or occupations, some address human capital through wages, arguing that wages are positively correlated with worker skills. For the United States, Baily, Hulten and Campbell [ □ · 15] found a positive link between wages and productivity, although the causality was not clear. Krueger [ □ · 16] used cross-sectional data and found that workers using computers were better paid than those that do not use computers. Dunne and Schmitz [ □ · 17] found that workers employed in establishments that use advanced technologies also pay higher wages. Doms, Dunne and Troske [ □ · 18] found no correlation between technology adoption and wages, however, and conclude that technologically advanced plants pay higher wages both before and after the adoption of new technologies. A more recent study by Luque and Miranda [ □ · 19] found that technological change in US manufacturing was skill-biased.

Some studies are also available for France. The French data include details about worker characteristics, which allows for a more detailed examination of the results. Entorf and Kramarz [ □ · 20] linked a variety of official statistics from the Institut National de la Statistique et des Etudes to examine the interaction between computer use and wages. They found that computer-based technologies are often used by workers with higher skills. These workers become more productive when they

□ · 15 Baily, M.N., C. Hulten, and D. Campbell (1992), "Productivity Dynamics in Manufacturing Plants", *Brookings Papers on Economic Activity: Microeconomics.*

□ · 16 Krueger, A.B. (1993), "How Computers Have Changed the Wage Structure: Evidence from Microdata, 1984-1989", *The Quarterly Journal of Economics*, February.

## Firm-level analysis

### The contribution of IT at the firm level

*Factors that affect the impact of IT*

*IT use is complementary to skills*

□ · 17 Dunne, T. and J. Schmitz (1995), "Wages, Employment Structure and Employer Size- Wage Premia: Their Relationship to Advanced-technology Usage at US Manufacturing Establishments", *Economica*, March.

□ · 18 Doms, M., T. Dunne and K.R. Troske (1997), "Workers, Wages and Technology", *Quarterly Journal of Economics*, 112, No. 1.

□ · 19 Luque, A. (2000), "An Option-Value Approach to Technology Adoption in US Manufacturing: Evidence from Plant-Level Data", *CES Working Papers*, No. 00-12, Center for Economic Studies.

□ · 20 Entorf, H. and F. Kramarz (1998), "The Impact of New Technologies on Wages: Lessons from Matching Panels on Employees and on their Firms", *Economic Innovation and New Technology*, Vol. 5.

[...] 21 Caroli, E. and J. van Reenen (1999), *"Organization, Skills and Technology: Evidence from a Panel of British and French Establishments"*, *IFS Working Paper Series* W99/23, Institute of Fiscal Studies, August.

## Firm-level analysis

### The contribution of IT at the firm level

*IT use is complementary to skills*

[...] 22 Greenan, N., J. Mairesse and A. Topiol-Bensaid (2001), "Information Technology and Research and Development Impacts on Productivity and Skills: Looking for Correlations on French Firm Level Data", *NBER Working Papers*, No. 8075.

[...] 23 Haskel, J. and Y. Heden (1999), "Computers and the Demand for Skilled Labour: Industry- and Establishment-Level Panel Evidence for the UK", *The Economic Journal*, 109, C68-C79, March.

[...] 24 Baldwin, J.R. and B. Diverty (1995), "Advanced Technology Use in Canadian Manufacturing Establishments", *Working Papers*, No. 85, Microeconomics Analysis Division, Statistics Canada.

[...] 25 Luque, A. and J. Miranda (2000), "Technology Use and Worker Outcomes: Direct Evidence from Linked Employee-Employer Data", *CES Working Papers*, No. 00-13, Center for Economic Studies.

get more experienced in using these technologies. The introduction of new technologies also contributes to a small increase in wage differentials within firms. Caroli and Van Reenen [[...] 21] found that French plants that introduce organisational change are more likely to reduce their demand for unskilled workers than those that do not. Shortages in skilled workers may reduce the probability of organisational changes. Moreover, the introduction of organisational changes in France would lead to significantly faster productivity growth. Greenan, *et al.* [[...] 22] also found evidence of a skill-bias in the use of computers. They found strong positive correlations between indicators of computerisation and research on the one hand, and productivity, average wages and the share of administrative managers on the other hand. They also found negative correlations between these indicators and the share of blue-collar workers.

For the United Kingdom, Haskel and Heden [[...] 23] used the UK's Annual Respondents Database together with a set of data on computerisation. They found that computerisation reduces the demand for manual workers, even when controlling for endogeneity, human capital upgrading and technological opportunities. Caroli and Van Reenen found evidence for the United Kingdom that human capital, technology and organisational change are complementary, and that organisational change reduces the demand for unskilled workers.

Studies for Canada also point to the complementarity between technology and skills. For example, Baldwin *et al.* [[...] 24] found that use of advanced technology was associated with a higher level of skill requirements. In Canadian plants using advanced technologies, this often led to a higher incidence of training. They also found that firms adopting advanced technologies increased their expenditure on education and training.

The majority of these micro-level studies thus confirm the complementarity between technology and skills in improving productivity performance. Many also found that computers are a skill-biased technology, *i.e.* increasing the demand for skilled workers and reducing the demand for unskilled workers.

A few studies have also looked at other worker-related impacts. For example, Luque and Miranda [[...] 25] find that the skill-biased technological change associated with the uptake of advanced technologies also affects worker mobility. The larger the number of advanced technologies adopted by a plant, the higher is the probability of exit of the worker. Their interpretation is that workers at technologically advanced plants have higher unobserved ability, and therefore can get a higher opportunity wage when they exit. The other mechanism at work is that less skilled workers tend to be pushed to plants that are less technologically advanced.

## Organisational change is key to making IT work

Closely linked to human capital is the role of organisational change. Studies typically find that the greatest benefits from IT are realised when IT investment is combined with other organisational changes, such as new strategies, new business processes and practices and new organisational structures. In the past, workers were required to perform specialised tasks within the framework of standardised production processes. In today's economy, they are often given responsibilities in different domains, for which multiple skills and the ability to work in teams are required. This phenomenon is reflected in the large variety of new work practices that are being implemented by firms. These include, inter alia, teamwork, flatter management structures, employee involvement and suggestion schemes. The common element among these practices is that they entail a greater degree of responsibility of individual workers regarding the content of their work and, to some extent, a greater proximity between management and labour. Because organisational change tends to be firm-specific, empirical studies show on average a positive return to IT investment, but with a huge variation across organisations.

For Germany, Bertschek and Kaiser [▯ · 26] draw on ZEW's quarterly Service Sector Business Survey to explore the impact of IT and organisational change on performance. The study finds that changes in human resource practices, such as the enhancement of team work and the flattening of hierarchies, do not significantly affect firm's output elasticities with respect to IT capital, non-IT capital and labour. The study does not find evidence of significant differences in returns to scale. It does, however, find that the introduction of organisational changes raises overall labour productivity. Studies at ZEW have also explored the link between IT use, organisational change and human capital. Falk [▯ · 27] used results from the 1995 and 1997 Mannheim Innovation Panel in Services (MIP-S), which is part of the Community Innovation Survey. He found that the introduction of IT and the share of training expenditures are important drivers of organisational changes, such as the introduction of total quality management, lean administration, flatter hierarchies and delegation of authority. The study finds that organisational changes have a positive impact on actual employment and on expected employment, apart from unskilled groups. Falk found that firms with a higher diffusion of IT employ a larger fraction of workers with a university degree as well as IT specialists. A greater penetration of IT is negatively related to the share of both medium- and low-skilled workers.

For France, Greenan and Guellec [▯ · 28] found that the use of advanced technologies and the skills of the workforce are both positively linked to organisational variables. An organisation that enables communication within the firm and that innovates at the organisational level seems better able to create the conditions for a successful uptake of advanced technologies. Moreover, these changes also seemed to increase the ability of firms to adjust to changing market conditions through technological innovation and the reduction of inventories.

### Firm-level analysis

**The Contribution of IT at the firm level**

*Organisational change is key to making IT work*

▯ · 26 Bertschek, I. and U. Kaiser (2001), "Productivity Effects of Organizational Change: Microeconometric Evidence", *ZEW Discussion Papers*, No. 01-32.

▯ · 27 Falk, M. (2001), "Organizational Change, New Information and Communication Technologies and the Demand for Labor in Services", *ZEW Discussion Papers*, No. 01-25.

▯ · 28 Greenan, N. and D. Guellec (1998), "Firm Organization, Technology and Performance: An Empirical Study", *Economics of Innovation and New Technology*, Vol. 6, No. 4.

## Firm size affects the impact of IT

A substantial number of studies have looked at the relationship between IT and firm size. This relationship can work in different ways. The first question is whether there is a difference in the uptake of IT by size classes. This question has been addressed in a large number of studies in many countries, which find that the adoption of advanced technologies, such as IT, increases with the size of firms and plants.

● ·Fig.4.9 confirms this result for the United Kingdom, with recent data for a variety of network technologies, used in different combinations. It shows that large firms of over 250 employees are more likely to use network technologies such as Intranet, Internet or Electronic Data Interchange (EDI) than small firms; they are also more likely to have their own website. However, small firms of between 10 and 49 employees are more likely to use Internet as their only IT network technology. Large firms are also more likely to use a combination of network technologies. For example, over 38% of all large UK firms use Intranet, EDI and Internet, and also have their own website, as opposed to less than 5% of small firms. Moreover, almost 45% of all large firms already use broadband technologies as opposed to less than 7% of small firms. These differences are linked to the different uses of the network technologies by large and small firms. Large firms may use the technologies to redesign information and communication flows within the firm, and to integrate these flows throughout the production process. Some small firms only use the Internet for marketing purposes.

There is also a question whether IT has an effect on the size of firms, or changes the boundaries of firms over time. This question is linked to the expectation that IT might help lower transaction costs and thus change the functions and tasks that should be carried out within firms and those that could be carried out outside the firm boundaries. This issue has been researched by fewer firm-level studies, most of which use private data. For example, Hitt [■ · 29] finds that increased use of IT is associated with decreases in vertical integration and an increase in diversification. Moreover, firms that are less vertically integrated and more diversified have a higher demand for IT capital. Motohashi [■ · 9] found that firms with computer networks outsource more activities.

## Ownership, competition and management are important

Firm-level studies also point to the importance of ownership changes and management in the uptake of technology. For example, a study by McGuckin and Nguyen [■ · 30] for the food processing industry found that plants with above-average productivity are more likely to change owners and that the acquiring firms also tended to have above-average productivity. Plants that changed owners generally improved productivity following the change. According to the authors, ownership changes appear associated with the purchase or integration of advanced technologies and better practices into new firms.

Firm-level analysis

**The contribution of IT at the firm level**

*Firm size affects the impact of IT*

*Ownership, competition and management are important*

■ · 29 Hitt, L.M. (1998), "Information Technology and Firm Boundaries: Evidence from Panel Data", University of Pennsylvania, *mimeo*.

■ · 30 McGuckin, R.H. and S.V. Nguyen (1995), "On Productivity and Plant Ownership Change: New Evidence from the LRD", *Rand Journal of Economics*, 26, No. 2.

Fig. 4.9

## Use of IT network technologies by size class, United Kingdom, 2000

Percentage of all firms business-weighted

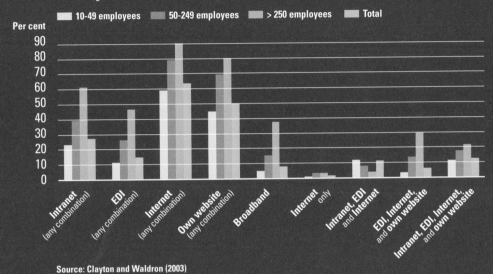

Source: Clayton and Waldron (2003)

Fig. 4.10

## Level of e-activity in 2000 as a percentage of all firms adopting IT in various years

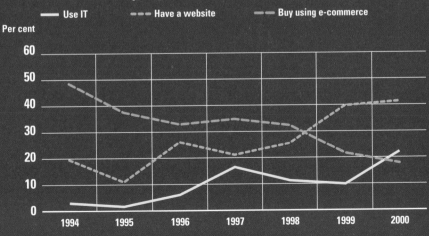

Source: Clayton and Waldron (2003)

Some studies also point to the impact of competition. A study by Baldwin and Diverty [🔲 · 31] found that foreign-owned plants were more likely to adopt advanced technologies than domestic plants. For Germany, Bertschek and Fryges [🔲 · 10] found that international competition was an important factor driving a firm's decision to implement B2B electronic commerce. These findings should be linked to the results of several firm-level studies that show that the implementation of advanced technologies can help firms to gain market share and to reduce the likelihood of plant exit.

## IT use is closely linked to innovation

Several studies point to an important link between the use of IT and the ability of a company to adjust to changing demand and to innovate. The clearest example of this link is found in work on Germany by ZEW, as this draws on innovation survey results. For example, Licht and Moch [🔲 · 32] found that information technology has important impacts on the qualitative aspects of service innovation, but not on productivity.

Hempell [🔲 · 33] also uses data from the MIP-S. The MIP-S not only contains data on innovation, but also on sales, employees, skills and investment (in both IT and non-IT capital). The study finds that firms that have introduced process innovations in the past are particularly successful in using IT; the output elasticity of IT capital for these firms is estimated to be about 12%, about four times that of other firms. This suggests that the productive use of IT is closely linked to innovation in general, and to the re-engineering of processes in particular. Moreover, the introduction of IT has many similarities with innovation, as it is risky and uncertain, with potentially positive outcomes.

Studies in other countries also confirm this link. For example, Greenan and Guellec [🔲 · 34] found that organisational change and the uptake of advanced technologies seemed to increase the ability of firms to adjust to changing market conditions through technological innovation.

## The impacts of IT use only emerge over time

Given the time it takes to adapt to IT, it should not be surprising that the benefits of IT may only emerge over time. This can be seen in the relationship between the use of IT and the year in which firms first adopted IT. ● · Fig.4.10 shows evidence for the United Kingdom. It shows that among the firms that had already adopted IT in or before 1995, close to 50% bought via electronic commerce in 2000. For firms that only adopted IT in 2000, less than 20% bought via e-commerce. The graph also suggests that firms move towards more complex forms of electronic activity over time; out of all firms starting to use IT prior to 1995, only 3% had not yet moved beyond the straightforward use of IT in 2000. Most had established an Internet site, or bought or sold through e-commerce. Out of the firms adopting IT in 2000, over 20% had not yet gone beyond the simple use of IT.

🔲 · 31 Baldwin, J.R.,
B. Diverty, and D. Sabourin (1995),
"Technology Use and Industrial
Transformation: Empirical Perspective",
Working Paper No. 75, Microeconomics
Analysis Division, Statistics Canada.

🔲 · 32 Licht, G. and D. Moch (1999),
"Innovation and Information
Technology in Services",
*Canadian Journal of Economics*,
Vol. 32, No. 2, April.

🔲 · 33 Hempell, T. (2002),
"Does Experience Matter? Productivity
Effects of ICT in the German Service Sector",
*Discussion Papers*, No. 02-43,
Centre for European Economic Research.

🔲 · 34 Greenan, N. and D. Guellec (1998),
"Firm Organization, Technology
and Performance: An Empirical Study",
*Economics of Innovation
and New Technology*, Vol. 6, No. 4.

Fig. 4.11

## Differences in productivity outcomes between Germany and the United States

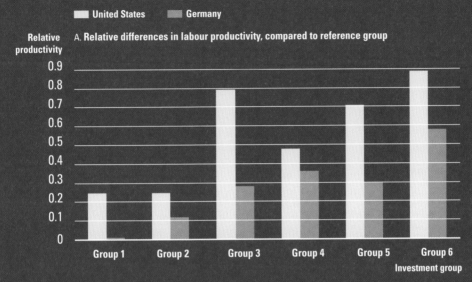

■ United States   ■ Germany

Relative
productivity

A. Relative differences in labour productivity, compared to reference group

Investment group

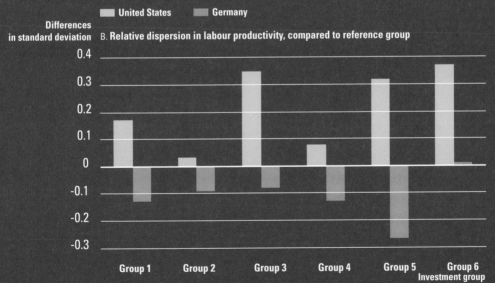

■ United States   ■ Germany

Differences
in standard deviation

B. Relative dispersion in labour productivity, compared to reference group

Investment group

Note:  Differences are in logs and are shown relative to a reference group of zero total investment and zero investment in IT. The groups are distinguished on the basis of total investment (0, low, high) and IT investment (0, low, high). Group 1 has low overall investment and zero IT investment. Group 2 has low overall investment and low IT investment. Group 3 has high overall investment and zero IT investment. Group 4 has low overall investment and high IT investment. Group 5 has high overall investment and low IT investment. Group 6 has high overall investment and high IT investment.

Source:  Haltiwanger, Jarmin and Schank (2002).

## Does the impact of IT at the firm level differ across countries?

■□ ▸ 35 Bartelsman,
E. A. Bassanini, J. Haltiwanger, R. Jarmin,
S. Scarpetta and T. Schank (2002),
"The Spread of ICT and Productivity
Growth – Is Europe Really Lagging
Behind in the New Economy?",
Fondazione Rodolfo DeBenedetti, *mimeo*.

## Firm-level analysis

### The contribution of IT at the firm level

*Does the impact of IT
at the firm level
differ across countries?*

Cross-country studies on the impact of IT at the firm level are still relatively rare, primarily since many of the original data sources were of an ad-hoc nature and not comparable across countries. In recent years, the growing similarity of official statistics is enabling more comparative work. An example is a recent comparison between the United States and Germany [■□ ▸ 35] that examines the relationship between labour productivity and measures of the choice of technology. ● · Fig.4.11 illustrates some of the empirical findings. The first panel shows that firms at any level of IT investment have much stronger productivity growth in the United States than in Germany. Moreover, firms with high IT investment have stronger productivity growth than firms with low IT investment.

The second panel of the graph shows that firms in the United States have much greater variation in their productivity performance than firms in Germany. This may suggest that US firms engage in much more experimentation than their German counterparts; they take greater risks and opt for potentially higher outcomes.

Firm-Level analysis:
# Key conclusions

Firm-level analysis

**Key conclusions**

- **Within-firm growth makes a smaller contribution to MFP growth than it does to labour productivity growth.**

- **The United States, the country at the forefront in adopting new technologies over the recent period, has also displayed greater variability of productivity levels amongst entering firms than other countries for which the data was available.**

- **Both European and US firms share these general features, but to a somewhat different extent. US entrant firms appear to be smaller and less productive than their European counterparts, but grow faster when successful.**

- **Overall, empirical evidence indicates that the use of IT has a positive influence on firm-performance. However, the use of IT does not guarantee success, seeing as most firms that improved performance thanks to their use of IT were already experiencing better performance than the average firm.**

# Macroeconomic indicators of economic growth

Annex 1

Macroeconomic Indicators of Economic Growth

A1.1. **Measurement of labour and capital inputs**

A1.2. **Estimates of trend output and trend labour productivity**

# Macroeconomic indicators of economic growth

## A1.1. Measurement of labour and capital inputs

Measures of factor use for the purpose of productivity analysis are constructed so as to reflect the role that each factor plays as input in the production process. In the case of labour input, different types of labour should be weighted by their marginal contribution to the production activity in which they are employed. Since these productivity measures are generally not observable, information on relative wages by characteristics is used to derive the required weights to aggregate different types of labour. Concerning physical capital, Jorgenson [▪▪·1] and Jorgenson and Griliches [▪▪·2] were the first to develop aggregate capital input measures that took the heterogeneity of assets into account. They defined the flow of quantities of capital services individually for each type of asset, and then applied asset-specific user costs as weights to aggregate across services from the different types of assets. User costs are prices for capital services and, under competitive markets and equilibrium conditions, these prices reflect marginal productivity of the different assets. User cost weights are thus a means to effectively incorporate differences in the productive contribution of heterogeneous investments as the composition of investment and capital changes. Changes in aggregate capital input, therefore, have two distinct sources – changes in the quantity of capital of a given type, and changes in the composition of the various types of assets with different marginal products and user costs [▪▪·3].

### Productivity growth measures without adjustment for different types of factor input

The following notation is used to discuss factor productivity with and without control for quality effects:

| | |
|---|---|
| $Y$ | Current price value-added; |
| $P$ | Price index of value-added; |
| $N$ | Total number of persons engaged; |
| $H$ | Average hours worked per person; |
| $N*H$ | Total hours worked; |
| $K$ | Aggregate gross capital stock. |

Letting lower case letters represent logarithms and $\Delta$ the first difference operator, $\Delta x$ approximates the (instantaneous) growth rate of any variable $x$. The standard measure of factor productivity growth rates, $\Delta\pi_L$ and $\Delta\pi_K$ are given by:

$$\Delta\pi_L = \Delta y - \Delta p - (\Delta n + \Delta h) \quad \text{Labour productivity}$$
$$\Delta\pi_K = \Delta y - \Delta p - \Delta k \quad \text{Capital productivity}$$

---

Sidebar:

Macroeconomic indicators of economic growth

A1.1. **Measurement of labour and capital inputs**

*Productivity growth measures without adjustment for different types of factor input*

▪▪·1 Jorgenson, D.W. (1963), "Capital Theory and Investment Behaviour", *American Economic Review*, Vol. 53, No. 2.

▪▪·2 Jorgenson, D.W. and Z. Griliches (1967), "The Explanation of Productivity Change", *Review of Economic Studies*, Vol. 34, No. 3.

▪▪·3 Ho, M.S., D.W. Jorgenson and K.J. Stiroh (1999), "U.S. High-Tech Investment and the Pervasive Slowdown in the Growth of Capital Services", *mimeo*.

This standard specification does not differentiate between different types of inputs: it attaches the same weight to each hour worked, and it does not differentiate between assets even though their marginal contribution to output may be quite different. Such differentiation can be introduced when there is information on quantities and prices of the different types of factor inputs. In the case of labour, prices will represent the skill-specific wage rate, and in the case of capital the asset specific rental price or user cost of capital. In what follows different types of labour and capital will be distinguished by the subscript $j$.

## Productivity growth measures with adjustment for different types of factor input

Given a set of observations on different types of labour or capital and a set of corresponding prices, $w_{j,t}$, it is possible to construct an aggregate variable $F$ that combines quantities of different types of inputs to a measure of total, quality-adjusted labour or capital input. In this regard, productivity studies often use the Törnqvist index and this practice is followed here. A Törnqvist index of factor input $F$ is given by the expression below, where $v_{j,t}$ stands for the share of the component $j$ in total costs of the factor. This is a conceptually correct measure for the flow of the total quantity of labour or capital services:

[A1.1]

$$\Delta f_t(adj) = \sum_j \overline{v}_{j,t} \cdot \Delta f_{j,t} \quad \text{où} \quad \overline{v}_{j,t} = \frac{1}{2}\left(v_{j,t} + v_{j,t-1}\right) \quad \text{et} \quad v_{j,t} = \frac{w_{j,t}\,F_{j,t}}{\sum_i w_{i,t}\,F_{i,t}}$$

Thus, the growth rate of total factor input $\Delta f$, using the Törnqvist index, is a weighted average of the growth rates of different components. Weights correspond to the current price share in the overall cost for each factor. Subtracting the unadjusted measure of factor input from the one adjusted for compositional changes yields an expression $\Delta cf$ for the effects of changing factor quality on total factor input services:

$$\Delta cl = \Delta l(adj) - (\Delta n + \Delta h) \qquad \text{[A1.2]}$$
$$\Delta ck = \Delta k(adj) - \Delta k \qquad \text{[A1.3]}$$

Equations [A1.2] and [A1.3] can be rearranged to yield a decomposition of the overall growth in factor input:

$$\Delta l(adj) = \Delta cl + \Delta n + \Delta h$$
$$\Delta k(adj) = \Delta ck + \Delta k$$

## Labour input

In order to consider changes in the composition of labour input, six different types of labour were considered, based on gender and three different educational levels: below upper secondary education;

upper secondary education and tertiary education. Thus, following equation [A1.1] and assuming that $L_j$ indicates the labour input $j$th with $j = 1, 2, \ldots 6$ and that each type of labour is remunerated with wage rate $w_j$, then a measure of adjusted labour input can be obtained. There are, however, a number of issues worth noting, including:

- First, it is assumed that the rate change in average weekly or yearly hours is identical between education and gender groups, *i.e.* $\Delta h_j = \Delta h$ for all $j$. This simplification can be used, in conjunction with the relation $\Delta l_j = \Delta n_j + \Delta h_j$.

## Macroeconomic Indicators of Economic Growth

### A1.1. **Measurement of labour and capital inputs**

*Capital input*

◻→ 4a Bassanini, A.,
S. Scarpetta and I. Visco (2000),
"Knowledge, Technology
and Economic Growth:
Recent Evidence from OECD Countries",
*OECD Economics Department
Working Papers*, No. 259.

4b Colecchia, A.,
and P. Schreyer (2002),
"ICT Investment and Economic Growth
in the 1990s: Is the United States
a Unique Case? A Comparative Study
of Nine OECD Countries"
*Review of Economic Dynamics*,
Vol. 5, No. 2.

- Second, data on relative wage rates by educational attainment and gender are only available for the 1990s, and relative wage rates were thus assumed to be constant over the period considered in the analysis. More specifically, for the six available categories of education and gender, the wage spread was computed as :

$$\frac{w_j}{w_{M,U\text{-}SE}} \quad, j = 2, 3, 4, 5, 6$$

as each education category's wage rate relative to wages of male workers with upper-secondary education ($w_{M,U\text{-}SE}$).

- Third, the weights $w_{j,c}$ from equation [A1.1] for country $c$ can be rewritten in terms of relative wages:

$$v_{j,c} = \frac{w_{j,c} N_{j,c}}{\sum\limits_{i=1}^{6} w_{i,c} N_{i,c}} = \frac{\dfrac{w_{j,c}}{w_{M,U-SE,c}} N_{j,c}}{\sum\limits_{i=1}^{6} \dfrac{w_{i,c}}{w_{M,U-SE,c}} N_{i,c}}$$

## *Capital input*

Standard measures of capital (based on aggregation of stocks made up of a moving sum of investment at real acquisition prices) rely on two assumptions [◻→ 4] :

- the flow of capital services is a constant proportion of an estimated measure of the capital stock and, thus, the rate of change of capital services over time coincides with the rate of change of the capital stock as estimated by cumulating measurable investment according to assumptions about asset lifetimes, physical depreciation, etc;
- the aggregate capital stock is made up of one homogenous type of asset or alternatively different assets that generate the same marginal revenues in production.

Alternatively, Jorgenson and Griliches (1967) [◻→ 2] proposed to compute growth rates of capital service of individual assets given information on investment flows, on the service life and on the profile of wear and tear of an asset. Then they suggested aggregating these different capital assets by their marginal productivities, proxied by user costs. User costs are composed of:

- the opportunity cost of investing money in financial (or other) assets rather than in a capital good;
- the physical depreciation, *i.e.* the loss in efficiency/productivity of the capital asset as it ages;
- the (expected) capital gain or loss (change in the real value of the asset unrelated to physical depreciation). These three components are reflected in the following expression, where $q_j$ is the asset's acquisition price, $r$ is the real rate of interest, and $d_j$ is the asset-specific rate of depreciation. Following the expression in [A1.1] above, the weighting factor for each asset $\mu_j$ is proxied by the user cost as:

[A1.4]

$$\mu_{j,t} = q_{j,t}\left(r_t + d_{j,t} - \frac{\Delta q^e_{j,t+1}}{q_{j,t}}\right) = q_{j,t}(r_t + d_{j,t}) - \Delta q^e_{j,t+1}$$

The inclusion of the market depreciation $(-\Delta q_j)$ as well as its exact quantification have been debated in the literature. Griliches himself suggests that only physical depreciation should be considered in the user cost, but not the market depreciation. The choice is in fact model dependent. In a putty-clay vintage model productivity is unchanged during the machine's whole lifetime; therefore, if the lifetime is sufficiently long, the marginal productivity of capital can be approximated by the right-hand side of equation [A1.4] without the market depreciation term. Alternatively, equation [A1.4] can be rationalised through the evolution along the balanced growth path of a putty-putty vintage model with perfect foresight (*i.e.*, $q^e_j = q_j$). However, outside the balanced growth path, market depreciation in a puttyputty vintage model should be introduced in equation [A1.4] in expected terms [● 1]. In practice, the expression proposed by Jorgenson and Griliches [◫ 2], the one more commonly used in the literature, assumes extrapolative expectations, while an expression without market depreciation could be rationalised through myopic expectations.

The capital service measure used here is taken from Colecchia and Schreyer [◫ 4b]. It is calculated for nine countries (including the G-7) on the basis of an aggregation across seven types of capital goods (including three IT capital goods – IT hardware, communications equipment and software), weighted with their user costs also considering capital gains or losses and hedonic deflators. Given the great heterogeneity of physical capital assets, this is still a fairly high level of aggregation. As a matter of comparison, Jorgenson generally uses a decomposition of capital into 69 different assets.

● 1 It should also be stressed that aggregation through (however defined) user costs assumes that assets are homogeneous. This implies that different vintages of the same machine should be counted as different assets, while their current prices (expressed in terms of the output deflator) appear in equation [A1.4]. In practice, however, this would introduce unsolvable problems in the construction of growth rates for new machines. As a solution, Jorgenson and Griliches (1967) suggest extending the foregoing procedure to aggregate different vintages of the same asset through the use of hedonic price indexes. In this way the aggregate flow of capital services of each asset across all vintages can be seen as proportional to the existing stock of that capital asset expressed in efficiency units.

[-> 5 Hodrick, R.
and E. Prescott (1997),
"Post-war US Business Cycles:
An Empirical Investigation",
*Journal of Money, Credit and Banking,*
Vol. 29.

[-> 6a Butler, L. (1996),
"A Semi-Structural Approach
to Estimate Potential Output:
Combining Economic Theory
with A Time-Series Filter",
Bank of Canada Technical Report, No. 76.

Macroeconomic Indicators
of Economic Growth

A1.2. **Estimates of trend
output and trend labour
productivity**

6b Conway, P. and B. Hunt (1997),
"Estimating Potential Output:
A Semi-Structural Approach",
*Bank of New Zealand
Discussion Papers,* No. G97/9.

[-> 7 Harvey, A.C.
and A. Jaeger (1993),
"Detrending, Stylized Facts
and the Business Cycle",
*Journal of Applied Econometrics,* Vol. 8.

[-> 8 Scarpetta, S., A. Bassanini,
D. Pilat and P. Schreyer (2000),
"Economic Growth in the OECD Area:
Recent Trends at the Aggregate
and Sectoral Level",
*OECD Economics Department
Working Papers,* No. 248.

[-> 9a Gordon, R.J. (1997),
"The Time-Varying NAIRU and Its
Implications for Economic Policy",
*Journal of Economic Perspectives,* Vol. 11.

9b OECD (1999),
*Implementing the OECD Jobs Strategy:
Assessing Performance and Policy.*

9c OECD (1999),
*OECD Economic Outlook,* No. 68.

Given the time series on $K_{j,t}^P$ and $\mu_{j,t}$, asset specific weights $v_{j,t}$ as in equation [A1.1] are given by:

$$v_{j,t} = \frac{\mu_{j,t} K_{j,t}^P}{\sum\limits_{i=1}^{6} \mu_{i,t} K_{i,t}^P}$$

## A1.2. **Estimates of trend output and trend labour productivity**

This section describes the method used to estimate trend time series: the extended Hodrick-Prescott filter [■ · 5]. Actual and trend figures for growth in GDP, GDP per capita and GDP per person employed (in the whole economy and in the business sector only) are presented in [● · Tables A1.1 to A1.8]. The Hodrick-Prescott (H-P) filter belongs to a family of stochastic approaches that treats the cyclical component of observed output as a stochastic phenomenon. The cyclical component (demand shocks) is separated from the permanent component (supply shocks) under the assumption that the former has only a temporary effect, while the latter persists. The H-P filter is derived by minimising the sum of squared deviations of the log variable (*e.g.* GDP) (*y*) from the estimated trend $\tau_y$, subject to a smoothness constraint that penalises squared variations in the growth of the estimated trend series. Thus, H-P trend values are those that minimise:

[A1.5]

$$HP(\lambda) = \Sigma \left(y_t - \tau_{y,t}\right)^2 + \lambda \Sigma \left[\left(\tau_{y,t+1} - \tau_{y,t}\right) - \left(\tau_{y,t} - \tau_{y,t-1}\right)\right]^2$$

The estimated trend variable $\tau_y$ is a function of $\lambda$ and both past and future values of $y$. Higher values of $\lambda$ imply a large weight on smoothness in the estimated trend series (for very large values the estimated trend series will converge to a linear time trend). Apart from the arbitrary choice of the $\lambda$ parameter (set to the standard value of 400 for semi-annual time series), the H-P filter may lead to "inaccurate" results if the temporary component contains a great deal of persistence. The distinction between temporary and permanent components then becomes particularly difficult, especially at the end of the sample when the H-P filter suffers from an in-sample phase shift problem.

In order to reduce the end-of-sample problem, the H-P filter is modified to take into account the information carried by the average historical growth rate [■ · 6]. Thus, trend values obtained through the Extended Hodrick-Prescott filter (EHP) would be those that minimise:

[A1.6]

$$EHP(w_1, w_2, \lambda) = \Sigma w_1\left(y_t - \tau_{y,t}\right)^2 + \Sigma w_2\left(\Delta\tau_{y,t} - g_{y,T_1,T_2}\right)^2 + \lambda \Sigma \left[\left(\tau_{y,t+1} - \tau_{y,t}\right) - \left(\tau_{y,t} - \tau_{y,t-1}\right)\right]^2$$

where the two w parameter vectors are the vectors of weights attached to the gap terms, $\Delta\tau_y$ is the growth rate of estimated trend output and $g$ is the historical growth rate between dates $T_1$ and $T_2$. The choice of weights determines the importance of the two gaps in the minimisation problem. In the estimations used earlier, $w_1$ is set equal to 1 in the sample period and to 0 afterwards, $w_2$ is set equal to 0 in the sample period and to 1 afterwards. Given the objective of estimating recent growth patterns, this way to solve the end-point problem can be considered as a prudent approach.

In fact it underestimates sharp deviations from the historical pattern in the neighbourhood of the end of the sample. On the other hand, its estimates can be considered as a lower bound in the case of acceleration of the growth rate in the most recent years (or vice versa in the case of deceleration) [● 2].

The end-point problem is not the only severe theoretical pitfall of the HP filter. When the supply-side components are subject to temporary stochastic shocks with greater variance than that of the demand-side component, or when the demand-side component has a significant degree of persistence, the decomposition of cycle and trend estimated by an H-P filter turns out to be inaccurate [■□··6b-7]. Scarpetta *et al.* [■□·8] also present a sensitivity analysis in which the extended H-P series of GDP growth are compared with those based on a Multivariate filter (MV). With the MV filter, information about the output-inflation process (Phillips Curve) and the employment-output process (Okun's law) is thus included in the optimisation problem [● 3]. To the extent that these two processes are well identified, data on inflation and employment help in the identification of trend output. The combined estimation of trend output, the Phillips curve and the Okun's curve guarantee consistent estimation of trend output and trend employment. Moreover, the ratio of the two series yields a consistent measure of trend labour productivity. Also in this case, estimates of trend GDP growth rates are broadly consistent with those obtained by the extended H-P filter discussed above.

■□··10 Moosa, I.A. (1997), "A Cross-country Comparison of Okun's Coefficient", *Journal of Comparative Economics*, Vol. 24.

■□··11a Laxton, D. and R. Tetlow (1992), "A Simple Multivariate Filter for the Measurement of Potential Output", *Bank of Canada Technical Report*, No. 59.

11b Apel, M. and P. Jansson (1999), "A Theory-Consistent Approach for Estimating Potential Output and the NAIRU", *Economics Letters*, No. 74.

## Macroeconomic indicators of economic growth

### A1.2. Estimates of trend output and trend labour productivity

● 2 Scarpetta *et al.* (2000) also compare trend series obtained with this approach with those obtained extending the time series by means of the OECD Medium Term Reference Scenario (MTRS). The results are broadly similar, although in a few instances estimated growth rates for the most recent years show some differences. Amongst the G-7 countries, trend GDP growth rates for Japan in 2000 will be somewhat lower using MTRS, while significant differences for 1999 and 2000 are also found for Ireland, Korea, Mexico and Turkey (with lower GDP growth rates obtained by using MTRS) as well as Greece (with higher GDP growth rate obtained by using MTRS).

● 3 The use of both is not frequent in the literature: the Phillips curve has been used more widely [■□··9], however Okun's law has been used by Moosa [■□··10]. Laxton and Tetlow, Conway and Hunt and Apel and Jansson [■□··6b-11] use both.

## Actual GDP growth in the OECD area

Total economy, percentage change at annual rate

| Total economy | 1970-00 | 1970-80 | 1980-90 | 1990[1]-00 | 1996-00 |
|---|---|---|---|---|---|
| United States | 3.2 | 3.2 | 3.2 | 3.2 | 4.2 |
| Japan | 3.3 | 4.4 | 4.1 | 1.3 | 0.7 |
| Germany | .. | .. | .. | 1.6 | 2.0 |
| *western Germany* | 2.5 | 2.7 | 2.2 | .. | .. |
| France | 2.5 | 3.3 | 2.4 | 1.8 | 2.9 |
| Italy | 2.5 | 3.6 | 2.2 | 1.6 | 2.1 |
| United Kingdom | 2.3 | 1.9 | 2.7 | 2.3 | 2.9 |
| Canada | 3.3 | 4.3 | 2.8 | 2.8 | 4.4 |
| Australia | 3.3 | 3.2 | 3.2 | 3.5 | 4.2 |
| Austria | 2.8 | 3.6 | 2.3 | 2.3 | 2.7 |
| Belgium | 2.5 | 3.4 | 2.1 | 2.1 | 3.2 |
| Czech Republic | .. | .. | .. | 1.5 | 0.1 |
| Denmark | 2.2 | 2.2 | 1.9 | 2.3 | 2.8 |
| Finland | 2.9 | 3.5 | 3.1 | 2.2 | 5.3 |
| Greece | 2.5 | 4.6 | 0.7 | 2.3 | 3.7 |
| Hungary | .. | .. | .. | 2.3 | 4.7 |
| Iceland | 3.9 | 6.3 | 2.7 | 2.6 | 4.6 |
| Ireland | 5.2 | 4.7 | 3.6 | 7.3 | 10.4 |
| Korea | 7.5 | 7.6 | 8.9 | 6.1 | 4.3 |
| Luxembourg | 4.3 | 2.6 | 4.5 | 5.9 | 7.1 |
| Mexico | 4.0 | 6.6 | 1.8 | 3.5 | 5.6 |
| Netherlands | 2.7 | 2.9 | 2.2 | 2.9 | 3.8 |
| New Zealand | 2.2 | 1.6 | 2.5 | 2.6 | 2.2 |
| Norway | 3.5 | 4.7 | 2.4 | 3.4 | 2.6 |
| *of which: Mainland* | 2.9 | 4.4 | 1.5 | 2.8 | 2.6 |
| Poland | .. | .. | .. | 3.6 | 4.9 |
| Portugal | 3.5 | 4.7 | 3.2 | 2.7 | 3.6 |
| Spain | 3.0 | 3.5 | 2.9 | 2.6 | 4.1 |
| Sweden | 1.9 | 1.9 | 2.2 | 1.7 | 3.3 |
| Switzerland | 1.4 | 1.4 | 2.1 | 0.9 | 2.2 |
| Turkey | 4.3 | 4.1 | 5.2 | 3.6 | 3.1 |
| | | | | | |
| Coefficient of variation | | | | | |
| OECD total | 0.38 | 0.41 | 0.51 | 0.51 | 0.83 |
| EU 15 | 0.30 | 0.28 | 0.34 | 0.58 | 0.80 |
| OECD 24[2] | 0.28 | 0.35 | 0.34 | 0.51 | 0.87 |

1. 1991 for Germany and Hungary, 1992 for Czech Republic.
2. Excluding Czech Republic, Hungary, Korea, Mexico, Poland and Slovak Republic.

Source: OECD (2001), OECD Economic Outlook, No. 70.

| 1990 | 1991 | 1992 | 1993 | 1994 | 1995 | 1996 | 1997 | 1998 | 1999 | 2000 |
|------|------|------|------|------|------|------|------|------|------|------|
| 1.8 | -0.5 | 3.1 | 2.7 | 4.0 | 2.7 | 3.6 | 4.4 | 4.3 | 4.1 | 4.1 |
| 5.3 | 3.1 | 0.9 | 0.4 | 1.0 | 1.6 | 3.5 | 1.8 | -1.1 | 0.8 | 1.5 |
| .. | .. | 1.8 | -1.1 | 2.3 | 1.7 | 0.8 | 1.4 | 2.0 | 1.8 | 3.0 |
| 5.7 | .. | .. | .. | .. | .. | .. | .. | .. | .. | .. |
| 2.6 | 1.0 | 1.3 | -0.9 | 1.8 | 1.9 | 1.1 | 1.9 | 3.5 | 3.0 | 3.4 |
| 2.0 | 1.4 | 0.8 | -0.9 | 2.2 | 2.9 | 1.1 | 2.0 | 1.8 | 1.6 | 2.9 |
| 0.8 | -1.4 | 0.2 | 2.5 | 4.7 | 2.9 | 2.6 | 3.4 | 3.0 | 2.1 | 2.9 |
| 0.2 | -2.1 | 0.9 | 2.4 | 4.7 | 2.8 | 1.6 | 4.3 | 3.9 | 5.1 | 4.4 |
| 1.3 | -0.6 | 2.4 | 3.9 | 4.7 | 4.1 | 4.1 | 3.5 | 5.4 | 4.5 | 3.4 |
| 4.7 | 3.3 | 2.3 | 0.4 | 2.6 | 1.6 | 2.0 | 1.6 | 3.5 | 2.8 | 3.0 |
| 2.9 | 1.8 | 1.6 | -1.5 | 2.8 | 2.6 | 1.2 | 3.6 | 2.2 | 3.0 | 4.0 |
| .. | .. | .. | -0.9 | 2.6 | 5.9 | 4.3 | -0.8 | -1.2 | -0.4 | 2.9 |
| 1.0 | 1.1 | 0.6 | 0.0 | 5.5 | 2.8 | 2.5 | 3.0 | 2.8 | 2.1 | 3.2 |
| 0.0 | -6.3 | -3.3 | -1.1 | 4.0 | 3.8 | 4.0 | 6.3 | 5.3 | 4.0 | 5.7 |
| 0.0 | 3.1 | 0.7 | -1.6 | 2.0 | 2.1 | 2.4 | 3.6 | 3.4 | 3.4 | 4.3 |
| .. | .. | -3.1 | -0.6 | 2.9 | 1.5 | 1.3 | 4.6 | 4.9 | 4.2 | 5.2 |
| 1.1 | 0.7 | -3.3 | 0.6 | 4.5 | 0.1 | 5.2 | 4.8 | 4.6 | 4.0 | 5.0 |
| 8.5 | 1.9 | 3.3 | 2.7 | 5.8 | 10.0 | 7.8 | 10.8 | 8.6 | 10.8 | 11.5 |
| 7.8 | 9.2 | 5.4 | 5.5 | 8.3 | 8.9 | 6.8 | 5.0 | -6.7 | 10.9 | 8.8 |
| 2.2 | 6.1 | 4.5 | 8.7 | 4.2 | 3.8 | 3.6 | 9.0 | 5.8 | 6.0 | 7.5 |
| 5.1 | 4.2 | 3.6 | 2.0 | 4.5 | -6.2 | 5.1 | 6.8 | 4.9 | 3.8 | 6.9 |
| 4.1 | 2.3 | 2.0 | 0.8 | 3.2 | 2.3 | 3.0 | 3.8 | 4.3 | 3.7 | 3.5 |
| 0.6 | -1.9 | 0.8 | 4.7 | 6.1 | 3.9 | 3.3 | 2.9 | -0.6 | 3.7 | 3.0 |
| 2.0 | 3.1 | 3.3 | 3.1 | 5.5 | 3.8 | 4.9 | 4.7 | 2.4 | 1.1 | 2.3 |
| 1.0 | 1.4 | 2.2 | 2.8 | 4.1 | 2.9 | 3.8 | 4.2 | 3.6 | 1.0 | 1.8 |
| .. | -7.0 | 2.5 | 3.7 | 5.2 | 7.0 | 6.0 | 6.8 | 4.9 | 4.0 | 4.0 |
| 4.4 | 2.3 | 2.5 | -1.1 | 2.2 | 2.8 | 3.7 | 3.8 | 3.8 | 3.3 | 3.3 |
| 3.8 | 2.5 | 0.9 | -1.0 | 2.4 | 2.8 | 2.4 | 4.0 | 4.3 | 4.1 | 4.1 |
| 1.1 | -1.1 | -1.7 | -1.8 | 4.1 | 3.7 | 1.1 | 2.1 | 3.6 | 4.1 | 3.5 |
| 3.7 | -0.8 | -0.1 | -0.5 | 0.5 | 0.5 | 0.3 | 1.7 | 2.4 | 1.6 | 3.0 |
| 9.3 | 0.9 | 6.0 | 8.0 | -5.5 | 7.2 | 7.0 | 7.5 | 3.1 | -4.7 | 7.2 |

## Actual GDP per capita growth in the OECD area

Total economy, percentage change at annual rate

| Total economy | 1970-00 | 1970-80 | 1980-90 | 1990[1]-00 | 1996-00 |
|---|---|---|---|---|---|
| United States | 2.2 | 2.1 | 2.2 | 2.2 | 3.3 |
| Japan | 2.6 | 3.3 | 3.5 | 1.1 | 0.5 |
| Germany | .. | .. | .. | 1.3 | 2.0 |
| *western Germany* | 1.5 | 2.6 | 2.0 | .. | .. |
| France | 2.0 | 2.7 | 1.8 | 1.4 | 2.6 |
| Italy | 2.2 | 3.1 | 2.2 | 1.4 | 1.9 |
| United Kingdom | 2.1 | 1.8 | 2.5 | 1.9 | 2.4 |
| Canada | 2.0 | 2.8 | 1.5 | 1.7 | 3.5 |
| Australia | 1.9 | 1.5 | 1.7 | 2.3 | 3.0 |
| Austria | 2.5 | 3.5 | 2.1 | 1.8 | 2.6 |
| Belgium | 2.3 | 3.2 | 2.0 | 1.8 | 3.0 |
| Czech Republic | .. | .. | .. | 1.6 | 0.2 |
| Denmark | 1.9 | 1.8 | 1.9 | 2.0 | 2.4 |
| Finland | 2.5 | 3.1 | 2.7 | 1.8 | 5.0 |
| Greece | 1.9 | 3.6 | 0.2 | 1.9 | 3.5 |
| Hungary | .. | .. | .. | 3.4 | 5.1 |
| Iceland | 2.8 | 5.2 | 1.6 | 1.6 | 3.4 |
| Ireland | 4.3 | 3.3 | 3.3 | 6.4 | 9.2 |
| Korea | 6.2 | 5.8 | 7.6 | 5.1 | 3.3 |
| Luxembourg | 3.4 | 1.9 | 3.9 | 4.5 | 5.7 |
| Mexico | 1.5 | 3.3 | -0.3 | 1.7 | 4.2 |
| Netherlands | 2.0 | 2.1 | 1.6 | 2.2 | 3.2 |
| New Zealand | 1.2 | 0.5 | 1.9 | 1.2 | 1.4 |
| Norway | 3.0 | 4.2 | 2.0 | 2.8 | 2.0 |
| *of which: Mainland* | 2.4 | 3.8 | 1.1 | 2.2 | 2.0 |
| Poland | .. | .. | .. | 3.5 | 4.9 |
| Portugal | 3.0 | 3.4 | 3.1 | 2.5 | 3.2 |
| Spain | 2.5 | 2.5 | 2.6 | 2.5 | 4.0 |
| Sweden | 1.6 | 1.6 | 1.9 | 1.4 | 3.2 |
| Switzerland | 1.0 | 1.2 | 1.5 | 0.2 | 1.8 |
| Turkey | 2.1 | 1.8 | 2.8 | 1.8 | 1.5 |
| Coefficient of variation | | | | | |
| OECD total | 0.44 | 0.43 | 0.61 | 0.58 | 0.55 |
| EU 15 | 0.31 | 0.26 | 0.38 | 0.60 | 0.52 |
| OECD 24[2] | 0.32 | 0.40 | 0.35 | 0.59 | 0.56 |

1. 1991 for Germany, 1992 for Czech Republic and Hungary.
2. Excluding Czech Republic, Hungary, Korea, Mexico, Poland and Slovak Republic.
Source: OECD (2001), OECD Economic Outlook, No. 70.

| 1990 | 1991 | 1992 | 1993 | 1994 | 1995 | 1996 | 1997 | 1998 | 1999 | 2000 |
|---|---|---|---|---|---|---|---|---|---|---|
| 0.7 | -1.5 | 1.9 | 1.6 | 3.0 | 1.7 | 2.6 | 3.4 | 3.3 | 3.2 | 3.2 |
| 5.0 | 2.8 | 0.6 | 0.2 | 0.8 | 1.1 | 3.2 | 1.6 | -1.4 | 0.6 | 1.4 |
| .. | .. | 1.5 | -1.8 | 2.0 | 1.4 | 0.5 | 1.2 | 2.0 | 1.8 | 2.9 |
| 3.7 | .. | .. | .. | .. | .. | .. | .. | .. | .. | .. |
| 2.1 | 0.6 | 0.8 | -1.3 | 1.5 | 1.5 | 0.7 | 1.6 | 3.2 | 2.6 | 2.9 |
| 3.4 | 1.3 | 0.6 | -1.2 | 1.9 | 2.7 | 0.9 | 1.8 | 1.7 | 1.5 | 2.7 |
| 0.4 | -1.8 | -0.1 | 2.2 | 4.3 | 2.5 | 2.3 | 3.1 | 2.6 | 1.7 | 2.4 |
| -1.3 | -3.3 | -0.4 | 1.2 | 3.5 | 1.7 | 0.5 | 3.2 | 3.0 | 4.2 | 3.6 |
| -0.2 | -1.9 | 1.2 | 2.9 | 3.6 | 2.9 | 2.8 | 2.3 | 4.3 | 3.4 | 2.2 |
| 3.4 | 1.9 | 1.5 | -1.0 | 2.1 | 1.4 | 1.8 | 1.4 | 3.4 | 2.6 | 2.8 |
| 2.6 | 1.4 | 1.2 | -1.9 | 2.4 | 2.2 | 1.2 | 3.3 | 2.0 | 2.8 | 3.8 |
| .. | .. | .. | -1.1 | 2.6 | 6.0 | 4.4 | -0.6 | -1.1 | -0.3 | 3.0 |
| 0.8 | 0.9 | 0.3 | -0.3 | 5.1 | 2.3 | 1.9 | 2.5 | 2.4 | 1.8 | 2.9 |
| -0.4 | -7.1 | -3.6 | -1.6 | 3.5 | 3.4 | 3.7 | 6.0 | 5.1 | 3.7 | 5.5 |
| -0.5 | 2.0 | -0.5 | -2.1 | 1.6 | 1.8 | 2.3 | 3.3 | 3.2 | 3.4 | 4.1 |
| .. | .. | .. | -0.3 | 3.3 | 1.8 | 1.7 | 5.0 | 5.3 | 4.6 | 5.6 |
| 0.3 | -0.5 | -4.5 | -0.4 | 3.6 | -0.4 | 4.6 | 4.0 | 3.5 | 2.7 | 3.5 |
| 8.8 | 1.3 | 2.6 | 2.3 | 5.2 | 9.4 | 7.0 | 9.8 | 7.3 | 9.7 | 10.2 |
| 6.8 | 8.1 | 4.3 | 4.4 | 7.2 | 7.8 | 5.7 | 4.0 | -7.6 | 9.9 | 7.8 |
| 0.6 | 4.7 | 3.0 | 7.2 | 2.7 | 2.2 | 2.9 | 7.6 | 4.5 | 4.5 | 6.0 |
| 3.0 | 2.2 | 1.6 | 0.0 | 2.4 | -8.1 | 2.9 | 4.8 | 3.0 | 1.8 | 7.1 |
| 3.4 | 1.4 | 1.3 | 0.1 | 2.6 | 1.7 | 2.6 | 3.3 | 3.7 | 3.0 | 2.7 |
| -0.4 | -5.1 | -0.2 | 3.5 | 4.7 | 2.4 | 1.7 | 1.6 | -1.5 | 3.2 | 2.5 |
| 1.6 | 2.6 | 2.7 | 2.5 | 4.9 | 3.3 | 4.4 | 4.1 | 1.8 | 0.4 | 1.6 |
| 0.6 | 0.9 | 1.6 | 2.2 | 3.5 | 2.4 | 3.3 | 3.6 | 3.0 | 0.4 | 1.2 |
| .. | -7.3 | 2.2 | 3.5 | 5.0 | 6.9 | 5.9 | 6.8 | 4.8 | 4.0 | 4.0 |
| 4.8 | 2.5 | 2.9 | -1.2 | 2.2 | 2.8 | 3.5 | 3.7 | 2.9 | 3.1 | 3.1 |
| 3.6 | 2.4 | 0.7 | -1.2 | 2.2 | 2.6 | 2.3 | 3.9 | 4.2 | 4.0 | 4.0 |
| 0.3 | -1.8 | -2.3 | -2.4 | 3.4 | 3.2 | 0.9 | 2.0 | 3.5 | 4.0 | 3.4 |
| 2.7 | -2.1 | -1.2 | -1.4 | -0.6 | 0.2 | -0.1 | 1.5 | 2.1 | 1.1 | 2.4 |
| 6.7 | -1.0 | 4.0 | 6.1 | -7.1 | 5.3 | 5.2 | 5.8 | 1.4 | -6.2 | 5.5 |

## Actual GDP per person employed in the OECD area

Total economy, percentage change at annual rate

| Total economy | 1970-00[1] | 1970-80 | 1980[2]-90 | 1990[3]-00[1] | 1996-00[1] |
|---|---|---|---|---|---|
| United States | 1.4 | 0.8 | 1.4 | 1.9 | 2.6 |
| Japan | 2.5 | 3.6 | 2.8 | 1.0 | 0.9 |
| Germany | .. | .. | .. | 1.5 | 1.1 |
| *western Germany* | 1.3 | 2.6 | 1.7 | .. | .. |
| France | 2.0 | 2.7 | 2.1 | 1.3 | 1.4 |
| Italy | 2.2 | 2.9 | 2.1 | 1.7 | 0.9 |
| United Kingdom | 1.9 | 1.7 | 2.0 | 2.0 | 1.5 |
| Canada | 1.1 | 0.8 | 1.1 | 1.4 | 1.8 |
| Australia | 1.6 | 1.7 | 1.0 | 2.1 | 2.2 |
| Austria | 2.3 | 3.0 | 2.1 | 1.9 | 1.8 |
| Belgium | 2.3 | 3.2 | 2.0 | 1.7 | 2.0 |
| Czech Republic | .. | .. | .. | .. | 1.4 |
| Denmark | 1.6 | 1.8 | 1.0 | 2.1 | 1.8 |
| Finland | 2.6 | 2.5 | 2.4 | 2.9 | 2.9 |
| Greece | 1.8 | 4.0 | -0.3 | 1.8 | 3.1 |
| Hungary | .. | .. | .. | 4.2 | 3.1 |
| Iceland | 2.1 | 3.6 | 1.0 | 1.5 | 2.2 |
| Ireland | 3.4 | 3.8 | 3.6 | 3.0 | 3.2 |
| Korea | 4.7 | 3.9 | 5.9 | 4.5 | 4.0 |
| Luxembourg | 3.3 | 1.5 | 3.7 | 4.6 | 4.8 |
| Mexico | .. | .. | 0.1 | 0.3 | 1.8 |
| Netherlands | 1.6 | 2.6 | 1.3 | 0.8 | 0.8 |
| New Zealand | 1.0 | 0.0 | 2.3 | 0.7 | 1.5 |
| Norway | 2.4 | 3.2 | 1.8 | 2.3 | 1.0 |
| *of which: Mainland* | 1.7 | 2.7 | 0.9 | 1.6 | 1.1 |
| Poland | .. | .. | .. | 5.8 | 5.7 |
| Portugal | 2.1 | 3.0 | 1.7 | 1.7 | 1.5 |
| Spain | 2.5 | 3.8 | 2.3 | 1.5 | 0.2 |
| Sweden | 1.7 | 1.0 | 1.6 | 2.5 | 2.1 |
| Switzerland | 0.7 | 1.2 | 0.3 | 0.6 | 1.6 |
| Turkey | 2.7 | 2.2 | 3.6 | 2.5 | 2.9 |
| **Coefficient of variation** | | | | | |
| EU 15 | 0.28 | 0.33 | 0.49 | 0.45 | 0.59 |
| OECD 24[4] | 0.34 | 0.46 | 0.53 | 0.46 | 0.52 |

1. 1999 for Ireland.
2. 1983 for Mexico.
3. 1991 for Hungary and Germany, 1992 for Czech Republic, 1993 for Poland.
4. Excluding Czech Republic, Hungary, Korea, Mexico, Poland and Slovak Republic.
Source: OECD (2001), OECD Economic Outlook, No. 70.

| 1990 | 1991 | 1992 | 1993 | 1994 | 1995 | 1996 | 1997 | 1998 | 1999 | 2000 |
|------|------|------|------|------|------|------|------|------|------|------|
| 0.5 | 0.4 | 2.4 | 1.1 | 1.7 | 1.2 | 2.1 | 2.1 | 2.8 | 2.5 | 2.8 |
| 3.3 | 1.2 | -0.1 | 0.2 | 0.9 | 1.5 | 3.0 | 0.7 | -0.4 | 1.6 | 1.8 |
| .. | .. | 3.8 | 0.3 | 2.5 | 1.5 | 1.1 | 1.6 | 0.9 | 0.6 | 1.3 |
| 2.7 | .. | .. | .. | .. | .. | .. | .. | .. | .. | .. |
| 1.8 | 1.0 | 1.9 | 0.3 | 1.7 | 1.0 | 0.9 | 1.3 | 2.1 | 1.2 | 1.1 |
| 0.7 | 0.7 | 1.8 | 2.3 | 3.9 | 3.6 | 0.6 | 1.6 | 0.7 | 0.4 | 1.0 |
| 0.5 | 1.7 | 2.4 | 2.9 | 3.7 | 1.5 | 1.5 | 1.4 | 1.8 | 0.9 | 1.8 |
| 0.2 | -0.4 | 1.6 | 1.6 | 2.7 | 0.9 | 0.8 | 1.9 | 1.2 | 2.2 | 1.8 |
| -0.2 | 1.5 | 3.1 | 3.5 | 1.5 | 0.0 | 2.7 | 2.6 | 3.6 | 2.2 | 0.4 |
| 3.0 | 1.9 | 2.1 | 1.1 | 2.7 | 1.6 | 2.6 | 1.1 | 2.7 | 1.4 | 2.1 |
| 2.0 | 1.7 | 2.1 | -0.8 | 3.1 | 1.9 | 0.8 | 2.8 | 1.0 | 1.6 | 2.4 |
| .. | .. | .. | 0.3 | 1.5 | 5.0 | 4.2 | -0.2 | 0.2 | 1.9 | 3.7 |
| 0.4 | 1.7 | 1.1 | 2.3 | 6.1 | 0.7 | 1.4 | 1.3 | 2.3 | 1.2 | 2.5 |
| 0.1 | -1.2 | 4.1 | 5.3 | 4.8 | 1.6 | 2.6 | 4.2 | 2.9 | 0.7 | 3.9 |
| -1.3 | 5.6 | -0.7 | -2.4 | 0.1 | 1.2 | 2.7 | 4.3 | -0.7 | 4.2 | 4.6 |
| .. | .. | 7.2 | 6.2 | 6.5 | 3.4 | 1.9 | 4.3 | 3.4 | 0.5 | 4.2 |
| 2.2 | 0.8 | -1.9 | 1.4 | 4.0 | -0.7 | 2.8 | 2.9 | 1.2 | 1.2 | 3.4 |
| 3.9 | 2.2 | 2.8 | 1.2 | 2.4 | 4.8 | 3.7 | 6.9 | -1.5 | 4.3 | .. |
| 4.7 | 5.8 | 3.5 | 3.9 | 5.1 | 6.1 | 4.8 | 3.6 | -1.5 | 9.3 | 4.8 |
| 0.7 | 4.7 | 4.3 | 9.0 | 3.4 | 2.8 | 2.6 | 7.7 | 3.8 | 3.3 | 4.6 |
| 2.2 | 1.4 | -0.1 | -1.7 | 1.2 | -6.2 | 1.1 | 0.7 | 1.5 | 2.6 | 2.2 |
| 1.0 | -0.3 | 0.4 | 0.1 | 3.3 | -0.2 | 1.0 | 0.4 | 1.0 | 0.7 | 1.2 |
| -0.3 | -0.6 | 0.0 | 2.0 | 1.3 | -1.2 | -0.4 | 2.5 | 0.0 | 2.2 | 1.4 |
| 2.9 | 4.2 | 3.6 | 3.1 | 3.9 | 1.6 | 2.3 | 1.7 | 0.0 | 0.7 | 1.8 |
| 2.1 | 2.8 | 2.4 | 2.7 | 2.5 | 0.5 | 1.2 | 1.1 | 1.1 | 0.7 | 1.2 |
| .. | .. | .. | .. | 6.9 | 6.1 | 4.8 | 5.4 | 3.6 | 8.2 | 5.7 |
| 2.1 | -0.6 | 1.6 | 0.9 | 2.4 | 3.4 | 3.2 | 1.9 | 1.3 | 1.4 | 1.5 |
| 1.1 | 2.3 | 2.9 | 3.4 | 3.3 | 0.9 | 1.0 | 1.1 | 0.8 | -0.5 | -0.6 |
| 0.1 | 0.9 | 2.6 | 4.2 | 5.1 | 2.1 | 1.7 | 3.2 | 2.1 | 1.8 | 1.3 |
| 0.6 | -3.2 | 1.2 | 0.1 | 2.3 | -0.1 | -0.1 | 2.1 | 0.9 | 1.2 | 2.0 |
| 7.4 | -1.6 | 5.6 | 14.1 | -11.9 | 4.6 | 4.5 | 7.7 | 0.6 | -7.1 | 11.4 |

Table A1.4

## Trend GDP growth in the OECD area

Total economy, percentage change at annual rate

| Total economy | 1970-00 | 1970-80 | 1980-90 | 1990[1]-00 | 1996-00 |
|---|---|---|---|---|---|
| United States | 3.1 | 3.0 | 3.1 | 3.3 | 3.7 |
| Japan | 3.4 | 4.7 | 3.9 | 1.7 | 1.1 |
| Germany | .. | .. | .. | 1.5 | 1.7 |
| *western Germany* | 2.6 | 2.7 | 2.2 | .. | .. |
| France | 2.5 | 3.3 | 2.2 | 1.9 | 2.3 |
| Italy | 2.5 | 3.5 | 2.3 | 1.7 | 1.8 |
| United Kingdom | 2.3 | 1.9 | 2.5 | 2.4 | 2.7 |
| Canada | 3.1 | 4.0 | 2.6 | 2.8 | 3.6 |
| Australia | 3.3 | 3.3 | 3.1 | 3.6 | 4.0 |
| Austria | 2.8 | 3.5 | 2.3 | 2.4 | 2.5 |
| Belgium | 2.5 | 3.2 | 2.1 | 2.2 | 2.6 |
| Denmark | 2.2 | 2.3 | 1.9 | 2.2 | 2.7 |
| Finland | 2.9 | 3.5 | 2.6 | 2.5 | 4.1 |
| Greece | 2.5 | 4.4 | 0.9 | 2.2 | 2.9 |
| Iceland | 3.6 | 5.5 | 2.8 | 2.5 | 3.7 |
| Ireland | 5.1 | 4.6 | 3.3 | 7.4 | 9.1 |
| Korea | 7.5 | 8.1 | 8.4 | 6.1 | 5.2 |
| Luxembourg | 4.2 | 2.4 | 4.5 | 5.8 | 6.0 |
| Mexico | 3.9 | 6.2 | 2.1 | 3.4 | 4.1 |
| Netherlands | 2.7 | 2.9 | 2.1 | 3.0 | 3.3 |
| New Zealand | 2.1 | 1.9 | 2.0 | 2.5 | 2.6 |
| Norway | 3.5 | 4.3 | 2.8 | 3.3 | 3.2 |
| *of which: Mainland* | 2.8 | 4.1 | 1.8 | 2.6 | 2.8 |
| Portugal | 3.5 | 4.3 | 3.1 | 3.0 | 3.1 |
| Spain | 3.0 | 3.4 | 2.6 | 2.8 | 3.3 |
| Sweden | 2.0 | 2.1 | 2.0 | 1.8 | 2.7 |
| Switzerland | 1.4 | 1.3 | 1.9 | 1.1 | 1.5 |
| Turkey | 4.3 | 4.5 | 4.5 | 3.9 | 3.5 |
| | | | | | |
| Coefficient of variation | | | | | |
| OECD total[2] | 0.38 | 0.40 | 0.49 | 0.49 | 0.48 |
| EU 15 | 0.29 | 0.26 | 0.32 | 0.56 | 0.56 |
| OECD 24[3] | 0.28 | 0.32 | 0.31 | 0.48 | 0.50 |

1. 1991 for Germany.
2. Excluding Czech Republic, Hungary, Poland and Slovak Republic.
3. Excluding Czech Republic, Hungary, Korea, Mexico, Poland and Slovak Republic.

Source: OECD (2001), OECD Economic Outlook, No. 70.

| 1990 | 1991 | 1992 | 1993 | 1994 | 1995 | 1996 | 1997 | 1998 | 1999 | 2000 |
|------|------|------|------|------|------|------|------|------|------|------|
| 2.7 | 2.6 | 2.6 | 2.8 | 3.0 | 3.3 | 3.5 | 3.7 | 3.8 | 3.8 | 3.7 |
| 3.7 | 3.2 | 2.6 | 2.1 | 1.8 | 1.5 | 1.4 | 1.2 | 1.1 | 1.0 | 1.1 |
| .. | .. | 1.2 | 1.2 | 1.3 | 1.4 | 1.5 | 1.6 | 1.7 | 1.8 | 1.8 |
| 3.2 | .. | .. | .. | .. | .. | .. | .. | .. | .. | .. |
| 2.2 | 1.9 | 1.6 | 1.5 | 1.5 | 1.6 | 1.8 | 2.0 | 2.3 | 2.4 | 2.5 |
| 2.0 | 1.8 | 1.6 | 1.5 | 1.5 | 1.6 | 1.6 | 1.7 | 1.8 | 1.9 | 1.9 |
| 2.1 | 1.9 | 1.9 | 2.1 | 2.3 | 2.5 | 2.7 | 2.7 | 2.7 | 2.7 | 2.6 |
| 1.9 | 1.7 | 1.8 | 2.0 | 2.4 | 2.7 | 3.1 | 3.3 | 3.6 | 3.7 | 3.7 |
| 2.9 | 2.9 | 3.0 | 3.2 | 3.5 | 3.7 | 3.9 | 4.0 | 4.0 | 4.0 | 3.8 |
| 2.9 | 2.8 | 2.6 | 2.4 | 2.3 | 2.2 | 2.2 | 2.3 | 2.4 | 2.5 | 2.6 |
| 2.4 | 2.2 | 2.0 | 1.9 | 1.9 | 2.0 | 2.2 | 2.4 | 2.5 | 2.7 | 2.7 |
| 1.3 | 1.4 | 1.5 | 1.8 | 2.1 | 2.4 | 2.6 | 2.7 | 2.7 | 2.7 | 2.6 |
| 0.7 | 0.2 | 0.3 | 0.8 | 1.6 | 2.4 | 3.2 | 3.8 | 4.2 | 4.3 | 4.2 |
| 1.4 | 1.4 | 1.4 | 1.5 | 1.7 | 2.0 | 2.4 | 2.7 | 2.9 | 3.0 | 3.0 |
| 1.2 | 1.0 | 1.0 | 1.3 | 1.8 | 2.4 | 3.0 | 3.4 | 3.7 | 3.9 | 3.9 |
| 4.6 | 4.8 | 5.2 | 5.7 | 6.5 | 7.3 | 8.1 | 8.7 | 9.1 | 9.3 | 9.4 |
| 8.4 | 7.9 | 7.4 | 6.9 | 6.5 | 6.0 | 5.6 | 5.2 | 5.0 | 5.2 | 5.4 |
| 6.1 | 6.0 | 5.9 | 5.7 | 5.6 | 5.6 | 5.7 | 5.8 | 6.0 | 6.0 | 6.0 |
| 2.6 | 2.8 | 2.8 | 2.7 | 2.7 | 2.9 | 3.2 | 3.7 | 4.1 | 4.3 | 4.5 |
| 2.9 | 2.8 | 2.7 | 2.7 | 2.7 | 2.9 | 3.1 | 3.2 | 3.3 | 3.4 | 3.4 |
| 1.4 | 1.6 | 2.0 | 2.4 | 2.8 | 3.0 | 2.9 | 2.8 | 2.7 | 2.6 | 2.5 |
| 2.5 | 2.8 | 3.1 | 3.4 | 3.6 | 3.7 | 3.7 | 3.5 | 3.2 | 3.0 | 2.9 |
| 1.2 | 1.5 | 1.9 | 2.4 | 2.7 | 3.0 | 3.1 | 3.0 | 2.9 | 2.7 | 2.5 |
| 3.7 | 3.3 | 2.9 | 2.7 | 2.6 | 2.7 | 2.9 | 3.0 | 3.1 | 3.2 | 3.2 |
| 3.2 | 2.8 | 2.4 | 2.3 | 2.3 | 2.5 | 2.8 | 3.1 | 3.3 | 3.4 | 3.5 |
| 1.1 | 0.8 | 0.8 | 1.0 | 1.3 | 1.7 | 2.1 | 2.4 | 2.7 | 2.8 | 2.8 |
| 1.7 | 1.3 | 0.9 | 0.7 | 0.7 | 0.8 | 1.0 | 1.2 | 1.4 | 1.6 | 1.7 |
| 4.6 | 4.4 | 4.2 | 4.0 | 3.9 | 3.9 | 3.9 | 3.8 | 3.6 | 3.4 | 3.4 |

# Table A1.5

## Trend GDP per capita growth in the OECD area

Total economy, percentage change at annual rate

| Total economy | 1970-00 | 1970-80 | 1980-90 | 1990[1]-00 | 1996-00 |
|---|---|---|---|---|---|
| United States | 2.1 | 1.9 | 2.1 | 2.3 | 2.8 |
| Japan | 2.8 | 3.6 | 3.3 | 1.4 | 0.9 |
| Germany | .. | .. | .. | 1.2 | 1.7 |
| *western Germany* | 1.5 | 2.5 | 1.9 | .. | .. |
| France | 1.9 | 2.7 | 1.6 | 1.5 | 1.9 |
| Italy | 2.3 | 3.0 | 2.3 | 1.5 | 1.7 |
| United Kingdom | 2.0 | 1.8 | 2.2 | 2.1 | 2.3 |
| Canada | 1.9 | 2.6 | 1.4 | 1.7 | 2.6 |
| Australia | 1.9 | 1.6 | 1.6 | 2.4 | 2.8 |
| Austria | 2.5 | 3.4 | 2.1 | 1.9 | 2.3 |
| Belgium | 2.3 | 3.0 | 2.0 | 1.9 | 2.3 |
| Denmark | 1.9 | 1.9 | 1.9 | 1.9 | 2.3 |
| Finland | 2.5 | 3.1 | 2.2 | 2.1 | 3.9 |
| Greece | 1.9 | 3.4 | 0.5 | 1.8 | 2.7 |
| Iceland | 2.5 | 4.3 | 1.7 | 1.5 | 2.6 |
| Ireland | 4.2 | 3.1 | 3.0 | 6.4 | 7.9 |
| Korea | 6.2 | 6.3 | 7.2 | 5.1 | 4.2 |
| Luxembourg | 3.4 | 1.7 | 4.0 | 4.5 | 4.6 |
| Mexico | 1.5 | 2.9 | 0.0 | 1.6 | 2.7 |
| Netherlands | 2.0 | 2.1 | 1.6 | 2.4 | 2.7 |
| New Zealand | 1.1 | 0.8 | 1.4 | 1.2 | 1.8 |
| Norway | 3.0 | 3.8 | 2.5 | 2.7 | 2.5 |
| *of which: Mainland* | 2.3 | 3.5 | 1.4 | 2.0 | 2.2 |
| Portugal | 3.0 | 3.0 | 3.1 | 2.8 | 2.7 |
| Spain | 2.4 | 2.3 | 2.3 | 2.7 | 3.2 |
| Sweden | 1.6 | 1.8 | 1.7 | 1.5 | 2.6 |
| Switzerland | 1.0 | 1.1 | 1.4 | 0.4 | 1.1 |
| Turkey | 2.1 | 2.2 | 2.1 | 2.1 | 1.9 |
| | | | | | |
| Coefficient of variation | | | | | |
| OECD total[2] | 0.44 | 0.42 | 0.60 | 0.57 | 0.49 |
| EU 15 | 0.30 | 0.24 | 0.37 | 0.56 | 0.52 |
| OECD 24[3] | 0.31 | 0.35 | 0.35 | 0.55 | 0.51 |

1. 1991 for Germany.
2. Excluding Czech Republic, Hungary, Poland and Slovak Republic.
3. Excluding Czech Republic, Hungary, Korea, Mexico, Poland and Slovak Republic.

Source: OECD (2001), OECD Economic Outlook, No. 70.

| 1990 | 1991 | 1992 | 1993 | 1994 | 1995 | 1996 | 1997 | 1998 | 1999 | 2000 |
|------|------|------|------|------|------|------|------|------|------|------|
| 1.6 | 1.5 | 1.5 | 1.7 | 2.0 | 2.3 | 2.5 | 2.7 | 2.8 | 2.9 | 2.8 |
| 3.4 | 2.8 | 2.3 | 1.9 | 1.6 | 1.1 | 1.1 | 0.9 | 0.8 | 0.9 | 0.9 |
| .. | .. | 0.4 | 0.5 | 1.0 | 1.1 | 1.2 | 1.4 | 1.7 | 1.7 | 1.8 |
| 1.2 | .. | .. | .. | .. | .. | .. | .. | .. | .. | .. |
| 1.7 | 1.4 | 1.2 | 1.1 | 1.2 | 1.3 | 1.5 | 1.7 | 1.9 | 2.0 | 2.0 |
| 3.5 | 1.7 | 1.4 | 1.1 | 1.2 | 1.4 | 1.5 | 1.5 | 1.7 | 1.8 | 1.7 |
| 1.8 | 1.5 | 1.6 | 1.8 | 2.0 | 2.2 | 2.3 | 2.4 | 2.4 | 2.2 | 2.2 |
| 0.3 | 0.5 | 0.5 | 0.9 | 1.2 | 1.6 | 1.9 | 2.3 | 2.7 | 2.8 | 2.8 |
| 1.4 | 1.6 | 1.7 | 2.2 | 2.4 | 2.5 | 2.5 | 2.8 | 2.9 | 2.8 | 2.6 |
| 1.7 | 1.4 | 1.8 | 1.0 | 1.8 | 2.0 | 2.1 | 2.2 | 2.4 | 2.3 | 2.4 |
| 2.1 | 1.8 | 1.6 | 1.5 | 1.6 | 1.6 | 2.2 | 2.1 | 2.3 | 2.4 | 2.5 |
| 1.1 | 1.1 | 1.2 | 1.5 | 1.8 | 1.9 | 1.9 | 2.2 | 2.4 | 2.3 | 2.3 |
| 0.2 | -0.6 | 0.0 | 0.3 | 1.1 | 2.0 | 2.9 | 3.5 | 3.9 | 3.9 | 4.0 |
| 0.9 | 0.3 | 0.2 | 1.0 | 1.3 | 1.8 | 2.3 | 2.3 | 2.7 | 3.0 | 2.8 |
| 0.4 | -0.3 | -0.2 | 0.3 | 1.0 | 1.9 | 2.4 | 2.7 | 2.6 | 2.6 | 2.4 |
| 4.9 | 4.2 | 4.4 | 5.3 | 5.9 | 6.8 | 7.3 | 7.7 | 7.8 | 8.2 | 8.2 |
| 7.3 | 6.8 | 6.3 | 5.8 | 5.4 | 5.0 | 4.5 | 4.2 | 4.1 | 4.2 | 4.5 |
| 4.5 | 4.5 | 4.4 | 4.2 | 4.2 | 4.0 | 5.0 | 4.5 | 4.6 | 4.6 | 4.6 |
| 0.6 | 0.8 | 0.8 | 0.8 | 0.7 | 0.8 | 1.0 | 1.7 | 2.2 | 2.3 | 4.7 |
| 2.2 | 1.9 | 1.9 | 1.9 | 2.1 | 2.4 | 2.6 | 2.7 | 2.7 | 2.7 | 2.7 |
| 0.4 | -1.7 | 0.9 | 1.3 | 1.4 | 1.5 | 1.3 | 1.5 | 1.8 | 2.1 | 1.9 |
| 2.1 | 2.3 | 2.5 | 2.8 | 3.0 | 3.2 | 3.2 | 2.9 | 2.6 | 2.3 | 2.2 |
| 0.9 | 1.0 | 1.4 | 1.8 | 2.1 | 2.4 | 2.5 | 2.5 | 2.3 | 2.1 | 1.9 |
| 4.2 | 3.4 | 3.3 | 2.6 | 2.6 | 2.6 | 2.7 | 2.9 | 2.2 | 3.0 | 2.9 |
| 3.0 | 2.6 | 2.2 | 2.1 | 2.1 | 2.3 | 2.6 | 2.9 | 3.2 | 3.3 | 3.4 |
| 0.3 | 0.2 | 0.2 | 0.4 | 0.6 | 1.2 | 1.9 | 2.3 | 2.6 | 2.7 | 2.6 |
| 0.7 | 0.0 | -0.2 | -0.2 | -0.5 | 0.5 | 0.5 | 0.9 | 1.1 | 1.1 | 1.1 |
| 2.1 | 2.4 | 2.2 | 2.1 | 2.1 | 2.1 | 2.2 | 2.1 | 1.9 | 1.8 | 1.8 |

## Trend GDP per person employed in the OECD area

Total economy, percentage change at annual rate

| Total economy | 1970-00[1] | 1970-80 | 1980[2]-90 | 1990[3]-00[1] | 1996-00[1] |
|---|---|---|---|---|---|
| United States | 1.3 | 0.7 | 1.3 | 1.8 | 2.2 |
| Japan | 2.6 | 3.9 | 2.6 | 1.2 | 1.0 |
| Germany | .. | .. | .. | 1.4 | 1.2 |
| *western Germany* | 1.3 | 2.7 | 1.6 | .. | .. |
| France | 2.0 | 2.8 | 2.0 | 1.4 | 1.3 |
| Italy | 2.3 | 2.9 | 2.2 | 1.7 | 1.3 |
| United Kingdom | 1.9 | 1.9 | 1.9 | 1.8 | 1.7 |
| Canada | 1.1 | 0.9 | 0.9 | 1.4 | 1.6 |
| Australia | 1.6 | 1.8 | 1.1 | 1.9 | 2.0 |
| Austria | 2.4 | 3.1 | 2.1 | 2.0 | 2.0 |
| Belgium | 2.3 | 3.2 | 2.0 | 1.7 | 1.7 |
| Denmark | 1.6 | 1.8 | 1.1 | 1.9 | 2.0 |
| Finland | 2.6 | 2.6 | 2.4 | 2.9 | 2.9 |
| Greece | 1.8 | 3.7 | 0.1 | 1.6 | 2.3 |
| Iceland | 1.9 | 2.8 | 1.2 | 1.6 | 1.9 |
| Ireland | 3.5 | 4.0 | 3.2 | 3.5 | 3.8 |
| Korea | 4.8 | 4.4 | 5.6 | 4.4 | 4.3 |
| Luxembourg | 3.3 | 1.5 | 3.8 | 4.5 | 4.2 |
| Mexico | .. | .. | -0.4 | 0.2 | 0.7 |
| Netherlands | 1.6 | 2.8 | 1.1 | 0.8 | 0.9 |
| New Zealand | 0.9 | 0.2 | 1.8 | 0.7 | 0.7 |
| Norway | 2.4 | 2.7 | 2.1 | 2.3 | 1.6 |
| *of which: Mainland* | 1.7 | 2.4 | 1.1 | 1.6 | 1.3 |
| Portugal | 2.1 | 2.6 | 1.8 | 1.9 | 1.8 |
| Spain | 2.5 | 3.8 | 2.4 | 1.4 | 0.7 |
| Sweden | 1.7 | 1.2 | 1.7 | 2.4 | 2.2 |
| Switzerland | 0.7 | 1.3 | 0.2 | 0.7 | 1.1 |
| Turkey | 2.7 | 2.7 | 2.9 | 2.6 | 2.6 |
| | | | | | |
| Coefficient of variation | | | | | |
| EU 15 | 0.28 | 0.30 | 0.44 | 0.45 | 0.50 |
| OECD 24[4] | 0.35 | 0.43 | 0.48 | 0.45 | 0.47 |

1. 1999 for Ireland.
2. 1983 for Mexico.
3. 1991 for Germany.
4. Excluding Czech Republic, Hungary, Korea, Mexico, Poland and Slovak Republic.

Source: OECD (2001), OECD Economic Outlook, No. 70.

| 1990 | 1991 | 1992 | 1993 | 1994 | 1995 | 1996 | 1997 | 1998 | 1999 | 2000 |
|------|------|------|------|------|------|------|------|------|------|------|
| 1.3 | 1.3 | 1.4 | 1.5 | 1.6 | 1.8 | 1.9 | 2.1 | 2.2 | 2.3 | 2.3 |
| 2.3 | 1.9 | 1.6 | 1.3 | 1.2 | 1.1 | 1.1 | 1.1 | 1.0 | 1.0 | 1.1 |
| .. | .. | 1.7 | 1.6 | 1.6 | 1.5 | 1.4 | 1.3 | 1.2 | 1.2 | 1.2 |
| 1.9 | .. | .. | .. | .. | .. | .. | .. | .. | .. | .. |
| 1.9 | 1.7 | 1.5 | 1.4 | 1.3 | 1.3 | 1.3 | 1.3 | 1.3 | 1.3 | 1.3 |
| 2.2 | 2.1 | 2.1 | 2.1 | 2.1 | 2.0 | 1.7 | 1.5 | 1.3 | 1.2 | 1.1 |
| 1.5 | 1.7 | 1.8 | 2.0 | 2.0 | 2.0 | 1.9 | 1.8 | 1.7 | 1.7 | 1.6 |
| 0.9 | 1.0 | 1.1 | 1.2 | 1.3 | 1.4 | 1.5 | 1.5 | 1.6 | 1.6 | 1.6 |
| 1.1 | 1.4 | 1.6 | 1.8 | 1.9 | 2.0 | 2.1 | 2.1 | 2.1 | 1.9 | 1.8 |
| 2.3 | 2.2 | 2.1 | 2.1 | 2.0 | 2.0 | 2.0 | 2.0 | 1.9 | 1.9 | 2.0 |
| 1.9 | 1.8 | 1.7 | 1.7 | 1.6 | 1.6 | 1.7 | 1.7 | 1.7 | 1.7 | 1.8 |
| 1.2 | 1.5 | 1.8 | 2.0 | 2.1 | 2.1 | 2.1 | 2.0 | 2.0 | 1.9 | 1.9 |
| 2.4 | 2.5 | 2.7 | 2.9 | 3.0 | 3.0 | 3.0 | 3.0 | 2.9 | 2.8 | 2.8 |
| 1.0 | 1.0 | 0.9 | 0.9 | 1.1 | 1.3 | 1.7 | 2.0 | 2.2 | 2.4 | 2.5 |
| 1.5 | 1.3 | 1.3 | 1.3 | 1.4 | 1.6 | 1.7 | 1.8 | 1.9 | 2.0 | 2.0 |
| 3.5 | 3.3 | 3.2 | 3.1 | 3.2 | 3.4 | 3.5 | 3.7 | 3.8 | 3.9 | .. |
| 5.0 | 4.8 | 4.6 | 4.5 | 4.4 | 4.3 | 4.2 | 4.2 | 4.2 | 4.3 | 4.4 |
| 5.1 | 5.0 | 5.0 | 4.9 | 4.7 | 4.5 | 4.4 | 4.4 | 4.3 | 4.2 | 4.1 |
| 0.0 | 0.0 | -0.1 | -0.3 | -0.3 | -0.3 | 0.0 | 0.3 | 0.6 | 0.9 | 1.1 |
| 0.8 | 0.8 | 0.8 | 0.8 | 0.8 | 0.8 | 0.8 | 0.8 | 0.9 | 0.9 | 0.9 |
| 1.3 | 1.0 | 0.8 | 0.7 | 0.6 | 0.6 | 0.6 | 0.7 | 0.7 | 0.8 | 0.7 |
| 2.8 | 2.9 | 3.0 | 2.9 | 2.7 | 2.4 | 2.1 | 1.8 | 1.6 | 1.5 | 1.5 |
| 1.6 | 1.8 | 1.9 | 1.9 | 1.8 | 1.6 | 1.5 | 1.4 | 1.3 | 1.2 | 1.2 |
| 2.2 | 2.1 | 2.0 | 2.0 | 2.0 | 2.1 | 2.1 | 2.0 | 1.8 | 1.7 | 1.6 |
| 2.1 | 2.1 | 2.2 | 2.1 | 1.9 | 1.7 | 1.4 | 1.1 | 0.8 | 0.6 | 0.5 |
| 1.9 | 2.1 | 2.3 | 2.6 | 2.7 | 2.7 | 2.6 | 2.5 | 2.3 | 2.1 | 2.0 |
| 0.2 | 0.2 | 0.3 | 0.4 | 0.6 | 0.7 | 0.9 | 1.0 | 1.1 | 1.1 | 1.2 |
| 2.9 | 2.8 | 2.8 | 2.6 | 2.4 | 2.3 | 2.4 | 2.5 | 2.5 | 2.6 | 2.9 |

# Table A1.7

## Trend GDP growth in the OECD area

Business sector, percentage change at annual rate

| Business sector | 1970[1]-00[2] | 1970[1]-80 | 1980-90 | 1990[3]-00[2] | 1996-00[2] |
|---|---|---|---|---|---|
| United States | 3.4 | 3.2 | 3.3 | 3.6 | 4.1 |
| Japan | 3.6 | 4.8 | 4.1 | 1.7 | 1.0 |
| Germany | .. | .. | .. | 1.8 | 2.1 |
| *western Germany* | 2.7 | 2.7 | 2.3 | .. | .. |
| France | 2.6 | 3.5 | 2.3 | 2.1 | 2.6 |
| Italy | 2.7 | 3.7 | 2.5 | 1.9 | 2.1 |
| United Kingdom | 2.4 | 2.0 | 3.1 | 2.0 | 2.6 |
| Canada | 3.3 | 4.1 | 2.7 | 3.1 | 4.0 |
| Australia | 3.6 | 2.9 | 3.5 | 4.1 | 4.5 |
| Austria | 2.9 | 3.6 | 2.4 | 2.7 | 2.6 |
| Belgium | 2.4 | 2.8 | 2.3 | 2.1 | 2.2 |
| Denmark | 2.0 | 1.3 | 2.2 | 2.6 | 3.1 |
| Finland | 2.8 | 2.8 | 2.6 | 2.9 | 4.9 |
| Greece | 2.2 | 3.9 | 0.7 | 2.1 | 2.8 |
| Iceland | 3.7 | 5.9 | 2.8 | 2.0 | 3.3 |
| Ireland | 5.2 | 4.7 | 4.0 | 7.4 | 8.7 |
| Korea | 7.7 | 7.5 | 9.2 | 6.1 | 4.1 |
| Luxembourg | .. | .. | .. | 6.2 | 6.4 |
| Mexico | .. | .. | 1.3 | 2.5 | .. |
| Netherlands | 2.7 | 2.8 | 2.2 | 3.1 | 3.4 |
| New Zealand | 2.2 | 2.2 | 1.3 | 2.9 | 3.3 |
| Norway[4] | 2.6 | 3.8 | 1.4 | 2.5 | 2.9 |
| Portugal | 3.2 | 4.2 | 2.8 | 2.1 | .. |
| Spain | 2.8 | 3.2 | 2.4 | 2.9 | 3.5 |
| Sweden | 2.0 | 1.4 | 2.1 | 2.4 | 3.4 |
| Switzerland | 1.2 | 1.1 | 1.7 | 0.5 | .. |
| Turkey | 4.6 | 3.4 | 5.5 | 5.0 | .. |
| | | | | | |
| Coefficient of variation | | | | | |
| OECD total[5] | 0.42 | 0.42 | 0.59 | 0.52 | 0.46 |
| EU 15 | 0.28 | 0.33 | 0.29 | 0.55 | 0.52 |
| OECD 24[6] | 0.30 | 0.36 | 0.39 | 0.51 | 0.47 |

1. 1971 for Denmark, 1972 for Turkey, 1975 for Australia and Korea.
2. 1993 for Turkey, 1995 for Portugal, 1996 for Mexico and Switzerland, 1997 for Austria,
   Belgium and New Zealand, 1998 for Iceland, Ireland, Korea and Netherlands,1999 for Japan,
   United Kingdom, Denmark, Greece and Luxembourg.
3. 1991 for Germany and Luxembourg.
4. Mainland only.
5. Excluding Czech Republic, Hungary, Poland and Slovak Republic.
6. Excluding Czech Republic, Hungary, Korea, Mexico, Poland and Slovak Republic.

Source: OECD (2001), OECD Economic Outlook, No. 70.

| 1990 | 1991 | 1992 | 1993 | 1994 | 1995 | 1996 | 1997 | 1998 | 1999 | 2000 |
|------|------|------|------|------|------|------|------|------|------|------|
| 2.8 | 2.8 | 2.9 | 3.1 | 3.4 | 3.6 | 3.9 | 4.1 | 4.1 | 4.2 | 4.1 |
| 4.0 | 3.4 | 2.7 | 2.2 | 1.8 | 1.5 | 1.3 | 1.1 | 1.0 | 1.0 | .. |
| .. | .. | 1.5 | 1.5 | 1.6 | 1.7 | 1.8 | 1.9 | 2.0 | 2.1 | 2.2 |
| 3.4 | .. | .. | .. | .. | .. | .. | .. | .. | .. | .. |
| 2.3 | 2.0 | 1.7 | 1.6 | 1.6 | 1.8 | 2.0 | 2.3 | 2.5 | 2.7 | 2.8 |
| 2.2 | 1.9 | 1.7 | 1.7 | 1.7 | 1.8 | 1.9 | 2.0 | 2.1 | 2.2 | 2.2 |
| 2.1 | 1.6 | 1.4 | 1.4 | 1.7 | 2.0 | 2.3 | 2.6 | 2.7 | 2.7 | .. |
| 1.8 | 1.7 | 1.8 | 2.2 | 2.7 | 3.1 | 3.5 | 3.8 | 4.1 | 4.1 | 4.1 |
| 3.3 | 3.3 | 3.4 | 3.7 | 4.0 | 4.3 | 4.5 | 4.6 | 4.5 | 4.4 | 4.3 |
| 3.2 | 3.1 | 2.9 | 2.7 | 2.6 | 2.5 | 2.6 | 2.6 | .. | .. | .. |
| 2.7 | 2.4 | 2.1 | 2.0 | 1.9 | 2.0 | 2.1 | 2.2 | .. | .. | .. |
| 1.5 | 1.6 | 1.8 | 2.1 | 2.5 | 2.8 | 3.0 | 3.1 | 3.1 | 3.1 | .. |
| 0.6 | 0.2 | 0.3 | 1.0 | 1.9 | 2.9 | 3.8 | 4.5 | 4.9 | 5.0 | 4.9 |
| 1.3 | 1.4 | 1.5 | 1.6 | 1.8 | 2.1 | 2.4 | 2.7 | 2.9 | 2.9 | .. |
| 1.1 | 0.8 | 0.8 | 1.2 | 1.7 | 2.3 | 2.8 | 3.2 | 3.3 | .. | .. |
| 5.6 | 5.7 | 6.0 | 6.5 | 7.1 | 7.8 | 8.4 | 8.7 | 8.8 | .. | .. |
| 8.9 | 8.3 | 7.8 | 7.2 | 6.6 | 5.9 | 5.1 | 4.4 | 3.9 | .. | .. |
| .. | 6.0 | 6.0 | 6.0 | 6.0 | 6.1 | 6.2 | 6.3 | 6.4 | 6.4 | .. |
| 2.9 | 3.0 | 2.9 | 2.6 | 2.3 | 2.2 | 2.2 | .. | .. | .. | .. |
| 3.1 | 3.0 | 2.9 | 2.9 | 2.9 | 3.1 | 3.2 | 3.3 | 3.4 | .. | .. |
| 1.2 | 1.6 | 2.2 | 2.8 | 3.3 | 3.5 | 3.5 | 3.3 | .. | .. | .. |
| 0.6 | 1.0 | 1.5 | 2.1 | 2.6 | 2.9 | 3.1 | 3.1 | 3.0 | 2.8 | 2.6 |
| 3.3 | 2.7 | 2.2 | 1.9 | 1.8 | 1.8 | .. | .. | .. | .. | .. |
| 3.1 | 2.7 | 2.4 | 2.3 | 2.4 | 2.6 | 2.9 | 3.2 | 3.5 | 3.6 | 3.6 |
| 1.4 | 1.1 | 1.1 | 1.3 | 1.8 | 2.3 | 2.7 | 3.1 | 3.4 | 3.5 | 3.5 |
| 1.3 | 1.0 | 0.7 | 0.4 | 0.3 | 0.3 | 0.3 | .. | .. | .. | .. |
| 9.8 | 0.7 | 6.2 | 8.3 | .. | .. | .. | .. | .. | .. | .. |

# Table A1.8

## Trend GDP per person employed in the OECD area

Business sector, percentage change at annual rate

| Business sector | 1970[1]-00[2] | 1970[1]-80 | 1980[3]-90 | 1990[4]-00[2] | 1996-00[2] |
|---|---|---|---|---|---|
| United States | 1.3 | 1.1 | 1.3 | 1.7 | 1.9 |
| Japan | 2.7 | 4.0 | 2.8 | 1.3 | 1.0 |
| Germany | .. | .. | .. | 1.5 | 1.3 |
| *western Germany* | 1.5 | 3.0 | 1.8 | .. | .. |
| France | 2.5 | 3.4 | 2.5 | 1.6 | 1.4 |
| Italy | 2.3 | 3.1 | 2.0 | 1.8 | 1.5 |
| United Kingdom | 1.9 | 2.5 | 1.9 | 1.2 | 1.2 |
| Canada | 1.2 | 1.1 | 1.1 | 1.5 | 1.7 |
| Australia | 1.8 | 1.9 | 1.3 | 2.1 | 2.2 |
| Austria | 2.8 | 3.4 | 2.5 | 2.5 | 2.5 |
| Belgium | 2.5 | 3.4 | 2.3 | 1.6 | 1.5 |
| Denmark | 2.0 | 2.4 | 1.4 | 2.4 | 2.4 |
| Finland | 3.4 | 3.3 | 3.4 | 3.6 | 3.3 |
| Greece | 1.7 | 3.5 | 0.2 | 1.5 | 2.1 |
| Iceland | 2.3 | 3.6 | 1.6 | 1.6 | 1.5 |
| Ireland | 4.0 | 4.6 | 3.9 | 3.5 | 3.1 |
| Korea | 5.3 | 4.8 | 6.3 | 4.4 | 3.5 |
| Luxembourg | .. | .. | .. | 2.6 | 2.5 |
| Mexico | .. | .. | -0.4 | -0.8 | .. |
| Netherlands | 2.0 | 3.1 | 1.5 | 1.2 | 1.0 |
| New Zealand | 0.9 | 0.8 | 1.3 | 0.7 | 0.8 |
| Norway[5] | 2.1 | 3.0 | 1.4 | 1.9 | 1.5 |
| Portugal | 2.3 | 2.9 | 2.0 | 2.0 | .. |
| Spain | 2.8 | 4.0 | 2.7 | 1.8 | 1.2 |
| Sweden | 2.2 | 1.9 | 2.0 | 2.7 | 2.4 |
| Switzerland | 0.2 | 0.5 | 0.1 | 0.1 | .. |
| Turkey | 3.2 | 1.8 | 3.9 | 4.9 | .. |
| | | | | | |
| Coefficient of variation | | | | | |
| EU 15 | 0.3 | 0.2 | 0.4 | 0.4 | 0.4 |
| OECD 24[6] | 0.4 | 0.4 | 0.5 | 0.5 | 0.4 |

1. 1971 for Denmark, 1972 for Turkey, 1975 for Australia and Korea.
2. 1993 for Turkey, 1995 for Portugal, 1996 for Mexico and Switzerland, 1997 for Austria, Belgium and New Zealand, 1998 for Iceland, Ireland, Korea and Netherlands, 1999 for Japan, United Kingdom, Denmark, Greece and Luxembourg.
3. 1983 for Mexico.
4. 1991 for Germany.
5. Mainland only.
6. Excluding Czech Republic, Hungary, Korea, Mexico, Poland and Slovak Republic.

Source: OECD (2001), OECD Economic Outlook, No. 70.

| 1990 | 1991 | 1992 | 1993 | 1994 | 1995 | 1996 | 1997 | 1998 | 1999 | 2000 |
|---|---|---|---|---|---|---|---|---|---|---|
| 1.3 | 1.3 | 1.4 | 1.4 | 1.5 | 1.6 | 1.7 | 1.8 | 1.9 | 2.0 | 2.0 |
| 2.5 | 2.1 | 1.7 | 1.4 | 1.2 | 1.1 | 1.0 | 1.0 | 1.0 | 1.0 | .. |
| .. | .. | 1.8 | 1.7 | 1.7 | 1.6 | 1.4 | 1.3 | 1.3 | 1.2 | 1.2 |
| 2.1 | .. | .. | .. | .. | .. | .. | .. | .. | .. | .. |
| 2.3 | 2.1 | 1.9 | 1.8 | 1.6 | 1.5 | 1.5 | 1.4 | 1.4 | 1.4 | 1.4 |
| 2.2 | 2.1 | 2.1 | 2.1 | 2.1 | 2.0 | 1.8 | 1.7 | 1.5 | 1.4 | 1.4 |
| 1.0 | 1.0 | 1.1 | 1.1 | 1.2 | 1.2 | 1.2 | 1.2 | 1.2 | 1.3 | .. |
| 1.1 | 1.1 | 1.3 | 1.4 | 1.5 | 1.5 | 1.6 | 1.6 | 1.7 | 1.7 | 1.7 |
| 1.3 | 1.5 | 1.8 | 2.0 | 2.2 | 2.2 | 2.3 | 2.3 | 2.3 | 2.1 | 2.0 |
| 2.6 | 2.6 | 2.5 | 2.5 | 2.5 | 2.5 | 2.5 | 2.5 | .. | .. | .. |
| 2.0 | 1.8 | 1.7 | 1.6 | 1.6 | 1.6 | 1.5 | 1.5 | .. | .. | .. |
| 1.5 | 1.8 | 2.2 | 2.5 | 2.6 | 2.6 | 2.6 | 2.5 | 2.4 | 2.4 | .. |
| 3.6 | 3.7 | 3.8 | 4.0 | 4.0 | 3.8 | 3.6 | 3.5 | 3.3 | 3.2 | 3.2 |
| 1.1 | 1.1 | 1.0 | 1.0 | 1.2 | 1.4 | 1.7 | 2.0 | 2.1 | 2.2 | .. |
| 1.9 | 1.7 | 1.6 | 1.6 | 1.6 | 1.6 | 1.6 | 1.5 | 1.4 | .. | .. |
| 4.1 | 3.9 | 3.7 | 3.5 | 3.5 | 3.5 | 3.4 | 3.2 | 3.0 | .. | .. |
| 5.6 | 5.3 | 5.1 | 4.8 | 4.6 | 4.3 | 4.0 | 3.6 | 3.4 | .. | .. |
| .. | 2.6 | 2.7 | 2.7 | 2.7 | 2.7 | 2.7 | 2.6 | 2.5 | 2.5 | .. |
| 0.2 | 0.0 | -0.3 | -0.6 | -1.0 | -1.3 | -1.4 | .. | .. | .. | .. |
| 1.4 | 1.4 | 1.3 | 1.3 | 1.3 | 1.2 | 1.1 | 1.0 | 1.0 | .. | .. |
| 0.9 | 0.8 | 0.7 | 0.6 | 0.6 | 0.6 | 0.7 | 0.8 | .. | .. | .. |
| 2.1 | 2.3 | 2.5 | 2.4 | 2.2 | 1.9 | 1.7 | 1.6 | 1.5 | 1.5 | 1.5 |
| 2.3 | 2.0 | 1.9 | 1.9 | 2.0 | 2.0 | .. | .. | .. | .. | .. |
| 2.4 | 2.5 | 2.5 | 2.4 | 2.3 | 2.0 | 1.7 | 1.4 | 1.2 | 1.1 | 1.1 |
| 2.2 | 2.5 | 2.8 | 3.1 | 3.2 | 3.1 | 3.0 | 2.7 | 2.5 | 2.3 | 2.2 |
| -0.2 | -0.2 | 0.0 | 0.1 | 0.2 | 0.2 | 0.2 | .. | .. | .. | .. |
| 8.7 | 0.1 | 6.1 | 8.7 | .. | .. | .. | .. | .. | .. | .. |

## Sensitivity analysis: MFP growth estimates (adjusted for hours worked), 1980-2000

Average annual growth rates

| | | 1980-1990[1] | 1990-2000[2] | 1996-2000[3] |
|---|---|---|---|---|
| United States | Average factor shares (actual series) | 1.05 | 1.20 | 1.53 |
| | Average factor shares (trend series) | 0.91 | 1.14 | 1.36 |
| | Time-varing factor shares (trend series) | 0.92 | 1.13 | 1.34 |
| Japan | Average factor shares (actual series) | 2.14 | 0.82 | 0.32 |
| | Average factor shares (trend series) | 2.03 | 1.17 | 0.86 |
| | Time-varing factor shares (trend series) | 2.15 | 1.02 | 0.71 |
| Germany[4] | Average factor shares (actual series) | 1.50 | 0.75 | 0.63 |
| | Average factor shares (trend series) | 1.45 | 0.96 | 0.86 |
| | Time-varing factor shares (trend series) | 1.49 | 0.94 | 0.81 |
| France | Average factor shares (actual series) | 1.92 | 1.02 | 1.53 |
| | Average factor shares (trend series) | 1.71 | 1.10 | 1.21 |
| | Time-varing factor shares (trend series) | 1.86 | 1.00 | 1.13 |
| Italy | Average factor shares (actual series) | 1.29 | 1.02 | 0.50 |
| | Average factor shares (trend series) | 1.50 | 1.10 | 0.87 |
| | Time-varing factor shares (trend series) | 1.55 | 1.03 | 0.75 |
| United Kingdom | Average factor shares (actual series) | 2.30 | 0.74 | .. |
| | Average factor shares (trend series) | 2.00 | 0.73 | .. |
| | Time-varing factor shares (trend series) | .. | 0.74 | .. |
| Canada | Average factor shares (actual series) | 0.76 | 1.34 | 1.96 |
| | Average factor shares (trend series) | 0.65 | 1.29 | 1.68 |
| | Time-varing factor shares (trend series) | 0.63 | 1.30 | 1.66 |
| Australia | Average factor shares (actual series) | 0.35 | 1.68 | 1.94 |
| | Average factor shares (trend series) | 0.53 | 1.34 | 1.46 |
| | Time-varing factor shares (trend series) | 0.57 | 1.31 | 1.43 |
| Austria | Average factor shares (actual series) | 2.09 | 1.39 | .. |
| | Average factor shares (trend series) | 1.78 | 1.67 | .. |
| | Time-varing factor shares (trend series) | 1.82 | 1.56 | .. |
| Belgium | Average factor shares (actual series) | 1.79 | 1.19 | .. |
| | Average factor shares (trend series) | 1.74 | 1.28 | .. |
| | Time-varing factor shares (trend series) | 1.72 | 1.24 | .. |
| Denmark | Average factor shares (actual series) | 1.25 | 1.44 | 0.93 |
| | Average factor shares (trend series) | 0.98 | 1.47 | 1.49 |
| | Time-varing factor shares (trend series) | 1.00 | 1.45 | 1.45 |

1. 1983-1990 for Belgium, Denmark, Greece and Ireland, 1985-1990 for Austria and New Zealand.
2. 1991-1996 for Switzerland, 1991-1998 for Iceland, 1991-2000 for Germany, 1990-1996 for Ireland and Sweden, 1990-1997 for Austria, Belgium, New Zealand and United Kingdom, 1990-1998 for Netherlands, 1990-1999 for Australia, Denmark, France, Greece, Italy and Japan.
3. 1996-1999 for Australia, Denmark, France, Greece, Italy and Japan.
4. Western Germany for 1980-1990.

| | | 1980-1990[1] | 1990-2000[2] | 1996-2000[3] |
|---|---|---|---|---|
| Finland | Average factor shares (actual series) | 2.39 | 2.94 | 3.86 |
| | Average factor shares (trend series) | 2.29 | 3.10 | 3.54 |
| | Time-varing factor shares (trend series) | 2.38 | 3.16 | 3.60 |
| Greece | Average factor shares (actual series) | 1.68 | 0.71 | 1.72 |
| | Average factor shares (trend series) | 0.59 | 0.91 | 1.04 |
| | Time-varing factor shares (trend series) | 0.64 | 0.84 | 0.92 |
| Iceland | Average factor shares (actual series) | .. | 1.48 | .. |
| | Average factor shares (trend series) | .. | 1.15 | .. |
| | Time-varing factor shares (trend series) | .. | 1.20 | .. |
| Ireland | Average factor shares (actual series) | 4.15 | 3.72 | .. |
| | Average factor shares (trend series) | 3.55 | 4.39 | .. |
| | Time-varing factor shares (trend series) | 3.60 | 4.41 | .. |
| Netherlands | Average factor shares (actual series) | 2.29 | 1.45 | .. |
| | Average factor shares (trend series) | 2.21 | 1.60 | .. |
| | Time-varing factor shares (trend series) | 2.26 | 1.58 | .. |
| New Zealand | Average factor shares (actual series) | 0.09 | 0.79 | .. |
| | Average factor shares (trend series) | 0.17 | 0.75 | .. |
| | Time-varing factor shares (trend series) | 0.20 | 0.76 | .. |
| Norway | Average factor shares (actual series) | 0.82 | 1.83 | 0.96 |
| | Average factor shares (trend series) | 1.11 | 1.79 | 1.39 |
| | Time-varing factor shares (trend series) | 1.19 | 1.74 | 1.34 |
| Spain | Average factor shares (actual series) | 2.07 | 0.81 | 0.43 |
| | Average factor shares (trend series) | 1.90 | 0.81 | 0.56 |
| | Time-varing factor shares (trend series) | 2.06 | 0.72 | 0.49 |
| Sweden | Average factor shares (actual series) | 1.02 | 1.38 | .. |
| | Average factor shares (trend series) | 1.01 | 1.44 | .. |
| | Time-varing factor shares (trend series) | 1.03 | 1.42 | .. |
| Switzerland | Average factor shares (actual series) | .. | -0.15 | .. |
| | Average factor shares (trend series) | .. | -0.49 | .. |
| | Time-varing factor shares (trend series) | .. | -0.41 | .. |

Annex 2
# The policy-and-institutions augmented growth model

# Annex 2 The policy-and-institutions augmented growth model

Following a standard approach (see *e.g.* Mankiw *et al.*; and Barro and Sala-i-Martin [■··1]), the standard neoclassical growth model is derived from a constant returns to scale production function with two inputs (capital and labour) that are paid their marginal products. Production at time *t* is given by:

$$Y(t) = K(t)^{\alpha} H(t)^{\beta} \left( A(t) L(t) \right)^{1-\alpha-\beta} \qquad [A2.1]$$

where $Y$, $K$, $H$, and $L$ are respectively output, physical capital, human capital and labour, $\alpha$ is the partial elasticity of output with respect to physical capital, $\beta$ is the partial elasticity of output with respect to human capital and $A(t)$ is the level of technological and economic efficiency. It can be assumed that the level of economic and technological efficiency $A(t)$ has two components: economic efficiency $I(t)$ dependent on institutions and economic policy (a vector $V(t)$) and the level of technological progress $\Omega(t)$ (see amongst others, Cellini *et al.* for a similar formulation [■··2]). In turn, $I(t)$ can be written as, *e.g.* a log-linear function of institutional and policy variables, while $\Omega(t)$ is assumed to grow at the rate $g(t)$.

■··1a Mankiw, G.N.,
D. Romer and D.N. Weil (1992),
"A Contribution to the Empirics of Economic Growth",
*Quarterly Journal of Economics*,
Vol. 107, No. 2.

1b Barro, R.J.
and X. Sala-I-Martin (1995),
*Economic Growth*,
McGraw-Hill.

■··2 Cellini, R.,
M. Cortese and N. Rossi (1999),
"Social Catastrophes and Growth",
University of Bologna, *mimeo*.

The time paths of the right-hand side variables are described by the following equations (hereafter dotted variables represent derivatives with respect to time):

$$\dot{k}(t) = s_k(t) A(t)^{1-\alpha-\beta} k(t)^{\alpha} h(t)^{\beta} - (n(t)+d) k(t) \qquad [A2.2]$$

$$\dot{h}(t) = s_h(t) A(t)^{1-\alpha-\beta} k(t)^{\alpha} h(t)^{\beta} - (n(t)+d) h(t)$$

$$A(t) = I(t) \Omega(t)$$

$$\ln I(t) = p_0 + \sum_j p_j \ln V_j(t)$$

$$\dot{\Omega}(t) = g(t) \Omega(t)$$

$$\dot{L}(t) = n(t) L(t)$$

where $k = K/L$, $h = H/L$, $y = Y/L$, stand for the capital labour ratio, average human capital and output per worker respectively; $s_k$ and $s_h$ stand for the investment rate in physical and human capital respectively; $d$ stands for the (constant) depreciation rate; and $n$ is the growth rate of the population. Under the assumption that $\alpha + \beta < 1$ (*i.e.* decreasing returns to reproducible factors), this system of equations can be solved to obtain steady-state values of $k^*$ and $h^*$ defined by:

$$[A2.3]$$

$$\ln k^*(t) = \ln A(t) + \frac{1-\beta}{1-\alpha-\beta} \ln s_k(t) + \frac{\beta}{1-\alpha-\beta} \ln s_h(t) - \frac{1}{1-\alpha-\beta} \ln(g(t)+n(t)+d)$$

$$\ln h^*(t) = \ln A(t) + \frac{\alpha}{1-\alpha-\beta} \ln s_k(t) + \frac{1-\alpha}{1-\alpha-\beta} \ln s_h(t) - \frac{1}{1-\alpha-\beta} \ln(g(t)+n(t)+d)$$

Substituting these two equations into the production function and taking logs yields the expression for the steady-state output in intensive form. The latter can be expressed either as a function of $s_h$ (investment in human capital) and the other variables or as a function of $h^*$ (the steady-state stock of human capital) and the other variables. Since human capital is proxied by the average years of education of the working age population, a formulation in terms of the stock of human capital was retained. The steady state path of output in intensive form can be written as: [● 1]

[A2.4]

$$\ln y^*(t) = \ln \Omega(t) + p_0 + \sum_j p_j \ln V_j(t)$$

$$+ \frac{\alpha}{1-\alpha} \ln s_k(t) + \frac{\beta}{1-\alpha} \ln h^*(t) - \frac{\alpha}{1-\alpha} \ln(g(t) + n(t) + d)$$

However, the steady-state stock of human capital is not observed. As shown by Bassanini and Scarpetta [■ ‣ 3], the expression for $h^*$ as a function of actual human capital is:

[A2.5]

$$\ln h^*(t) = \ln h(t) + \frac{1-\psi}{\psi} \Delta \ln(h(t)/A(t))$$

where $\psi$ is a function of $(\alpha, \beta)$ and $n + g + d$.

Equation [A2.4] would be a valid specification in the empirical cross-country analysis if countries were in their steady states or if deviations from the steady state were independent and identically distributed. If observed growth rates include out-of-steady-state dynamics, then the transitional dynamics have to be modelled explicitly. A linear approximation of the transitional dynamics can be expressed as follows [■ ‣ 1a]:

[A2.6]

$$\Delta \ln y(t) = -\phi(\lambda) \ln(y(t-1)) + \phi(\lambda) \frac{\alpha}{1-\alpha} \ln s_k(t) + \phi(\lambda) \frac{\beta}{1-\alpha} \ln h(t) + \sum_j p_j \phi(\lambda) \ln V_j(t)$$

$$+ \frac{1-\psi}{\psi} \frac{\beta}{1-\alpha} \Delta \ln h(t) - \phi(\lambda) \frac{\alpha}{1-\alpha} \ln(g(t) + n(t) + d) + \left(1 - \frac{\phi(\lambda)}{\psi}\right) g(t) + \phi(\lambda)(p_0 + \ln \Omega(0)) + \phi(\lambda) g(t)t$$

where $\lambda = (1 - \alpha - \beta)(g(t) + n(t) + d)$. Adding short-term dynamics to equation [A2.6] yields:

[A2.7]

$$\Delta \ln y(t) = a_0 - \phi \ln y(t-1) + a_1 \ln s_k(t) + a_2 \ln h(t) - a_3 n(t) + a_4 t + \sum_j a_{j+4} \ln V_j$$

$$+ b_1 \Delta \ln s_k(t) + b_2 \Delta \ln h(t) + b_3 \Delta \ln n(t) + \sum_j b_{j+4} \Delta \ln V_j + \varepsilon(t)$$

Equation [A2.7] represents the generic functional form. Estimates of steady state coefficients as well as of the parameters of the production function can be retrieved on the basis of the estimated coefficients of this equation by comparing it with equation [A2.6]. For instance, an estimate of the elasticity of steady state output to the investment rate (that is the long-run effect of the investment rate on output) is given by $\hat{a}_1/\hat{\phi}$ where ^ identifies estimated coefficients. Conversely, an estimate of the share of physical capital in output (the parameter $\alpha$ of the production function) can be obtained as $\hat{a}_1/(\hat{\phi} + \hat{a}_1)$.

The policy-and-institutions augmented growth model

● 1 Strictly speaking, equation [A2.4] is written under the simplifying assumption that policy and institutional variables do not change persistently in the long-run. If this is not the case, $\ln(g+n+d)$ must be augmented by a term reflecting the rate of change of policy and institutional variables. As the estimable equation is linearised and contains short-run dynamics anyway, this term will be omitted hereafter for simplicity.

■ ‣ 3 Bassanini, A. and S. Scarpetta (2002), "Does Human Capital Matter for Growth in OECD Countries? A Pooled Mean Group Approach", *Economics Letters*, Vol. 74, No. 3.

# Methodological details on the empirical analysis of industry multi-factor productivity

Annex

3

Methodological details
on the empirical analysis
of industry multi-factor
productivity

A3.1. **The theorical framework**

### A3.1. **The theoretical framework**

The basic framework of the analysis starts with a standard production function (in country $i$ and sector $j$), under perfect competition and constant returns to scale. This can be formalised as follows:

$$Y_{ijt} = A_{ijt} \cdot F_{ij}\left(L_{ijt}, K_{ijt}\right)$$

where $Y$ is output [1], $A$ is a Hicks-neutral parameter of technical change [2], $F_{ij}$ is a country/sector-specific production function, $K$ is physical capital and $L$ labour. Assuming a Cobb-Douglas production function and taking logs yield:

$$y_{ijt} = a_{ijt} + \alpha_{ijt} \cdot l_{ijt} + \left(1 - \alpha_{ijt}\right) \cdot k_{ijt}$$

Methodological details on the empirical analysis of industry multi-factor productivity

A3.1. **The theorical framework**

*The convergence equation*

In this context, multi-factor productivity growth can be proxied by the so called Solow residual as follows:

$$\Delta MFP_{ijt} = \Delta y_{ijt} - \alpha_{ijt} \cdot \Delta l_{ijt} - \left(1 - \alpha_{ijt}\right) \cdot \Delta k_{ijt}$$

### *The convergence equation*

In order to assess the driving forces of MFP growth, the models adopts a catch-up specification, whereby, within each industry, the production possibility set is influenced by technological and organisational transfer from the technology-frontier country to other countries. The co-integration model of MFP may also account for the international transmission of business cycles across OECD countries (for instance trade and financial channels). In this context, multi-factor productivity for a given industry $j$ of country $i$ at date $t$ ($MFP_{ijt}$) can be modelled as an auto-regressive distributed lag ADL(1,1) process in which the level of MFP is co-integrated with the level of MFP of the technological frontier country $F$. Formally:

[A3.1]

$$\ln MFP_{ijt} = \beta_1 \ln MFP_{ijt-1} + \beta_2 \ln MFP_{Fjt} + \beta_3 \ln MFP_{Fjt-1} + \omega_{ijt}$$

where $\omega$ stands for all observable and non-observable factors influencing the level of MFP. Under the assumption of long-run homogeneity $(1 - \beta_1 = \beta_2 + \beta_3)$ and rearranging equation [A3.1] yields the convergence equation:

[A3.2]

$$\Delta \ln MFP_{ijt} = \beta_2 \Delta \ln MFP_{Fjt} - \left(1 - \beta_1\right) RMFP_{ijt} + \omega_{ijt}$$

where $RMFP_{ijt} = \ln(MFP_{ijt}) - \ln(MPF_{Fjt})$ is the technological gap between country $i$ and the leading country $F$. This is the specification used in the

[1] The analysis follows a value-added concept of output, which does not require measures of intermediate consumption. This is the proper approach because the industries that we use may have different levels of aggregation.

[2] Technical change is "Hicks neutral", or "output augmenting", when it can be represented as an outward shift of the production function that affects all factors of production in the same proportion.

empirical analysis. Moreover, the following (productivity) index is used as a measure of the MFP level:

[A3.3]

$$MFP_{ijt} = \frac{Y_{ijt}}{\overline{Y}_{jt}} \cdot \left( \frac{\overline{L}_{jt}}{L_{ijt}} \right)^{\alpha_{ijt}} \cdot \left( \frac{\overline{K}_{jt}}{K_{ijt}} \right)^{1-\alpha_{ijt}}$$

where a *bar* denotes a geometric average over all the countries for a given industry $j$ and year $t$. The index has the desirable properties of superlativeness and transitiveness which makes it possible to compare national productivity levels [◼→ 1]. However, the comparison of productivity levels also requires the conversion of underlying data into a common currency, while also taking into account differences in purchasing powers across countries. These issues are discussed in the next section.

The residual in equation [A3.2] is modelled as follows:

[A3.4]

$$\omega_{ijt} = \sum_{k} \gamma_k V_{kijt-1} + f_i + g_j + d_t + \varepsilon_{ijt}$$

where $(V_{ijt})$ is a vector of covariates (*e.g.* product and labour market regulations, human capital, or R&D) affecting the level of MFP; $f_i$, $g_j$, and $d_t$ are respectively country, industry and year fixed effects. $\varepsilon$ is an *2d* shock. Moreover, equation [A3.2] can be solved for steady-state MFP in country $i$ relative to the frontier in industry $j$ which gives insights on the effects of these country and/or country-industry specific factors on the steady-state level of MFP.

## The steady-state equilibrium

At a steady-state equilibrium, the independent variables are constant over time ($\omega_{ijt} = \omega_{ij}$) and the multi-factor productivity in sector $j$ grows at the same constant rate in all countries: $\Delta \ln MFP_{ijt} = \Delta \ln MFP_{Fj}$.

For the ease of exposition, the residual in equation [A3.2] is redefined as follows:

[A3.5]

$$\omega_{ijt} = \omega'_{ijt} + \omega''_{ijt} \cdot RMFP_{ijt}$$

where $\omega'$ and $\omega''$ correspond to the factors affecting the rate of growth of MFP respectively, directly or through the diffusion of technology and organisational practises. Solving for the steady-state, one can obtain the following expression for the level of MFP in country $i$ relative to the frontier in industry $j$:

[A3.6]

$$RMFP_{ij} = \frac{\omega'_{ij} - (1 - \beta_2) \Delta MFP_{Fj}}{(1 - \beta)_1 - \omega''_{ij}}$$

For details on the method of estimation (approach followed, diagnostic tests, sensitivity analysis, etc.) see Scarpetta and Tressel [◼→ 2]

**Methodological details on the empirical analysis of industry multi-factor productivity**

A3.1. **The theorical framework**

*The steady-state equilibrium*

◼→ 1 Caves, D., L. Christensen and E. Diewert (1982), "Multilateral Comparisons of Output, Input, and Productivity Using Superlative Index Numbers", *Economic Journal*, Vol. 92, No. 365.

◼→ 2 Scarpetta, S. and T. Tressel (2002), "Productivity and Convergence in a Panel of OECD Industries: Do Regulations and Institutions Matter?", *OECD Economics Department Working Papers*, No. 342.

Understanding Economic Growth | © OECD 2004

# Details on firm-level data

## A4.1. **The data and indicators of firm dynamics and survival**

### *Raw data on firm dynamics and survival*

The analysis of firm entry and exit and firm survival presented earlier is based on business registers (Canada, Denmark, France, Finland, Netherlands, United Kingdom and United States) or social security databases (Germany and Italy). Data for Portugal are drawn from an employee-based register containing information on both establishments and firms.

The key features of these data on firm dynamics and survival are as follows:

Unit of observation: Data used in the study refer to the firm as the unit of reference, with the exception of Germany where data are only available with reference to establishments. More specifically, most of the data used conform to the following definition [▪▪→1] "an organisational unit producing goods or services which benefits from a certain degree of autonomy in decisionmaking, especially for the allocation of its current resources". Generally, this will be above the establishment level. However, firms that have operating units in multiple countries in the EU will have at least one unit counted in each country. Of course, it may well be that the national boundaries that generate a statistical split-up of a firm, in fact split a firm in a "real" sense as well. Also related to the unit of analysis is the issue of mergers and acquisitions. Only in some countries does the business register keep close track of such organisational changes within and between firms. In addition, ownership structures themselves may vary across countries because of tax considerations or other factors that influence how business activities are organised within the structure of defined legal entities.

Size threshold: While some registers include even single-person businesses, others omit firms smaller than a certain size, usually in terms of the number of employees, but sometimes in terms of other measures such as sales (as is the case in the data for France and Italy). Data used in this study exclude single-person businesses. However, because smaller firms tend to have more volatile firm dynamics, remaining differences in the threshold across different country datasets should be taken into account in the international comparison.

▪▪→ 1 EUROSTAT (1995),
*"Recommendation Manual:*
*Business Register"*,
http://europa.eu.int/comm/eurostat

**Period of analysis:** Data on firm dynamics and survival are compiled on an annual basis, covering varying time spans. The German, Danish and Finnish register data cover the longest time periods, while data for the other countries are available for shorter periods of time or, although available for longer periods, include significant breaks in definitions or coverage. In most of the analysis presented, data refer to the period 1989-94, which guarantees the largest country coverage.

**Sectoral coverage:** Special efforts have been made to organise the data in a common industry classification (ISIC Rev.3, [● Table A4.1] that matches the OECD STAN database. In the panel data constructed to generate the tabulations, firms were allocated to the STAN industry that most closely fitted their operations over the complete time-span. Note that in countries where the data collection by the statistical agency varied across major sectors (*e.g.*, construction, industry, services), a firm that switched between major sectors could not be tracked as a continuing firm, but ended up creating an exit in one sector and an entry in another. Most countries have been able to provide firm demographic data across most sectors of the economy, with the exception that public services are often not included (the United Kingdom is a special case, where data only refer only to manufacturing).

### Details on Firm-level Data

A4.1. **The data and indicators of firm dynamics and survival**

*Indicators collected for firm dynamics and survival*

## Indicators collected for firm dynamics and survival

The use of annual data on firm dynamics implies a significant volatility in the resulting indicators. In order to limit the possible impact of measurement problems, it was decided to use definitions of continuing, entering and exiting firms on the basis of three (rather than the usual two) time periods. Thus, the tabulations of firm dynamics contained the following variables:

- Firm entry, comprising firms observed as (out, in, in) the register in time $(t - 1, t, t + 1)$.
- Firm exit, comprising firms observed as (in, in, out) the register in time $(t - 1, t, t + 1)$.
- Continuing firms, comprising firms observed as (in, in, in) the register in time $(t - 1, t, t + 1)$.
- One-year firms, comprising firms observed as (in, out, in) the register in time $(t - 1, t, t + 1)$.

This method of defining continuing, entering and exiting firms implies that a change in the stock of continuing firms $(C)$ relates to entry $(E)$ and exit $(X)$ in the following way:

[A4.1]

$$C_t - C_{t-1} = E_{t-1} - X_t$$

This has implications for the appropriate measure of firm "turnover". Given that continuing, entering, exiting and "one-year" firms ($O$) all exist in time $t$ then the total number of firms ($T$) is:

$$T_t = C_t + E_t + X_t + O_t \qquad [A4.2]$$

From this, the change in the total number of firms between two years, taking into account equation [A4.1], can be written as:

$$[A4.3]$$

$$T_t - T_{t-1} = E_t - X_{t-1} + O_t - O_{t-1}$$

● 1 It should be noted that the gross employment flows tabulated from the statistical register files do not necessarily coincide with gross job flow data tabulated from production surveys, such as those used by Davis *et al.* [■→ 2].

■→ 2 Davis, S.J., J. Haltiwanger and S. Schu (1996), "Small Business and Job Creation: Dissecting the Myth and Reassessing the Facts", *Small Business Economics*, Vol. 8.

Thus, a turnover measure that is consistent with the contribution of net entry to changes in the total number of firms should be based on the sum of contemporaneous entry with lagged exit.

In practice, a number of complications arise in constructing and interpreting data that conform to the definitions of continuing, entering and exiting firms described above. In particular, the "one-year" category, in principle, represents short-lived firms that are observed in time t but not in adjacent time periods and could therefore be treated as an additional piece of information in evaluating firm demographics. However, in some databases this category also includes measurement errors and possibly ill-defined data. Thus, the total number of firms in the analysis for the main text excludes these "one-year" firms.

Available data also allowed to track entering firms over time and to assess the contribution of firm dynamics to the overall job turnover by industry and over time. In particular, the following indicators were constructed:

- The analysis of survival: Entering cohorts of firms were tracked down which allowed assessment of the probability of failure and survivor rates by duration. Moreover, information was collected on employment in these firms, both in the year of entry and in subsequent years.
- Job creation and destruction: Additional information on employment changes in continuing firms also permitted the calculation of the overall job turnover by industry and over time and assessment of the contribution of firm dynamics to this process [● 1].

## A4.2. **Productivity decomposition data**

Using mainly longitudinal business surveys, analysis provides a decomposition of industry productivity growth into the contribution of within-firm growth and that due to reallocation of resources across firms – which includes reallocation amongst incumbents, as well as reallocation due to the entry of new units and/or the exit of other units. Detailed results are presented in ● · Tables A4.2 to A4.8 at the end of this **Annex**.

They are based on the approach developed by Griliches and Regev [■·· 3] (referred to hereafter as the GR method), but alternative calculations were also made in order to check the robustness of the results, based on the method developed by Foster, Haltiwanger, and Krizan [■·· 4] (referred hereafter as the FHK method). This section of the Annex aims to provide methodological details on both approaches. Full details on their results can be found in Scarpetta *et al.* [■·· 5].

## Definition of entry and exit

Following standard practice, the productivity decompositions were based on a fairly long time interval (in this case 5 years). Thus, unlike the annual firm-demographics data, a more conventional method of defining continuing, entering and exiting firms was used:

- Continuing firms: observed both in the first year $(t - k)$ and the last year $(t)$ of the period.
- Entering firms: observed in the last year $(t)$, but not in the first year $(t - k)$.
- Exiting firms: observed in the first year $(t - k)$, but not in the last year $(t)$.

## Decomposition methods

The GR method can best be understood by examining first the FHK method, as it is essentially a simplification of the latter. The FHK method decomposes aggregate productivity growth into five components, commonly called the "within effect", "between effect", "cross effect", "entry effect", and "exit effect", as follows:

$$\Delta P_t = \sum_{i \in C} \theta_{it-k} \Delta p_{it} + \sum_{i \in C} \Delta \theta_{it} \left( p_{it-k} - P_{t-k} \right) + \sum_{i \in C} \Delta \theta_{it} \Delta p_{it} \qquad [A4.4]$$
$$+ \sum_{i \in N} \theta_{it} \left( p_{it} - P_{t-k} \right) - \sum_{i \in X} \theta_{it-k} \left( p_{it-k} - P_{t-k} \right)$$

where $\Delta$ means changes over the k-years' interval between the first year $(t - k)$ and the last year $(t)$; $\theta_{it}$ is the share of firm $i$ in the given sector at time $t$; $C$, $N$, and $X$ are sets of continuing, entering, and exiting firms, respectively; and $P_{t-k}$ is the aggregate (*i.e.*, weighted average) productivity level of the sector as of the first year $(t - k)$ [● 2].

Thus, the components of the FHK decomposition are defined as follows:

- The *within-firm effect* is within-firm productivity growth weighted by initial output shares.
- The *between-firm effect* captures the gains in aggregate productivity coming from the expanding market of high productivity firms, or from lowproductivity firms' shrinking shares weighted by *initial* shares.

**Details on firm-level data**

A4.2. **Productivity decomposition data**

*Definition of entry and exit*

*Decomposition methods*

● 2 The shares are usually based on employment in decompositions of labour productivity and on output in decompositions of total factor productivity.

■·· 3 Griliches, Z. and H. Regev (1995), "Firm Productivity in Israeli Industry, 1979-1988", *Journal of Econometrics*, Vol. 65.

■·· 4 Foster, L., J.C. Haltiwanger and C.J. Krizan (1998), "Aggregate Productivity Growth: Lessons from Microeconomic Evidence", *NBER Working Papers*, No. 6803.

■·· 5 Scarpetta, S., P. Hemmings, T. Tressel and J. Woo (2002), "The Role of Policy and Institutions for Productivity and Firm Dynamics: Evidence from Micro and Industry Data", *OECD Economics Department Working Papers*, No. 329.

- The *"cross effect"* reflects gains in productivity from high-productivity growth firms' expanding shares or from low-productivity *growth* firms' shrinking shares.
- The *entry effect* is the sum of the differences between each entering firm's productivity and *initial* productivity in the industry, weighted by its market share.
- The *exit effect* is the sum of the differences between each exiting firm's productivity and *initial* productivity in the industry, weighted by its market share.

**Details on firm-level data**

A4.2. **Productivity decomposition data**

*Decomposition methods*

While the FHK method uses the first year's values for a continuing firm's share ($\theta_{it-k}$), its productivity level ($p_{it-k}$) and the sector-wide average productivity level ($P_{t-k}$), the GR method uses the time averages of the first and last years for them ($\overline{\theta}_i$, $\overline{p}_i$ and $\overline{P}$). As a result the, "cross-effect" or ("covariance") term in the FHK method, disappears from the decomposition. The resulting formula is:

$$\Delta P_t = \sum_{i \in C} \overline{\theta}_i \Delta p_{it} + \sum_{i \in C} \Delta \theta_{it} \left( \overline{p}_i - \overline{P} \right)$$
$$+ \sum_{i \in N} \theta_{it} \left( p_{it} - \overline{P} \right) - \sum_{i \in X} \theta_{it-k} \left( p_{it-k} - \overline{P} \right)$$

[A4.5]

where a bar over a variable indicates the average of the variable over the first year ($t - k$) and the last year ($t$). Thus, the components of the GR decomposition can be described as follows:

- The *within effect* describes the productivity growth within firms weighted by the *average* firm share over the time interval of the calculation.
- The *between-firm effect* captures the gains in aggregate productivity which comes from high-productivity firms' expanding shares, or from low-productivity firms' shrinking shares weighted by *average* shares over the time interval of the calculation.
- The *entry effect* is the sum of the differences between each entering firm's productivity and *average* productivity in the industry, weighted by its market share.
- The *exit effect* is the sum of the differences between each exiting firm's productivity and *average* productivity in the industry, weighted by its market share.

Certain aspects of the decomposition need to be borne in mind when interpreting the data:

The FHK "within effect" reflects the pure contribution of continuing individual firms' productivity growth, as it is weighted by the *initial* shares. The "between effect" reflects the contribution of changes in market share, given initial productivity level and the "cross effect" or "covariance term" reveals whether firms with increasing productivity also tend to increase market share or not.

By contrast, in the GR method the distinction between the within and between effects is somewhat blurred in the sense that time averaging makes the within effect term affected by changes in the firms' shares over time and the between effect term affected by changes in productivity over time.

Although disadvantageous in some respects, it has been suggested that the GR method is less sensitive than the FHK method to annual fluctuations in the underlying data and, possibly, measurement errors. For example, firms with overestimated labour input in a given year will have spuriously low measured labour productivity and spuriously high measured employment share in that year, potentially producing negative covariance between productivity and share changes. In this case, the within effect in the FHK method could be misleadingly high [● 3].

**Details on firm-level data**

A4.2. **Productivity decomposition data**

*Decomposition methods*

● 3 Similarly, in the case of total factor productivity decomposition using output shares, random measurement errors in output could yield a positive covariance between productivity changes and share changes, and hence, the within effect could be spuriously low.

## The STAN industry list (based on ISIC Rev. 3)

| ISIC Rev. 3 codes | Industry name | ISIC Rev. 3 codes | Industry name |
|---|---|---|---|
| Total | Total | Total | Total |
| 01-05 | Agriculture, hunting, forestry and fishing | 40-41 | Electricity gas and water supply |
| 10-14 | Mining and quarrying | 45 | Construction |
| 15-37 | Total manufacturing | 50-99 | Total services |
| 15-16 | Food products, beverages and tobacco | 50-74 | Business sector services |
| 17-19 | Textiles, textile products, leather and footwear | 50-55 | Wholesale and retail trade; restaurants and hotels |
| 20 | Wood, products of wood and cork | 50-52 | Wholesale and retail trade; repairs |
| 21-22 | Pulp paper, paper products, printing and publishing | 55 | Hotels and restaurants |
| 23-25 | Chemical, rubber, plastics and fuel products | 60-64 | Transport and storage and communication |
| 23-24 | Chemical and fuel products | 60-63 | Transport and storage |
| 23 | Coke refined, petroleum products and nuclear fuel | 64 | Post and telecommunications |
| 24 | Chemicals and chemical products | 65-74 | Finance, insurance, real estate and business services |
| 24 ex 2423 | Chemicals excluding pharmaceuticals | 65-67 | Financial intermediation |
| 2423 | Pharmaceuticals | 65 | Financial intermediation except insurance and pension funding |
| 25 | Rubber and plastics products | 66 | Insurance and pension funding except compulsory social securit |
| 26 | Other non-metallic mineral products | 67 | Activities related to financial intermediation |
| 27-35 | Basic metals, metal products, machinery and equipment | 70-74 | Real estate renting and business activities |
| 27-33 | Basic metals, metal products, machinery and equipment, excluding transport | 70 | Real estate activities |
| 27-28 | Basic metals and fabricated metal products | 71 | Renting of machinery and equipment |
| 27 | Basic metals | 72 | Computer and related activities |
| 28 | Fabricated metal products except machinery and equipment | 73 | Research and development |
| 29-33 | Machinery and equipment | 74 | Other business activities |
| 29 | Machinery and equipment n.e.c. | 75-99 | Community social and personal services |
| 30-33 | Electrical and optical equipment | 75 | Public admin. and defence; compulsory social security |
| 30 | Office accounting and computing | 80 | Education |
| 31 | Electrical machinery and apparatus n.e.c. | 85 | Health and social work |
| 32 | Radio, television and communication equipment | 90-93 | Other community social and personal services |
| 33 | Medical precision and optical instruments | 95 | Private households with employed persons |
| 34-35 | Transport equipment | 99 | Extra-territorial organisations and bodies |
| 34 | Motor vehicles, trailers and semi-trailers | | |
| 35 | Other transport equipment | | |
| 351 | Building and repairing of ships and boats | | |
| 353 | Aircraft and spacecraft | | |
| 352+359 | Railroad equipment and transport | | |
| 36-37 | Manufacturing n.e.c.; recycling | | |

## Labour productivity decompositions: France

Decomposition based on the Griliches and Regev (1995) approach

Average period: **1987-1992**

| Industries | Productivity growth (annual % change) | Decomposition | | | | |
|---|---|---|---|---|---|---|
| | | Within | Between | Net entry | of which | |
| | | | | | Entry | Exit |
| Total manufacturing | 2.3 | 2.0 | 0.0 | 0.2 | -0.2 | 0.4 |
| Food products, beverages and tobacco | 2.6 | 2.4 | -0.3 | 0.4 | 0.2 | 0.2 |
| Textiles, textile products, leather and footwear | 1.8 | 1.5 | 0.3 | -0.1 | -0.8 | 0.7 |
| Wood and products of wood and cork | 1.9 | 1.6 | 0.6 | -0.3 | -0.1 | -0.2 |
| Pulp paper, paper products, printing and publishing | 2.3 | 1.3 | 0.2 | 0.8 | 0.4 | 0.4 |
| Chemical and fuel products | 2.6 | 2.0 | 0.2 | 0.4 | 0.2 | 0.3 |
| Coke refined, petroleum products and nuclear fuel | -1.1 | -0.9 | -0.3 | 0.1 | -0.1 | 0.2 |
| Chemicals and chemical products | 3.0 | 2.3 | 0.3 | 0.4 | 0.2 | 0.2 |
| Chemicals excluding pharmaceuticals | 2.3 | 1.9 | 0.1 | 0.4 | 0.3 | 0.1 |
| Pharmaceuticals | 4.2 | 3.0 | 0.7 | 0.5 | 0.1 | 0.4 |
| Rubber and plastics products | 2.4 | 1.7 | 0.5 | 0.2 | 0.3 | -0.1 |
| Other non-metallic mineral products | 0.6 | 1.2 | -0.4 | -0.2 | -0.1 | -0.1 |
| Basic metals, metal products, machinery and equipment excl. transport | 1.3 | 2.0 | -0.2 | -0.4 | -0.1 | -0.3 |
| Basic metals and fabricated metal products | -0.1 | 1.7 | -0.4 | -1.4 | -0.4 | -1.0 |
| Machinery and equipment | 2.4 | 2.2 | -0.1 | 0.4 | 0.2 | 0.3 |
| Machinery and equipment n.e.c. | 2.4 | 2.1 | -0.1 | 0.4 | 0.2 | 0.2 |
| Electrical and optical equipment | 2.5 | 2.3 | -0.1 | 0.4 | 0.1 | 0.3 |
| Electrical machinery and apparatus n.e.c. | 2.6 | 2.0 | -0.0 | 0.7 | 0.5 | 0.2 |
| Radio, television and communication equipment | 2.9 | 3.1 | -0.3 | 0.1 | -0.4 | 0.5 |
| Medical precision and optical instruments | 2.4 | 1.7 | -0.1 | 0.9 | 0.3 | 0.6 |
| Transport equipment | 3.2 | 3.2 | -0.3 | 0.3 | -0.3 | 0.5 |
| Motor vehicles, trailers and semi-trailers | 3.5 | 3.2 | -0.1 | 0.4 | -0.3 | 0.6 |
| Other transport equipment | 2.6 | 3.1 | -0.6 | 0.1 | -0.1 | 0.2 |
| Manufacturing n.e.c.; recycling | 2.7 | 1.8 | 0.1 | 0.8 | 0.6 | 0.2 |

# Table A4.3

## Labour productivity decompositions: Finland

Decomposition based on the Griliches and Regev (1995) approach

Average period: **1987-1992**

| Industries | Productivity growth (annual % change) | Decomposition | | | | |
|---|---|---|---|---|---|---|
| | | Within | Between | Net entry | of which | |
| | | | | | Entry | Exit |
| Total manufacturing | 5.0 | 2.6 | 0.9 | 1.5 | 0.0 | 1.5 |
| Food products, beverages and tobacco | 4.4 | 3.4 | 0.1 | 1.0 | 0.3 | 0.7 |
| Textiles, textile products, leather and footwear | 3.1 | 0.0 | 0.8 | 2.3 | 0.1 | 2.2 |
| Wood and products of wood and cork | 4.8 | 3.5 | 0.3 | 1.0 | 0.2 | 0.8 |
| Pulp paper, paper products, printing and publishing | 4.9 | 3.1 | 0.7 | 1.0 | -0.2 | 1.2 |
| Chemical, rubber, plastics and fuel products | 4.0 | 3.4 | 0.0 | 0.6 | 0.1 | 0.5 |
| Chemical and fuel products | 2.8 | 3.3 | -1.2 | 0.7 | 0.3 | 0.5 |
| Coke refined, petroleum products and nuclear fuel | 4.4 | 7.3 | -0.9 | .. | -2.0 | .. |
| Chemicals and chemical products | 3.2 | 2.7 | -0.1 | 0.6 | 0.4 | 0.2 |
| Chemicals excluding pharmaceuticals | 3.2 | 2.5 | -0.0 | 0.7 | 0.3 | 0.4 |
| Pharmaceuticals | 3.5 | 3.4 | -0.2 | 0.3 | 0.6 | -0.4 |
| Rubber and plastics products | 4.3 | 3.6 | 0.3 | 0.5 | 0.2 | 0.3 |
| Other non-metallic mineral products | 2.4 | 1.5 | 0.2 | 0.7 | 0.5 | 0.3 |
| Basic metals, metal products, machinery and equipment | 4.6 | 2.7 | 0.8 | 1.1 | -0.0 | 1.1 |
| Basic metals, metal products, machinery and equipment excl. transport | 4.6 | 2.5 | 0.9 | 1.2 | -0.0 | 1.2 |
| Basic metals and fabricated metal products | 4.9 | 2.8 | 1.2 | 1.0 | -0.4 | 1.4 |
| Basic metals | 6.3 | 3.8 | 1.4 | 1.1 | 0.2 | 0.8 |
| Fabricated metal products excl. machinery and equipment | 2.7 | 2.0 | 0.1 | 0.6 | -0.4 | 1.0 |
| Machinery and equipment | 4.4 | 2.4 | 0.8 | 1.2 | 0.2 | 1.1 |
| Machinery and equipment n.e.c. | 1.8 | 0.5 | 0.5 | 0.8 | -0.1 | 0.9 |
| Electrical and optical equipment | 7.8 | 4.9 | 1.1 | 1.8 | 0.4 | 1.5 |
| Office accounting and computing machinery | 9.6 | 3.0 | 0.4 | 6.2 | 4.7 | 1.6 |
| Electrical machinery and apparatus n.e.c. | 7.5 | 4.0 | 0.8 | 2.7 | 0.8 | 1.9 |
| Radio, television and communication equipment | 8.1 | 6.6 | 1.2 | 0.2 | 0.0 | 0.2 |
| Medical precision and optical instruments | 5.7 | 4.8 | 0.3 | 0.6 | -0.1 | 0.7 |
| Transport equipment | 4.4 | 3.5 | 0.3 | 0.6 | -0.2 | 0.8 |
| Motor vehicles, trailers and semi-trailers | 3.4 | 1.6 | 0.5 | 1.3 | -0.4 | 1.7 |
| Other transport equipment | 4.9 | 4.5 | 0.1 | 0.2 | -0.0 | 0.3 |
| Building and repairing of ships and boats | 5.7 | 4.6 | 0.3 | 0.7 | -0.2 | 0.9 |
| Railroad equipment and transport equipment n.e.c. | 2.1 | 4.2 | -0.4 | -1.7 | 0.6 | -2.3 |
| Manufacturing n.e.c.; recycling | 3.3 | 2.0 | 0.3 | 1.0 | 0.3 | 0.7 |

## Labour productivity decompositions: Finland

Decomposition based on the Griliches and Regev (1995) approach

Average period: **1989-1994**

| Industries | Productivity growth (annual % change) | Decomposition | | | | |
|---|---|---|---|---|---|---|
| | | Within | Between | Net entry | of which | |
| | | | | | Entry | Exit |
| Total manufacturing | 5.2 | 3.0 | 0.9 | 1.3 | -0.1 | 1.4 |
| Food products, beverages and tobacco | 5.0 | 3.8 | 0.4 | 0.8 | 0.2 | 0.6 |
| Textiles, textile products, leather and footwear | 5.8 | 2.5 | 0.8 | 2.5 | 0.2 | 2.3 |
| Wood and products of wood and cork | 4.7 | 3.7 | 0.0 | 1.0 | 0.2 | 0.9 |
| Pulp paper, paper products, printing and publishing | 6.0 | 3.8 | 1.0 | 1.2 | -0.1 | 1.3 |
| Chemical, rubber, plastics and fuel products | 3.4 | 2.9 | -0.2 | 0.7 | 0.1 | 0.6 |
| Chemical and fuel products | 3.2 | 2.8 | -0.5 | 0.9 | 0.4 | 0.5 |
| Coke refined, petroleum products and nuclear fuel | 6.4 | 6.5 | -0.1 | -0.0 | -1.3 | 1.3 |
| Chemicals and chemical products | 2.4 | 2.4 | -0.6 | 0.6 | 0.3 | 0.3 |
| Chemicals excluding pharmaceuticals | 4.0 | 3.7 | -0.5 | 0.8 | 0.2 | 0.6 |
| Pharmaceuticals | -3.1 | -2.4 | -0.4 | -0.3 | -0.0 | -0.3 |
| Rubber and plastics products | 3.6 | 3.0 | 0.3 | 0.3 | -0.1 | 0.4 |
| Other non-metallic mineral products | 2.2 | 1.8 | -0.4 | 0.8 | 0.6 | 0.3 |
| Basic metals, metal products, machinery and equipment | 4.4 | 2.8 | 1.1 | 0.6 | -0.4 | 1.0 |
| Basic metals, metal products, machinery and equipment excl. transport | 4.7 | 2.9 | 1.3 | 0.5 | -0.5 | 1.0 |
| Basic metals and fabricated metal products | 4.5 | 2.6 | 1.2 | 0.7 | -0.7 | 1.4 |
| Basic metals | 4.4 | 3.3 | 0.9 | 0.2 | -0.2 | 0.4 |
| Fabricated metal products excl. machinery and equipment | 2.7 | 2.2 | -0.2 | 0.6 | -0.3 | 0.9 |
| Machinery and equipment | 4.9 | 3.0 | 1.4 | 0.5 | -0.3 | 0.8 |
| Machinery and equipment n.e.c. | 1.7 | 0.7 | 0.6 | 0.4 | -0.4 | 0.8 |
| Electrical and optical equipment | 8.5 | 5.8 | 2.1 | 0.6 | -0.2 | 0.9 |
| Office accounting and computing machinery | 9.0 | 4.9 | 2.6 | 1.5 | 0.3 | 1.2 |
| Electrical machinery and apparatus n.e.c. | 5.6 | 3.8 | 1.1 | 0.7 | -0.3 | 1.0 |
| Radio, television and communication equipment | 12.2 | 9.4 | 1.4 | 1.3 | -0.7 | 2.0 |
| Medical precision and optical instruments | 4.3 | 3.4 | 0.2 | 0.7 | 0.2 | 0.5 |
| Transport equipment | 2.4 | 1.7 | -0.1 | 0.8 | -0.1 | 0.9 |
| Motor vehicles, trailers and semi-trailers | -0.5 | -0.4 | -0.8 | 0.6 | -0.2 | 0.8 |
| Other transport equipment | 4.2 | 2.8 | 0.5 | 1.0 | 0.1 | 0.9 |
| Building and repairing of ships and boats | 5.5 | 4.4 | -0.0 | 1.1 | -0.0 | 1.2 |
| Railroad equipment and transport equipment n.e.c. | -1.0 | -2.6 | 1.0 | 0.6 | -0.1 | 0.7 |
| Manufacturing n.e.c.; recycling | 3.0 | 1.7 | 0.4 | 1.0 | 0.3 | 0.7 |

## Labour productivity decompositions: Italy

Decomposition based on the Griliches and Regev (1995) approach

Average period: **1987-1992**

| Industries | Productivity growth (annual % change) | Decomposition | | | | |
|---|---|---|---|---|---|---|
| | | Within | Between | Net entry | of which | |
| | | | | | Entry | Exit |
| Total manufacturing | 3.9 | 2.0 | 0.5 | 1.4 | 0.8 | 0.6 |
| Food products, beverages and tobacco | 5.1 | 2.6 | 0.3 | 2.3 | 0.8 | 1.5 |
| Textiles, textile products, leather and footwear | 3.8 | 1.7 | 0.7 | 1.5 | 1.3 | 0.2 |
| Wood and products of wood and cork | 4.5 | 3.4 | 0.3 | 0.8 | 0.6 | 0.2 |
| Pulp paper, paper products, printing and publishing | 2.7 | 2.1 | 0.3 | 0.3 | 0.6 | -0.3 |
| Chemical, rubber, plastics and fuel products | 4.6 | 2.2 | 0.6 | 1.8 | 0.8 | 1.0 |
| Coke refined, petroleum products and nuclear fuel | -3.1 | -1.7 | 0.1 | -1.5 | -1.5 | -0.1 |
| Chemicals and chemical products | 5.5 | 2.6 | 0.7 | 2.2 | 1.1 | 1.1 |
| Chemicals excluding pharmaceuticals | 4.8 | 1.4 | 0.7 | 2.6 | 1.4 | 1.2 |
| Pharmaceuticals | 6.7 | 4.8 | 0.6 | 1.3 | 0.7 | 0.7 |
| Rubber and plastics products | 4.0 | 2.1 | 0.4 | 1.5 | 0.5 | 1.0 |
| Other non-metallic mineral products | 4.5 | 2.8 | 0.1 | 1.6 | 0.4 | 1.3 |
| Basic metals, metal products, machinery and equipment | 3.5 | 1.9 | 0.4 | 1.3 | 0.6 | 0.7 |
| Basic metals and fabricated metal products | 4.1 | 2.2 | 0.4 | 1.5 | 1.0 | 0.5 |
| Basic metals | 4.7 | 2.0 | 0.6 | 2.2 | 1.1 | 1.1 |
| Fabricated metal products excl. machinery and equipment | 3.9 | 2.3 | 0.4 | 1.2 | 0.6 | 0.6 |
| Machinery and equipment | 4.1 | 2.7 | 0.0 | 1.5 | 0.9 | 0.6 |
| Machinery and equipment n.e.c. | 2.9 | 1.4 | 0.4 | 1.0 | 0.2 | 0.8 |
| Electrical and optical equipment | 5.2 | 3.7 | -0.4 | 1.9 | 1.5 | 0.4 |
| Transport equipment | 1.5 | -0.3 | 1.2 | 0.6 | -0.2 | 0.9 |
| Motor vehicles, trailers and semi-trailers | -1.1 | -2.2 | 0.9 | 0.2 | -0.3 | 0.5 |
| Other transport equipment | 5.4 | 3.3 | 0.6 | 1.6 | 1.0 | 0.6 |
| Building and repairing of ships and boats | 7.8 | 6.3 | 0.6 | 0.9 | 0.7 | 0.3 |
| Aircraft and spacecraft | 3.0 | 2.5 | -0.2 | 0.7 | 0.7 | 0.0 |
| Manufacturing n.e.c.; recycling | 4.7 | 2.4 | 0.5 | 1.7 | 0.8 | 0.9 |

## Labour productivity decompositions: Italy

Decomposition based on the Griliches and Regev (1995) approach

### Average period: **1992-1997**

| Industries | Productivity growth (annual % change) | Decomposition | | | | |
|---|---|---|---|---|---|---|
| | | Within | Between | Net entry | of which | |
| | | | | | Entry | Exit |
| Total manufacturing | 4.3 | 2.5 | 0.5 | 1.3 | 0.4 | 0.9 |
| Food products, beverages and tobacco | 1.2 | 1.0 | 0.5 | -0.4 | -0.2 | -0.1 |
| Textiles, textile products, leather and footwear | 5.2 | 2.2 | 0.8 | 2.2 | 0.8 | 1.4 |
| Wood and products of wood and cork | 3.8 | 1.9 | 0.4 | 1.6 | -0.0 | 1.6 |
| Pulp paper, paper products, printing and publishing | 4.6 | 2.5 | 0.4 | 1.7 | 1.1 | 0.6 |
| Chemical, rubber, plastics and fuel products | 3.1 | 1.6 | 0.5 | 1.0 | 0.5 | 0.6 |
| Coke refined, petroleum products and nuclear fuel | 7.3 | 2.3 | 2.7 | 2.2 | -1.6 | 3.9 |
| Chemicals and chemical products | 4.0 | 1.2 | 0.8 | 2.0 | 0.7 | 1.3 |
| Chemicals excluding pharmaceuticals | 5.5 | 1.5 | 1.0 | 2.9 | 1.2 | 1.8 |
| Pharmaceuticals | 1.6 | 0.6 | 0.5 | 0.5 | -0.1 | 0.5 |
| Rubber and plastics products | 3.5 | 2.2 | 0.3 | 1.1 | 0.4 | 0.7 |
| Other non-metallic mineral products | 3.7 | 1.6 | 0.5 | 1.6 | 0.5 | 1.1 |
| Basic metals, metal products, machinery and equipment | 4.7 | 3.2 | 0.3 | 1.2 | 0.4 | 0.8 |
| Basic metals and fabricated metal products | 4.6 | 2.7 | 0.1 | 1.7 | 0.6 | 1.2 |
| Basic metals | 6.4 | 3.1 | 0.0 | 3.3 | 1.1 | 2.2 |
| Fabricated metal products excl. machinery and equipment | 4.2 | 2.4 | 0.1 | 1.6 | 0.4 | 1.2 |
| Machinery and equipment | 4.8 | 3.4 | 0.4 | 1.0 | 0.4 | 0.6 |
| Machinery and equipment n.e.c. | 4.4 | 2.7 | 0.2 | 1.6 | 0.5 | 1.0 |
| Electrical and optical equipment | 5.3 | 4.3 | 0.5 | 0.5 | 0.3 | 0.3 |
| Transport equipment | 4.6 | 2.9 | 0.1 | 1.7 | 0.2 | 1.5 |
| Motor vehicles, trailers and semi-trailers | -1.1 | -2.2 | 0.9 | 0.2 | -0.3 | 0.5 |
| Other transport equipment | 5.4 | 3.3 | 0.6 | 1.6 | 1.0 | 0.6 |
| Building and repairing of ships and boats | 7.8 | 6.3 | 0.6 | 0.9 | 0.7 | 0.3 |
| Aircraft and spacecraft | 3.0 | 2.5 | -0.2 | 0.7 | 0.7 | 0.0 |
| Manufacturing n.e.c.; recycling | 4.7 | 2.4 | 0.5 | 1.7 | 0.8 | 0.9 |

## Labour productivity decompositions: Netherlands

Decomposition based on the Griliches and Regev (1995) approach

Average period: **1987-1992**

| Industries | Productivity growth (annual % change) | Decomposition | | | | |
|---|---|---|---|---|---|---|
| | | Within | Between | Net entry | of which | |
| | | | | | Entry | Exit |
| Total manufacturing | 2.3 | 1.8 | 0.1 | 0.4 | 0.7 | -0.3 |
| Food products, beverages and tobacco | 1.7 | 0.9 | 0.2 | 0.6 | 0.1 | 0.5 |
| Textiles, textile products, leather and footwear | 2.5 | 1.2 | 0.7 | 0.6 | 0.5 | 0.1 |
| Wood and products of wood and cork | 0.7 | 0.4 | 0.1 | 0.2 | 0.3 | -0.2 |
| Pulp paper, paper products, printing and publishing | 1.8 | 1.3 | 0.2 | 0.4 | 0.6 | -0.2 |
| Chemical and fuel products | 2.4 | 1.5 | 0.0 | 0.9 | 0.8 | 0.1 |
| Chemical, rubber, plastics and fuel products | 1.9 | 1.5 | 0.2 | 0.3 | 1.1 | -0.8 |
| Chemicals and chemical products | 2.6 | 1.4 | 0.4 | 0.9 | 1.0 | -0.1 |
| Chemicals excluding pharmaceuticals | 2.6 | 1.4 | 0.4 | 0.9 | 1.0 | -0.1 |
| Rubber and plastics products | 1.9 | 1.2 | 0.5 | 0.3 | 0.4 | -0.1 |
| Other non-metallic mineral products | 2.4 | 1.9 | -0.1 | 0.6 | 0.3 | 0.3 |
| Basic metals, metal products machinery and equipment excl. transport | 2.6 | 2.7 | -0.5 | 0.4 | 0.1 | 0.4 |
| Basic metals and fabricated metal products | 1.6 | 0.5 | 0.2 | 0.9 | 0.5 | 0.4 |
| Basic metals, metal products, machinery and equipment | 3.0 | 2.4 | -0.4 | 1.0 | 0.6 | 0.3 |
| Fabricated metal products excl. machinery and equipment | 1.6 | 0.9 | 0.2 | 0.6 | 0.1 | 0.5 |
| Machinery and equipment n.e.c. | 2.4 | 1.5 | 0.2 | 0.6 | 0.6 | 0.1 |
| Machinery and equipment | 3.2 | 3.8 | -0.8 | 0.2 | -0.1 | 0.3 |
| Electrical and optical equipment | 4.2 | 5.0 | -0.7 | -0.1 | -0.4 | 0.3 |
| Electrical machinery and apparatus n.e.c. | 2.6 | 1.9 | 0.1 | 0.6 | -0.1 | 0.7 |
| Radio, television and communication equipment | 6.0 | 7.0 | -0.3 | -0.7 | -0.7 | 0.0 |
| Medical precision and optical instruments | 2.9 | 0.3 | 0.0 | 2.5 | 2.2 | 0.3 |
| Transport equipment | 4.7 | 0.9 | 0.1 | 3.7 | 3.0 | 0.7 |
| Motor vehicles, trailers and semi-trailers | .. | .. | .. | .. | .. | .. |
| Other transport equipment | 4.7 | 0.9 | 0.1 | 3.7 | 3.0 | 0.7 |
| Building and repairing of ships and boats | .. | .. | .. | .. | .. | .. |
| Manufacturing n.e.c.; recycling | 1.4 | 1.2 | 0.1 | 0.1 | -1.5 | 1.7 |

## Labour productivity decompositions: Netherlands

Decomposition based on the Griliches and Regev (1995) approach

Average period: **1992-1997**

| Industries | Productivity growth (annual % change) | Decomposition | | | | |
|---|---|---|---|---|---|---|
| | | Within | Between | Net entry | of which | |
| | | | | | Entry | Exit |
| Total manufacturing | 4.1 | 2.8 | -0.3 | 1.5 | 0.7 | 0.8 |
| Food products, beverages and tobacco | 3.1 | 2.6 | -0.4 | 0.9 | 0.8 | 0.1 |
| Textiles, textile products, leather and footwear | 5.7 | 2.2 | 0.4 | 3.1 | 1.2 | 1.9 |
| Wood and products of wood and cork | 4.6 | 1.6 | 0.2 | 2.8 | 0.5 | 2.3 |
| Pulp paper, paper products, printing and publishing | 3.5 | 2.2 | -0.0 | 1.3 | 0.6 | 0.7 |
| Chemical and fuel products | 6.0 | 5.8 | -1.6 | 1.7 | 0.9 | 0.9 |
| Chemical, rubber, plastics and fuel products | 5.3 | 5.0 | -1.4 | 1.8 | 0.8 | 1.0 |
| Chemicals and chemical products | 6.2 | 6.1 | -1.8 | 1.9 | 1.2 | 0.7 |
| Chemicals excluding pharmaceuticals | 6.5 | 6.0 | -1.7 | 2.2 | 1.2 | 1.0 |
| Rubber and plastics products | 4.2 | 2.7 | 0.1 | 1.4 | 1.1 | 0.3 |
| Other non-metallic mineral products | 3.5 | 2.5 | 0.3 | 0.8 | 0.0 | 0.8 |
| Basic metals, metal products, machinery and equipment excl. transport | 4.2 | 3.0 | 0.1 | 1.1 | -0.0 | 1.1 |
| Basic metals and fabricated metal products | 3.9 | 3.2 | -0.1 | 0.8 | 0.1 | 0.7 |
| Basic metals, metal products, machinery and equipment | 4.0 | 2.5 | 0.1 | 1.3 | 0.7 | 0.7 |
| Fabricated metal products excl. machinery and equipment | 3.6 | 2.3 | 0.0 | 1.3 | 0.5 | 0.8 |
| Machinery and equipment n.e.c. | 5.0 | 3.2 | 0.5 | 1.3 | 0.5 | 0.8 |
| Machinery and equipment | 4.4 | 2.9 | 0.3 | 1.3 | -0.1 | 1.4 |
| Electrical and optical equipment | 4.3 | 2.6 | 0.2 | 1.5 | -0.3 | 1.8 |
| Electrical machinery and apparatus n.e.c. | 5.8 | 2.9 | 0.5 | 2.4 | 0.1 | 2.2 |
| Radio, television and communication equipment | 2.0 | 1.0 | -0.1 | 1.0 | -0.2 | 1.2 |
| Medical precision and optical instruments | 6.6 | 5.1 | 0.6 | 0.9 | 0.4 | 0.6 |
| Transport equipment | 3.0 | -0.1 | -0.3 | 3.4 | 3.7 | -0.2 |
| Motor vehicles, trailers and semi-trailers | 6.1 | -2.2 | 2.1 | .. | 6.2 | .. |
| Other transport equipment | 0.3 | 1.4 | -0.4 | -0.7 | 0.3 | -1.0 |
| Building and repairing of ships and boats | 3.9 | 2.4 | 0.7 | .. | 0.7 | .. |
| Manufacturing n.e.c.; recycling | 4.2 | 2.3 | 0.1 | 1.9 | 0.8 | 1.1 |

## Labour productivity decompositions: Portugal

Decomposition based on the Griliches and Regev (1995) approach

Average period: **1987-1992**

| Industries | Productivity growth (annual % change) | Decomposition | | | | |
|---|---|---|---|---|---|---|
| | | Within | Between | Net entry | of which | |
| | | | | | Entry | Exit |
| Total manufacturing | 5.3 | 4.0 | -0.5 | 1.8 | -0.4 | 2.2 |
| Food products, beverages and tobacco | 3.9 | 2.2 | 1.2 | 0.6 | -0.5 | 1.0 |
| Textiles, textile products, leather and footwear | 5.8 | 4.2 | 0.1 | 1.5 | -0.6 | 2.1 |
| Wood and products of wood and cork | 5.6 | 3.2 | 0.4 | 2.1 | -0.1 | 2.1 |
| Pulp paper, paper products, printing and publishing | 6.3 | 4.2 | -0.1 | 2.2 | 0.1 | 2.2 |
| Chemical, rubber, plastics and fuel products | 4.6 | 6.3 | -3.3 | 1.5 | 0.5 | 1.1 |
| Chemical and fuel products | 5.1 | 8.1 | -3.7 | 0.6 | 0.6 | 0.0 |
| Chemicals and chemical products | 5.2 | 8.2 | -3.7 | 0.6 | 0.6 | 0.0 |
| Chemicals excluding pharmaceuticals | 5.1 | 9.9 | -4.3 | -0.5 | -0.5 | -0.0 |
| Pharmaceuticals | 6.4 | 5.8 | -0.4 | 1.0 | 0.7 | 0.4 |
| Rubber and plastics products | 5.5 | 1.4 | 1.1 | 3.0 | 0.0 | 3.0 |
| Other non-metallic mineral products | 7.9 | 4.7 | 0.5 | 2.7 | 1.2 | 1.6 |
| Basic metals, metal products, machinery and equipment | 4.8 | 2.9 | -0.1 | 2.1 | 0.2 | 1.9 |
| Basic metals, metal products, machinery and equipment excl. transport | 4.0 | 3.0 | -0.3 | 1.4 | 0.2 | 1.1 |
| Basic metals and fabricated metal products | 3.5 | 2.8 | -0.1 | 0.9 | -0.1 | 1.0 |
| Basic metals | 3.5 | 3.9 | -1.0 | 0.5 | -0.4 | 1.0 |
| Fabricated metal products excl. machinery and equipment | 4.0 | 2.4 | 0.6 | 1.1 | 0.2 | 0.9 |
| Machinery and equipment | 4.0 | 3.3 | -0.7 | 1.4 | 0.3 | 1.2 |
| Machinery and equipment n.e.c. | 7.0 | 3.3 | 1.2 | 2.5 | 0.7 | 1.8 |
| Electrical and optical equipment | 1.0 | 3.7 | -2.6 | -0.1 | -0.4 | 0.3 |
| Office accounting and computing machinery | 7.9 | 4.7 | 0.2 | 3.0 | 0.4 | 2.6 |
| Electrical machinery and apparatus n.e.c. | -3.8 | 3.4 | -4.3 | -2.9 | -3.6 | 0.7 |
| Radio, television and communication equipment | 5.6 | 4.4 | -0.9 | 2.1 | 1.8 | 0.3 |
| Medical precision and optical instruments | -2.3 | -0.6 | -0.3 | -1.3 | -1.5 | 0.2 |
| Transport equipment | 7.4 | 2.2 | 1.0 | 4.3 | 0.2 | 4.0 |
| Motor vehicles, trailers and semi-trailers | 3.9 | 3.1 | 1.0 | -0.2 | -1.7 | 1.5 |
| Other transport equipment | 8.8 | 1.6 | 0.5 | 6.7 | 2.4 | 4.3 |
| Building and repairing of ships and boats | 9.7 | -2.0 | 0.4 | 11.3 | 3.9 | 7.4 |
| Railroad equipment and transport equipment n.e.c. | 7.8 | 6.4 | 0.7 | 0.8 | 1.4 | -0.6 |
| Manufacturing n.e.c.; recycling | 6.1 | 4.4 | 0.3 | 1.4 | -0.2 | 1.5 |

## Labour productivity decompositions: Portugal

Decomposition based on the Griliches and Regev (1995) approach

Average period: **1992-1997**

| Industries | Productivity growth (annual % change) | Decomposition Within | Between | Net entry | of which Entry | Exit |
|---|---|---|---|---|---|---|
| Total manufacturing | 4.7 | 3.1 | -0.3 | 1.9 | 0.0 | 1.9 |
| Food products, beverages and tobacco | -2.4 | 1.3 | -1.9 | .. | -1.8 | .. |
| Textiles textile, products, leather and footwear | 4.7 | 3.0 | 0.2 | 1.5 | -0.5 | 2.0 |
| Wood and products of wood and cork | -0.4 | -3.3 | 0.6 | 2.4 | -0.5 | 2.8 |
| Pulp paper, paper products, printing and publishing | 0.8 | 0.4 | 0.1 | 0.3 | 1.4 | -1.1 |
| Chemical, rubber, plastics and fuel products | 2.9 | 2.9 | -0.4 | 0.4 | -1.0 | 1.3 |
| Chemical and fuel products | 2.7 | 2.7 | -0.7 | 0.7 | -1.3 | 2.1 |
| Chemicals and chemical products | 3.4 | 3.4 | -0.8 | 0.7 | -1.3 | 2.0 |
| Chemicals excluding pharmaceuticals | 0.6 | 2.9 | -0.9 | -1.4 | -2.0 | 0.6 |
| Pharmaceuticals | 5.8 | 2.8 | 0.5 | 2.5 | -0.7 | 3.2 |
| Rubber and plastics products | 4.3 | 3.1 | 1.0 | 0.3 | -0.1 | 0.4 |
| Other non-metallic mineral products | 6.0 | 3.3 | 0.0 | 2.6 | 0.4 | 2.2 |
| Basic metals, metal products, machinery and equipment | 8.7 | 6.2 | -0.7 | 3.2 | 1.8 | 1.4 |
| Basic metals, metal products, machinery and equipment excl. transport | 7.9 | 5.9 | -0.2 | 2.1 | 1.0 | 1.1 |
| Basic metals and fabricated metal products | 7.1 | 4.2 | 0.2 | 2.7 | 1.6 | 1.1 |
| Basic metals | 4.2 | 0.2 | -0.4 | 4.4 | 3.8 | 0.6 |
| Fabricated metal products excl. machinery and equipment | 8.8 | 5.7 | 0.3 | 2.8 | 1.3 | 1.5 |
| Machinery and equipment | 8.1 | 7.2 | -0.7 | 1.6 | 0.7 | 0.9 |
| Machinery and equipment n.e.c. | 6.6 | 5.3 | 0.1 | 1.2 | 0.2 | 1.0 |
| Electrical and optical equipment | 8.6 | 8.5 | -1.5 | 1.7 | 1.0 | 0.7 |
| Electrical machinery and apparatus n.e.c. | 10.1 | 9.3 | -2.0 | 2.8 | 0.5 | 2.2 |
| Radio, television and communication equipment | 8.8 | 7.2 | -0.8 | 2.4 | 1.5 | 0.8 |
| Medical precision and optical instruments | 9.7 | 7.6 | -0.3 | 2.4 | 0.5 | 1.8 |
| Transport equipment | 12.8 | 7.6 | -1.7 | 6.9 | 4.3 | 2.6 |
| Motor vehicles, trailers and semi-trailers | 13.6 | 7.5 | -3.2 | 9.2 | 6.0 | 3.2 |
| Other transport equipment | 7.4 | 8.9 | -0.3 | -1.2 | -0.3 | -0.9 |
| Building and repairing of ships and boats | 8.4 | 21.1 | -8.9 | -3.8 | -0.4 | -3.5 |
| Railroad equipment and transport equipment n.e.c. | 1.4 | 3.8 | -0.3 | -2.1 | -0.5 | -1.6 |
| Manufacturing n.e.c.; recycling | -9.7 | -7.4 | -0.1 | -2.2 | -2.2 | -0.0 |

# Table A4.7

## Labour productivity decompositions: United Kingdom

Decomposition based on the Griliches and Regev (1995) approach

### Average period: **1987-1992**

| Industries | Productivity growth (annual % change) | Decomposition | | | | |
|---|---|---|---|---|---|---|
| | | Within | Between | Net entry | of which | |
| | | | | | Entry | Exit |
| Total manufacturing | 2.5 | 1.5 | 0.3 | 0.8 | 0.0 | 0.7 |
| Food products, beverages and tobacco | 1.2 | 1.5 | -0.1 | -0.3 | -0.6 | 0.3 |
| Textiles, textile products, leather and footwear | 2.8 | 1.6 | 0.1 | 1.1 | -0.1 | 1.1 |
| Wood and products of wood and cork | -0.9 | -0.4 | -0.7 | 0.2 | 0.1 | 0.1 |
| Pulp paper, paper products, printing and publishing | 3.1 | 1.7 | 0.2 | 1.2 | 0.1 | 1.1 |
| Chemical, rubber, plastics and fuel products | 1.2 | 1.4 | -0.3 | 0.1 | -0.0 | 0.1 |
| Chemical and fuel products | 2.3 | 1.8 | -0.6 | 1.1 | 0.9 | 0.2 |
| Chemicals and chemical products | 2.5 | 1.8 | -0.6 | 1.3 | 0.9 | 0.3 |
| Chemicals excluding pharmaceuticals | 2.0 | 1.5 | -0.7 | 1.2 | 0.8 | 0.4 |
| Pharmaceuticals | 4.0 | 2.6 | 0.1 | 1.3 | 1.1 | 0.2 |
| Rubber and plastics products | 0.5 | 0.7 | 0.2 | -0.4 | -0.7 | 0.3 |
| Other non-metallic mineral products | 0.2 | -0.4 | 0.3 | 0.3 | 0.8 | -0.5 |
| Basic metals, metal products, machinery and equipment | 2.8 | 1.7 | 0.5 | 0.6 | 0.0 | 0.6 |
| Basic metals, metal products, machinery and equipment excl. transport | 2.9 | 1.7 | 0.4 | 0.8 | 0.2 | 0.7 |
| Basic metals and fabricated metal products | 1.2 | 1.1 | -0.2 | 0.4 | -0.5 | 0.8 |
| Basic metals | 2.8 | 2.2 | -0.4 | 1.0 | 0.1 | 0.9 |
| Fabricated metal products excl. machinery and equipment | 1.1 | 0.4 | 0.1 | 0.6 | -0.4 | 1.0 |
| Machinery and equipment | 3.7 | 2.0 | 0.7 | 1.1 | 0.5 | 0.6 |
| Machinery and equipment n.e.c. | 2.0 | 1.5 | -0.1 | 0.6 | 0.0 | 0.6 |
| Electrical and optical equipment | 4.8 | 2.3 | 1.2 | 1.4 | 0.8 | 0.5 |
| Office accounting and computing machinery | 7.8 | 0.9 | 3.2 | 3.7 | 2.7 | 1.0 |
| Electrical machinery and apparatus n.e.c. | 3.4 | 2.6 | 0.3 | 0.5 | 0.3 | 0.2 |
| Radio, television and communication equipment | 4.1 | 2.7 | 0.9 | 0.5 | -0.1 | 0.7 |
| Medical precision and optical instruments | 3.4 | 2.4 | 0.2 | 0.8 | -0.0 | 0.8 |
| Transport equipment | 2.8 | 1.7 | 0.8 | 0.3 | -0.4 | 0.7 |
| Motor vehicles, trailers and semi-trailers | 1.4 | 0.6 | 0.5 | 0.2 | -0.6 | 0.8 |
| Other transport equipment | 3.3 | 3.0 | 0.5 | -0.2 | 0.2 | -0.4 |
| Building and repairing of ships and boats | 6.3 | 4.5 | 0.7 | 1.2 | 0.6 | 0.7 |
| Aircraft and spacecraft. | 2.6 | 2.6 | 0.0 | 0.1 | 0.2 | -0.1 |
| Railroad equipment and transport equipment n.e.c. | 3.9 | 3.3 | 0.4 | 0.1 | 0.2 | -0.0 |
| Manufacturing n.e.c.; recycling | 0.7 | 0.4 | 0.3 | -0.0 | -0.5 | 0.5 |

## Labour productivity decompositions: United Kingdom

Decomposition based on the Griliches and Regev (1995) approach

Average period: **1992-1997**

| Industries | Productivity growth (annual % change) | Decomposition | | | | |
|---|---|---|---|---|---|---|
| | | Within | Between | Net entry | of which | |
| | | | | | Entry | Exit |
| Total manufacturing | 3.1 | 2.4 | -0.2 | 0.9 | -0.1 | 1.1 |
| Food products, beverages and tobacco | -1.0 | 0.4 | -0.8 | -0.6 | -0.2 | -0.4 |
| Textiles, textile products, leather and footwear | 2.8 | 2.2 | -0.5 | 1.1 | 0.2 | 1.0 |
| Wood and products of wood and cork | 2.2 | 1.5 | 0.9 | -0.2 | -1.2 | 1.0 |
| Pulp paper, paper products, printing and publishing | 0.5 | 1.3 | -0.2 | -0.7 | -1.6 | 0.9 |
| Chemical, rubber, plastics and fuel products | 1.3 | 2.5 | -0.6 | -0.6 | -0.9 | 0.3 |
| Chemical and fuel products | 1.6 | 3.0 | -0.4 | -1.0 | -1.1 | 0.2 |
| Chemicals and chemical products | 2.1 | 3.0 | -0.4 | -0.5 | -1.0 | 0.5 |
| Chemicals excluding pharmaceuticals | 1.5 | 3.1 | -0.8 | -0.7 | -1.3 | 0.6 |
| Pharmaceuticals | 3.4 | 2.9 | 0.7 | -0.1 | -0.3 | 0.2 |
| Rubber and plastics products | 1.2 | 1.8 | -0.2 | -0.4 | -0.7 | 0.2 |
| Other non-metallic mineral products | 2.4 | 1.8 | -0.3 | 0.9 | 0.7 | 0.2 |
| Basic metals, metal products, machinery and equipment | 5.4 | 3.5 | 0.1 | 1.8 | 0.2 | 1.6 |
| Basic metals, metal products, machinery and equipment excl. transport | 5.2 | 3.0 | 0.3 | 1.8 | 0.7 | 1.1 |
| Basic metals and fabricated metal products | 3.1 | 2.4 | 0.2 | 0.6 | -0.9 | 1.5 |
| Basic metals | 4.4 | 3.0 | -0.1 | 1.5 | -0.2 | 1.7 |
| Fabricated metal products excl. machinery and equipment | 1.8 | 1.9 | -0.0 | -0.1 | -0.7 | 0.5 |
| Machinery and equipment | 6.0 | 3.3 | 0.4 | 2.3 | 1.3 | 1.0 |
| Machinery and equipment n.e.c. | 3.8 | 2.8 | 0.1 | 0.9 | 0.0 | 0.9 |
| Electrical and optical equipment | 7.4 | 3.7 | 0.6 | 3.2 | 2.1 | 1.1 |
| Office accounting and computing machinery | 14.9 | 4.6 | -0.1 | 10.4 | 5.6 | 4.8 |
| Electrical machinery and apparatus n.e.c. | 6.0 | 3.8 | -0.1 | 2.4 | 0.7 | 1.7 |
| Radio, television and communication equipment | 8.6 | 4.0 | 1.0 | 3.7 | 1.7 | 2.0 |
| Medical precision and optical instruments | 2.8 | 2.7 | -0.1 | 0.1 | 0.2 | -0.1 |
| Transport equipment | 6.3 | 4.5 | -0.2 | 1.9 | -0.5 | 2.4 |
| Motor vehicles, trailers and semi-trailers | 4.9 | 4.8 | -0.6 | 0.7 | -1.0 | 1.7 |
| Other transport equipment | 7.6 | 4.2 | -0.0 | 3.4 | 0.8 | 2.6 |
| Building and repairing of ships and boats | 4.1 | 3.8 | 0.1 | 0.2 | -1.0 | 1.2 |
| Aircraft and spacecraft. | 9.2 | 4.9 | -0.1 | 4.5 | 1.8 | 2.7 |
| Railroad equipment and transport equipment n.e.c. | 2.0 | 0.6 | 0.6 | 0.9 | -1.1 | 2.0 |
| Manufacturing n.e.c.; recycling | 2.0 | 0.8 | 0.3 | 0.9 | -0.4 | 1.3 |

## Labour productivity decompositions: United States

Decomposition based on the Griliches and Regev (1995) approach

Average period: **1987-1992**

| Industries | Productivity growth (annual % change) | Decomposition | | | | |
|---|---|---|---|---|---|---|
| | | Within | Between | Net entry | of which | |
| | | | | | Entry | Exit |
| Total manufacturing | 1.6 | 1.4 | -0.1 | 0.3 | -0.9 | 1.2 |
| Food products, beverages and tobacco | 0.6 | 0.7 | -0.4 | 0.3 | -0.4 | 0.7 |
| Textiles, textile products, leather and footwear | 1.4 | 0.7 | 0.7 | -0.0 | -1.4 | 1.4 |
| Wood and products of wood and cork | -1.2 | -0.8 | 0.3 | -0.6 | -0.7 | 0.1 |
| Pulp paper, paper products, printing and publishing | 0.2 | 0.3 | 0.1 | -0.2 | -0.8 | 0.6 |
| Coke refined, petroleum products and nuclear fuel | 2.1 | 1.2 | 0.8 | 0.2 | 0.1 | 0.0 |
| Chemicals and chemical products | 0.6 | 1.1 | -0.4 | -0.2 | -0.7 | 0.6 |
| Rubber and plastics products | 1.6 | 1.4 | -0.0 | 0.3 | -0.4 | 0.6 |
| Other non-metallic mineral products | 0.5 | 0.6 | -0.3 | 0.2 | -0.6 | 0.8 |
| Basic metals | 1.2 | 0.8 | -0.2 | 0.5 | -0.2 | 0.7 |
| Fabricated metal products excl. machinery and equipment | 0.7 | 0.3 | 0.3 | 0.1 | -0.3 | 0.4 |
| Machinery and equipment n.e.c. | 1.2 | 1.1 | -0.1 | 0.3 | -0.3 | 0.6 |
| Office accounting and computing machinery | 11.2 | 9.0 | -0.7 | 2.9 | 0.7 | 2.2 |
| Electrical machinery and apparatus n.e.c. | 4.2 | 3.4 | 0.0 | 0.8 | -0.3 | 1.1 |
| Radio, television and communication equipment | 6.8 | 4.6 | 0.4 | 1.7 | 0.1 | 1.7 |
| Medical precision and optical instruments | 3.0 | 2.7 | -0.1 | 0.3 | -0.4 | 0.8 |
| Motor vehicles, trailers and semi-trailers | 1.7 | 2.2 | -0.9 | 0.4 | -0.8 | 1.2 |
| Building and repairing of ships and boats | -0.2 | -0.6 | 0.3 | 0.1 | -1.0 | 1.0 |
| Aircraft and spacecraft. | 3.0 | 3.0 | 0.2 | -0.2 | -0.3 | 0.2 |
| Railroad equipment and transport equipment n.e.c. | 3.2 | 2.5 | -0.2 | 1.0 | -0.2 | 1.1 |
| Manufacturing n.e.c.; recycling | 1.3 | 0.4 | 0.3 | 0.6 | -0.3 | 0.9 |

## Labour productivity decompositions: United States

Decomposition based on the Griliches and Regev (1995) approach

Average period: **1992-1997**

| Industries | Productivity growth (annual % change) | Decomposition | | | | |
|---|---|---|---|---|---|---|
| | | Within | Between | Net entry | of which | |
| | | | | | Entry | Exit |
| Total manufacturing | 3.0 | 3.0 | -0.6 | 0.6 | -0.8 | 1.4 |
| Food products, beverages and tobacco | 0.8 | 2.1 | -1.3 | -0.1 | -1.1 | 1.0 |
| Textiles, textile products, leather and footwear | 4.2 | 2.4 | 0.6 | 1.2 | -1.2 | 2.5 |
| Wood and products of wood and cork | -0.3 | -0.4 | 0.4 | -0.3 | -0.8 | 0.5 |
| Pulp paper, paper products, printing and publishing | 0.9 | 1.0 | -0.3 | 0.2 | -0.6 | 0.7 |
| Coke refined, petroleum products and nuclear fuel | 6.7 | 6.2 | 0.3 | 0.3 | -0.2 | 0.4 |
| Chemicals and chemical products | 2.9 | 3.3 | -0.7 | 0.2 | -0.2 | 0.4 |
| Rubber and plastics products | 2.3 | 2.1 | -0.1 | 0.4 | -0.4 | 0.8 |
| Other non-metallic mineral products | 2.3 | 1.8 | -0.1 | 0.6 | -0.4 | 1.0 |
| Basic metals | 2.4 | 3.1 | -1.0 | 0.4 | -0.2 | 0.6 |
| Fabricated metal products excl. machinery and equipment | 2.1 | 2.0 | -0.2 | 0.3 | -0.2 | 0.5 |
| Machinery and equipment n.e.c. | 3.0 | 2.7 | -0.1 | 0.3 | -0.4 | 0.7 |
| Office accounting and computing machinery | 18.7 | 16.3 | 0.0 | 2.4 | 0.5 | 1.9 |
| Electrical machinery and apparatus n.e.c. | 4.5 | 3.0 | -0.3 | 1.8 | 1.0 | 0.8 |
| Radio, television and communication equipment | 13.0 | 11.7 | -0.5 | 1.7 | 0.0 | 1.7 |
| Medical precision and optical instruments | 3.7 | 3.3 | -0.5 | 0.9 | -0.0 | 0.9 |
| Motor vehicles, trailers and semi-trailers | 2.9 | 4.3 | -1.6 | 0.2 | -0.8 | 1.1 |
| Building and repairing of ships and boats | -0.6 | 0.2 | -1.0 | 0.2 | -0.9 | 1.1 |
| Aircraft and spacecraft. | 2.9 | 2.2 | 0.0 | 0.6 | -0.3 | 0.9 |
| Railroad equipment and transport equipment n.e.c. | 2.5 | 2.3 | 0.0 | 0.3 | -0.5 | 0.8 |
| Manufacturing n.e.c.; recycling | 0.1 | 0.6 | -0.8 | 0.3 | -0.7 | 1.0 |

# Fig. A4.1a

## The evolution of labour productivity and its components, total manufacturing

Decomposition based on the Griliches and Regev (1995) approach

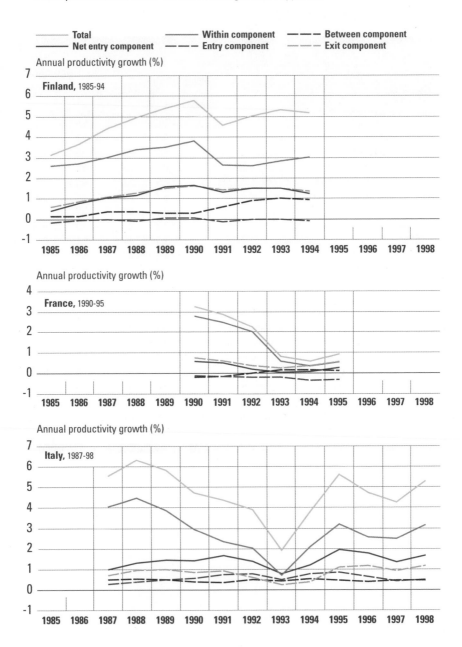

## The evolution of labour productivity and its components, total manufacturing

Decomposition based on the Griliches and Regev (1995) approach

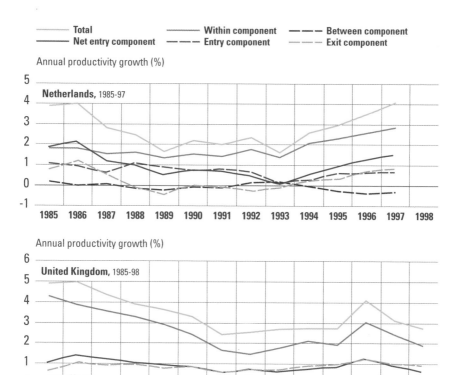

## The evolution of multi-factor productivity growth, total manufacturing

Decomposition based on the Griliches and Regev (1995) approach

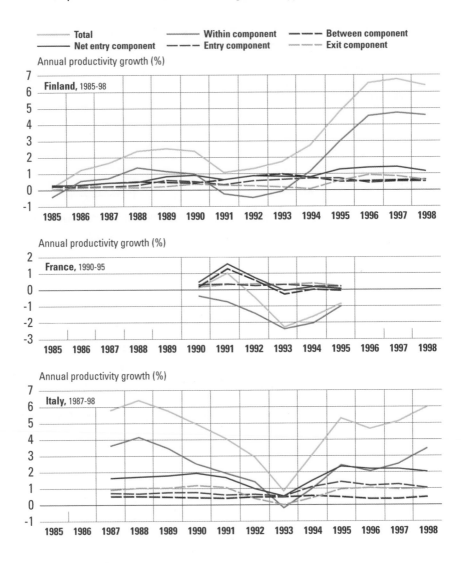

## The evolution of multi-factor productivity growth, total manufacturing

Decomposition based on the Griliches and Regev (1995) approach

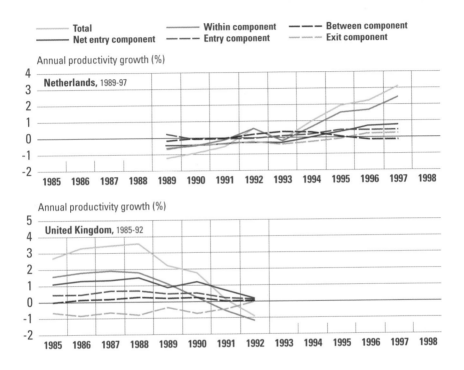

# Bibliography

◼→ Ahmad, N. (2003),
   "Measuring Investment in Software", *OECD STI Working Papers*, No. 2003/6, Paris.

◼→ Akerlof, G.A., W.T. Dickens and G.L. Perry. (1996),
   "The Macroeconomics of Low Inflation", *Brookings Papers on Economic Activity*, Vol. 1, pp. 1-59.

◼→ Apel, M. and P. Jansson (1999),
   "A Theory-Consistent Approach for Estimating Potential Output and the NAIRU",
   *Economics Letters*, No. 74, pp. 271-75.

◼→ Armstrong, P., T.M. Harchaoui, C. Jackson and F. Tarkhani (2002),
   "A Comparison of Canada − US Economic Growth in the Information Age, 1981-2000:
   The Importance of Investment in Information and Communication Technologies",
   *Economic Analysis Research Paper Series*, No. 001, Statistics Canada, Ottawa.

◼→ Atrostic, B.K. and J. Gates (2001),
   "US Productivity and Electronic Processes in Manufacturing", *CES Working Papers*, No. 01-11,
   Center for Economic Studies, Washington DC.

◼→ Atrostic, B.K. and S. Nguyen (2002),
   "Computer Networks and US Manufacturing Plant Productivity: New Evidence from the
   CNUS Data", *CES Working Papers*, No. 02-01, Center for Economic Studies, Washington DC.

◼→ Baily, M.N. (2002),
   "The New Economy: Post Mortem or Second Wind", *Journal of Economic Perspectives*, Vol. 16,
   No. 2, Spring 2002, pp. 3-22.

◼→ Baily, M.N., C. Hulten, and D. Campbell (1992),
   "Productivity Dynamics in Manufacturing Plants", *Brookings Papers on Economic Activity:
   Microeconomics*, pp. 187-267.

◼→ Baldwin, J.R. and B. Diverty (1995),
   "Advanced Technology Use in Canadian Manufacturing Establishments", *Working Papers*, No. 85,
   Microeconomics Analysis Division, Statistics Canada, Ottawa.

◼→ Baldwin, J.R., B. Diverty, and D. Sabourin (1995),
   "Technology Use and Industrial Transformation: Empirical Perspective", *Working Papers*, No. 75,
   Microeconomics Analysis Division, Statistics Canada, Ottawa.

◼→ Baldwin, J.R., T. Gray, and J. Johnson (1995),
   "Technology Use, Training and Plant-Specific Knowledge in Manufacturing Establishments",
   *Working Papers*, No. 86, Microeconomics Analysis Division, Statistics Canada, Ottawa.

◼→ Baldwin, J.R. and D. Sabourin (2002),
   "Impact of the Adoption of Advanced Information and Communication Technologies on Firm
   Performance in the Canadian Manufacturing Sector", *OECD STI Working Papers*, No. 2002/1,
   Paris.

◼→ Barro, R.J. (1991),
   "Economic Growth in a Cross section of Countries", *Quarterly Journal of Economics*, Vol. 106,
   No. 2, pp.407-433.

◼→ Barro, R.J. and X. Sala-i-Martin (1995),
   *Economic Growth*, McGraw-Hill, New York.

▪▭→ Bartelsman, E. A. Bassanini, J. Haltiwanger, R. Jarmin, S. Scarpetta and T. Schank (2002),
"The Spread of ICT and Productivity Growth – Is Europe Really Lagging Behind in the New Economy?", Fondazione Rodolfo DeBenedetti, *mimeo*.

▪▭→ Bassanini, A. and S. Scarpetta (2002),
"Does Human Capital Matter for Growth in OECD Countries? A Pooled Mean Group Approach", *Economics Letters*, Vol. 74, No. 3, pp. 399-405.

▪▭→ Bassanini, A., S. Scarpetta and I. Visco (2000),
"Knowledge, Technology and Economic Growth: Recent Evidence from OECD Countries", *OECD Economics Department Working Papers*, No. 259.

▪▭→ Bayoumi, T. and M. Haacker (2002),
"It's Not What You Make, It's How You Use It: Measuring the Welfare Benefits of the IT Revolution Across Countries", *CEPR Discussion Papers*, No. 3555, Center for Economic Policy Research, London.

▪▭→ Bertschek, I. and H. Fryges (2002),
"The Adoption of Business-to-Business E-Commerce: Empirical Evidence for German Companies", *ZEW Discussion Papers*, No. 02-05, ZEW, Mannheim.

▪▭→ Bertschek, I. and U. Kaiser (2001),
"Productivity Effects of Organizational Change: Microeconometric Evidence", *ZEW Discussion Papers*, No. 01-32, ZEW, Mannheim.

▪▭→ BLS (Bureau of Labor Statistics) (2002),
www.bls.gov

▪▭→ Bresnahan, T.F. and S. Greenstein (1996),
"Technical Progress and Co-Invention in Computing and the Use of Computers", *Brookings Papers on Economic Activity: Microeconomics*, pp. 1-77.

▪▭→ Broersma, L. and R.H. McGuckin (2000),
"The Impact of Computers on Productivity in the Trade Sector: Explorations with Dutch Microdata", *Research Memorandum* GD-45, Groningen Growth and Development Centre, June.

▪▭→ Bruno, M. and W. Easterly (1998),
"Inflation Crises and Long-run Growth", *Journal of Monetary Economics*, Vol. 41, pp. 3-26.

▪▭→ Brynjolfsson, E. and S. Yang (1996),
Information Technology and Productivity: A Review of the Literature, *mimeo*, http://ebusiness.mit.edu/erik

▪▭→ Bureau of Economic Analyses,
U.S. Department of Commerce, *Fixed Assets Tables*, www.bea.doc.gov

▪▭→ Butler, L. (1996),
"A Semi-Structural Approach to Estimate Potential Output: Combining Economic Theory with A Time-Series Filter", *Bank of Canada Technical Report*, No. 76.

▪▭→ Caroli, E. and J. van Reenen (1999),
"Organization, Skills and Technology: Evidence from a Panel of British and French Establishments", *IFS Working Paper Series* W99/23, Institute of Fiscal Studies, August.

■⊐→ Caves, D., L. Christensen and E. Diewert (1982),
"Multilateral Comparisons of Output, Input, and Productivity Using Superlative Index Numbers",
*Economic Journal*, Vol. 92, No. 365, pp. 73-86.

■⊐→ Cellini, R., M. Cortese and N. Rossi (1999),
"Social Catastrophes and Growth", University of Bologna, Bologne, *mimeo*.

■⊐→ Cette, G., J. Mairesse and Y. Kocoglu (2002),
"Diffusion of ICTs and Growth of the French Economy over the Long Term, 1980-2000",
*International Productivity Monitor*, No. 4, Spring, pp. 27-38.

■⊐→ Clayton, T. and K. Waldron (2003),
"E-Commerce Adoption and Business Impact, A Progress Report", *Economic Trends*,
No. 591, February.

■⊐→ Cohen, W. and D. Levinthal (1989),
"Innovation and Learning: The Two Faces of R&D", *Economic Journal*, Vol. 99, pp. 569-596.

■⊐→ Colecchia, A., and P. Schreyer (2002),
"ICT Investment and Economic Growth in the 1990s: Is the United States a Unique Case?
A Comparative Study of Nine OECD Countries" *Review of Economic Dynamics*,
Vol. 5, No. 2, pp. 408-442.

■⊐→ Colecchia, A. and P. Schreyer (2001),
"The Impact of Information Communications Technology on Output Growth",
*OECD STI Working Papers*, No. 2001/7, Paris.

■⊐→ Conway, P. and B. Hunt (1997),
"Estimating Potential Output: A Semi-Structural Approach",
*Bank of New Zealand Discussion Paper*, No. G97/9.

■⊐→ David, P.A., B.H. Hall, and A.A. Toole (1999),
"Is Public R&D a Complement or Substitute for Private R&D? A Review of the Econometric
Evidence", *NBER Working Papers*, No. 7373.

■⊐→ Davis, S.J., J. Haltiwanger and S. Schu (1996),
"Small Business and Job Creation: Dissecting the Myth and Reassessing the Facts",
*Small Business Economics*, Vol. 8, pp. 297-315.

■⊐→ Doms, M., R. Jarmin and S. Klimek (2002),
"IT Investment and Firm Performance in US Retail Trade", *CES Working Papers*, No. 02-14,
Center for Economic Studies, Washington DC.

■⊐→ Doms, M., T. Dunne and K.R. Troske (1997),
"Workers, Wages and Technology", *Quarterly Journal of Economics*, 112, No. 1, pp. 253-290.

■⊐→ Doms, M., T. Dunne, and M.J. Roberts (1995),
"The Role of Technology Use in the Survival and Growth of Manufacturing Plants",
*International Journal of Industrial Organization*, Vol 13, No. 4, December, pp. 523-542.

■⊐→ Dunne, T. and J. Schmitz (1995),
"Wages, Employment Structure and Employer Size- Wage Premia: Their Relationship to
Advanced-technology Usage at US Manufacturing Establishments", *Economica*,
March, pp. 89-107.

■□→ Edey, M. (1994),
"Costs and Benefits From Moving from Low Inflation to Price Stability", *OECD Economic Studies*, No. 23, Paris, pp. 109-130.

■□→ Entorf, H. and F. Kramarz (1998),
"The Impact of New Technologies on Wages: Lessons from Matching Panels on Employees and on their Firms", *Economic Innovation and New Technology*, Vol. 5, pp. 165-197.

■□→ EUROSTAT (1995),
"*Recommendation Manual: Business Register*", http://europa.eu.int/comm/eurostat

■□→ Falk, M. (2001),
"Organizational Change, New Information and Communication Technologies and the Demand for Labor in Services", *ZEW Discussion Papers*, No. 01-25, ZEW, Mannheim.

■□→ Feldstein, M. (1996),
"The Costs and Benefits of Going from Low Inflation to Price Stability", *NBER Working Papers*, No. 5469.

■□→ Foster, L., J.C. Haltiwanger and C.J. Krizan (1998),
"Aggregate Productivity Growth: Lessons from Microeconomic Evidence", *NBER Working Papers*, No. 6803.

■□→ Geroski, P.A. (1991),
*Market Dynamics and Entry*, Basil Blackwell, Oxford.

■□→ Gordon, R.J. (1997),
"The Time-Varying NAIRU and Its Implications for Economic Policy", *Journal of Economic Perspectives*, Vol. 11, pp. 11-32.

■□→ Gordon, R.J. (2002),
"Technology and Economic Performance in the American Economy", *NBER Working Papers*, No. 8771, National Bureau of Economic Research, February.

■□→ Gordon, R.J. (2003),
"Hi-Tech Innovation and Productivity Growth: Does Supply Create Its Own Demand?", *NBER Working Papers*, No. 9437, National Bureau of Economic Research, January.

■□→ Greenan, N. and D. Guellec (1998),
"Firm Organization, Technology and Performance: An Empirical Study", *Economics of Innovation and New Technology*, Vol. 6, No. 4, pp. 313-347.

■□→ Greenan, N., J. Mairesse and A. Topiol-Bensaid (2001),
"Information Technology and Research and Development Impacts on Productivity and Skills: Looking for Correlations on French Firm Level Data", *NBER Working Papers*, No. 8075, Cambridge, MA.

■□→ Gretton, P., J. Gali and D. Parham (2002),
"Uptake and Impacts of ICT in the Australian Economy: Evidence from Aggregate, Sectoral and Firm Levels", *paper presented at OECD Workshop on ICT and Business Performance*, Productivity Commission, Canberra, December.

■□→ Griliches, Z. (1990),
"Patent Statistics as Economic Indicators: A Survey", *Journal of Economic Literature*, Vol. 28, pp. 1661-1797.

**Bibliography**

Griliches, Z. and H. Regev (1995),
"Firm Productivity in Israeli Industry, 1979-1988", *Journal of Econometrics*, Vol. 65, pp. 175-203.

Guellec, D. and B. van Pottelsberghe (2000),
"The Impact of Public R&D Expenditure on Business R&D", *OECD STI Working Papers*,
No. 2000/4, Paris.

Gust, C. and J. Marquez (2002),
"International Comparisons of Productivity Growth: The Role of Information Technology
and Regulatory Practices", *International Finance Discussion Papers*, No. 727,
Federal Reserve Board, May.

Haltiwanger, J., R. Jarmin and T. Schank (2002),
"Productivity, Investment in ICT and Market Experimentation: Micro Evidence from Germany
and the United States.", paper presented at OECD Workshop on ICT and Business Performance,
December.

Harvey, A.C. and A. Jaeger (1993),
"Detrending, Stylized Facts and the Business Cycle", *Journal of Applied Econometrics*,
Vol. 8, pp. 231-47.

Haskel, J. and Y. Heden (1999),
"Computers and the Demand for Skilled Labour: Industry- and Establishment-Level Panel
Evidence for the UK", *The Economic Journal*, 109, C68-C79, March.

Hempell, T. (2002),
"Does Experience Matter? Productivity Effects of ICT in the German Service Sector",
*Discussion Papers*, No. 02-43, Centre for European Economic Research, Mannheim.

Hitt, L.M. (1998),
"Information Technology and Firm Boundaries: Evidence from Panel Data",
University of Pennsylvania, *mimeo*.

Ho, M.S., D.W. Jorgenson and K.J. Stiroh (1999),
"U.S. High-Tech Investment and the Pervasive Slowdown in the Growth of Capital Services",
*mimeo*.

Hodrick, R. and E. Prescott (1997),
"Post-war US Business Cycles: An Empirical Investigation", *Journal of Money,
Credit and Banking*, Vol. 29, pp. 1-16.

Jalava, J., and M. Pohjola (2002).
"Economic Growth in the New Economy, Evidence from Advanced Economies."
*Information Economics and Policy* 14, 189–210.

Jorgenson, D.W. (1963),
"Capital Theory and Investment Behaviour", *American Economic Review*, Vol. 53, No. 2.

Jorgenson, D.W. and Z. Griliches (1967),
"The Explanation of Productivity Change", *Review of Economic Studies*, Vol. 34, No. 3.

Jorgenson D.W. (2001),
"Information Technology and the U.S. Economy", *American Economic Review*, Vol. 91,
No. 1, pp. 1-32.

**Bibliography**

◼▭→ Jorgenson, D.W., M.S. Ho and K.J. Stiroh (2002),
  "Projecting Productivity Growth: Lessons from the US Growth Resurgence",
  *Federal Reserve Bank of Atlanta Economic Review*, third quarter, pp. 1-13.

◼▭→ Kegels, C., M. Van Overbeke and W. Van Zandweghe (2002),
  "ICT Contribution to Economic Performance in Belgium: Preliminary Evidence",
  *Working Papers*, No. 8-02, Federal Planning Bureau, Brussels, September.

◼▭→ Khan, H. and M. Santos (2002),
  "Contribution of ICT Use to Output and Labour: Productivity Growth in Canada",
  *Working Papers*, No. 2002-7, Bank of Canada, Ottawa, March.

◼▭→ Kim, S.J. (2002),
  *The Digital Economy and the Role of Government: Information Technology and Economic
  Performance in Korea*, Program on Information Resources Policy, Harvard University, January.

◼▭→ Krueger, A.B. (1993),
  "How Computers Have Changed the Wage Structure: Evidence from Microdata, 1984-1989",
  *The Quarterly Journal of Economics*, February, pp. 33-60.

◼▭→ Laxton, D. and R. Tetlow (1992),
  "A Simple Multivariate Filter for the Measurement of Potential Output",
  *Bank of Canada Technical Report*, No. 59.

◼▭→ Levine, R. (1997),
  "Financial Development and Economic Growth: Views and Agendas",
  *Journal of Economic Literature*, Vol. 35, No. 2, pp. 688-726.

◼▭→ Levine, R., N. Loayza and T. Beck (2000),
  "Financial Intermediation and Growth: Causality and Causes",
  *Journal of Monetary Economics*, Vol. 46, No. 1, pp. 31-77.

◼▭→ Licht, G. and D. Moch (1999),
  "Innovation and Information Technology in Services", *Canadian Journal of Economics*,
  Vol. 32, No. 2, April.

◼▭→ Luque, A. (2000),
  "An Option-Value Approach to Technology Adoption in US Manufacturing: Evidence from
  Plant-Level Data", *CES Working Papers*, No. 00-12, Center for Economic Studies, Washington, DC.

◼▭→ Luque, A. and J. Miranda (2000),
  "Technology Use and Worker Outcomes: Direct Evidence from Linked Employee-Employer Data",
  *CES Working Papers*, No. 00-13, Center for Economic Studies, Washington, DC.

◼▭→ Mankiw, G.N., D. Romer and D.N. Weil (1992),
  "A Contribution to the Empirics of Economic Growth", *Quarterly Journal of Economics*,
  Vol. 107, No. 2, pp. 407-37.

◼▭→ McGuckin, R.H. and S.V. Nguyen (1995),
  "On Productivity and Plant Ownership Change: New Evidence from the LRD",
  *Rand Journal of Economics*, 26, No. 2, pp. 257- 276.

◼▭→ McGuckin, R.H. and K.J. Stiroh (2001),
  "Do Computers Make Output Harder to Measure?", *Journal of Technology Transfer*,
  Vol. 26, pp. 295-321.

■□→ McKinsey (2001),
*US Productivity Growth 1995-2000: Understanding the Contribution of Information Technology Relative to Other Factors*, McKinsey Global Institute, Washington, DC, October.

■□→ Miyagawa, T., Y. Ito and N. Harada (2002),
"Does the IT Revolution Contribute to Japanese Economic Growth?",
*JCER Discussion Papers*, No. 75, Japan Center for Economic Research, Tokyo.

■□→ Moosa, I.A. (1997),
"A Cross-country Comparison of Okun's Coefficient", *Journal of Comparative Economics*,
Vol. 24, pp. 335-56.

■□→ Motohashi, K. (2001),
"Economic Analysis of Information Network Use: Organisational and Productivity Impacts on Japanese Firms", Research and Statistics Department, METI, *mimeo*.

■□→ Motohashi, K. (2002),
"IT Investment and Productivity Growth of the Japanese Economy and A Comparison with the United States" (in Japanese), *RIETI Discussion Papers*, 02-J-018, Research Institute of Economy, Trade and Industry, November.

■□→ OECD,
*OECD Productivity Database*

■□→ OECD,
*OECD Structural Analysis (STAN) Database*

■□→ OECD (1999),
*Implementing the OECD Jobs Strategy: Assessing Performance and Policy*, Paris.

■□→ OECD (1999),
*OECD Economic Outlook*, No. 68, Paris.

■□→ OECD (2001),
*OECD Economic Outlook*, No 70, Paris.

■□→ OECD (2001),
*OECD Science, Technology and Industry Scoreboard – Towards a Knowledge-Based Economy*, Paris.

■□→ OECD (2001),
*The New Economy: Beyond the Hype*, Paris.

■□→ OECD (2002),
*Measuring the Information Economy* 2002, Paris, www.oecd.org/sti/measuring-infoeconomy

■□→ Oliner, S.D. and D.E. Sichel (2002),
"Information Technology and Productivity: Where Are We Now and Where Are We Going?",
*Federal Reserve Bank of Atlanta Economic Review*, third quarter, pp. 15-44.

■□→ Oulton, N. (2001),
"ICT and Productivity Growth in the United Kingdom", *Working Papers*, No. 140,
Bank of England, London.

■□→ Parham, D., P. Roberts and H. Sun (2001),
"Information Technology and Australia's Productivity Surge", *Staff Research Paper*, Productivity Commission, AusInfo, Canberra.

■→ Pilat, D., F. Lee and B. Van Ark (2002),
"Production and use of ICT: A sectoral perspective on productivity growth in the OECD area",
*OECD Economic Studies*, No. 35, Paris.

■→ RWI (Rheinisch-Westfälisches Institute), **www.rwi-essen.de**

■→ Scarpetta, S., P. Hemmings, T. Tressel and J. Woo (2002),
"The Role of Policy and Institutions for Productivity and Firm Dynamics: Evidence from Micro
and Industry Data", *OECD Economics Department Working Papers*, No. 329, Paris.

■→ Scarpetta, S., A. Bassanini, D. Pilat and P. Schreyer (2000),
"Economic Growth in the OECD Area: Recent Trends at the Aggregate and Sectoral Level",
*OECD Economics Department Working Papers*, No. 248.

■→ Scarpetta, S. and T. Tressel (2002),
"Productivity and Convergence in a Panel of OECD Industries: Do Regulations and Institutions
Matter?", *OECD Economics Department Working Papers*, No. 342.

■→ Schreyer, P., P.E. Bignon and J. Dupont,
"OECD Capital Services Estimates: Methodology and a First Set of Results",
*OECD Statistics Working Papers*, Paris, forthcoming.

■→ Simon, J. and S. Wardrop (2002),
"Australian Use of Information Technology and Its Contribution to Growth", *Research Discussion
Papers,* RDP2002-02, Reserve Bank of Australia, Sydney, January.

■→ Solow, R.M. (1987),
"We'd Better Watch Out", *New York Times*, July 12, *Book Review*, No. 36, New York.

■→ Temple, J. (1999),
"The New Growth Evidence", *Journal of Economic Literature*, Vol. 37, No. 1, pp. 112-156.

■→ Teulings, C. and J. Hartog (1998),
*Corporatism or Competition? Labour Contracts, Institutions and Wage Structures in International
Comparison*, Cambridge University Press, Cambridge, Mass.

■→ Triplett, J.E. and B.B. Bosworth (2002),
"'Baumol's Disease' has Been Cured: IT and Multi-Factor Productivity in U.S. Services Industries",
paper prepared for Brookings workshop on services industry productivity, Brookings Institution,
Washington, DC, September.

■→ United States Council of Economic Advisors (2001),
*Economic Report of the President*, 2001, United States Government Printing Office,
Washington, DC, February.

■→ Van Ark, B., R. Inklaar and R.H. McGuckin (2002),
"'Changing gear' Productivity, ICT and Service Industries: Europe and the United States",
Research Memorandum GD-60, Groningen Growth and Development Centre, Groningen,
www.eco.rug.nl/ggdc/homeggdc.html.

■→ Van Der Wiel, H. (2001),
"Does ICT boost Dutch Productivity Growth?", CPB Document No. 016, CPB Netherlands Bureau
of Economic Policy Analysis, December.

**Bibliography**